Practical Financial Management

Practical Financial Management

RICHARD DOBBINS and
STEPHEN F. WITT

Basil Blackwell

Copyright©Richard Dobbins and Stephen F. Witt 1988

First published 1988

Basil Blackwell Ltd
108 Cowley Road, Oxford, OX4 1JF, UK

Basil Blackwell Inc.
432 Park Avenue South, Suite 1503
New York, NY 10016, USA

British Library Cataloguing in Publication Data
Dobbins, Richard
  Practical financial management.
  1. Financial management.
  I. Title   II. Witt, Stephen F.
  658.1′5
  ISBN 0-631-14095-6
  ISBN 0-631-14096-4 Pbk

Library of Congress Cataloging in Publication Data
Dobbins, Richard.
  Practical financial management.
  Bibliography: p.
  Includes index.
  1. Business enterprises – Finance.   2. Corporations – Finance.
  I. Witt, Stephen F.   II. Title.
  HC4026.D58   1988   658.1′5   88-5044
  ISBN 0-631-14095-6
  ISBN 0-631-14096-4 (pbk.)

Phototypeset in 10 on 12 point Times
by Dobbie Typesetting Service, Plymouth, Devon
Printed in Great Britain by Page Bros (Norwich) Ltd

For Chris Martin and Marie P. Robson

Contents

Preface

Financial theory has been extensively developed in the past twenty years. A casual glance at the finance journals reveals a great many equations with no mention of balance sheets, profit and loss accounts, management accounting, or ratio analysis. Indeed, we have seen many finance courses around the world on which the subject was taught almost entirely as a mathematical subject. On the other hand, the financial managers of commercial enterprises continue to base their decisions on return on capital employed, effect on earnings per share, effect on the balance sheet and profit and loss account. Many are sceptical of the value of new ideas.

We believe that the objective of an education in financial management should be to help managers and potential managers to make sensible investment and financing decisions with a view to making money satisfying consumer wants in competitive markets. In this book, we acknowledge that financial theory teaches that investment and financing decisions should be based on cash flow and risk. At the same time, we provide information on the payback period, return on capital employed, earnings per share effect, working capital, profit planning, standard costing, financial statement planning, and ratio analysis. These practical tools are used in the real world as rules of thumb in making sensible investment and financing decisions.

Financial theorists may not approve of the practical rules of thumb. Traditionalists may not approve of some of the ideas in financial theory. We hope that we have provided a balanced approach to practical financial management for MBA students, financial managers, and undergraduates.

We thank Sylvia Ashdown, Sue Crawford, and Kay Sutcliffe for their assistance. For services beyond the scope of practical financial management, additional thanks go to Bernard and Jean, Hugh and Anne, Louise . . . and little Lucy.

Richard Dobbins and Stephen F. Witt

Part I

Investment Decisions

1

Project and Product Decisions

The Theory of Project and Product Decisions

The objective of the firm is assumed to be to maximize the wealth of its shareholders, that is to maximize the current value of the firm. In practice, the separation of ownership from management in many companies results in shareholders only exerting limited influence over the investment and financial strategies of companies. Thus managers may pursue objectives relating to their own welfare rather than that of their shareholders, and hence adopt low-risk survival strategies and *satisficing* rather than *maximizing* decision behaviour, that is seek satisfactory rather than optimal solutions. However, shareholders can encourage managers to act optimally from the shareholders' point of view by offering appropriate incentives and instituting necessary controls.

Firms create wealth by making successful investment decisions which generate positive net cash flows. They make money satisfying consumer wants by matching the resources of the organization to the needs of the market place. Investment decisions are discussed in chapters 1–4. These are far more important than financing decisions because it is the investment decisions which decide the level of future cash flows generated from successful trading. However, financing decisions also have an impact on the value of the firm, and hence appropriate financing policies should be adopted. Financing decisions are discussed in chapters 5–9.

The goal of firms has traditionally been regarded as profit maximization. Profits are created when the market value of the firm's outputs is greater than the market value of its inputs. However, profit is essentially a single-period measure of company performance. By equating maximization of profit with maximization of the current value of the firm several problems are overcome, for example the trade-off between short-term and long-term profits, the valuation of inflows and outflows of cash at different points in time, and the incorporation of risk into the analysis.

3

In order to calculate the present value of the firm it is necessary to use the technique of *discounting*. The value of money is time-dependent–£1 now is worth more than £1 at some future date – and this needs to be taken into account in valuing the firm. A future sum of money may be transformed into an equivalent present sum of money by applying a discount rate. Thus selection of an appropriate discount rate allows the present values of all the firm's forecast cash flows at various future dates to be obtained. As the cash flows are valued on a consistent basis, they may now be compared. Thus the forecast cash flow profiles attaching to firms may be evaluated in terms of their present values in order to determine the value of the firm. The discount rate chosen to value a firm depends upon the riskiness of its forecast cash flows; those which are subject to considerable variability (risk) need to be discounted at a higher rate than less risky cash flows. As investors can diversify their shareholdings across companies, they only need compensation for the risk which cannot be diversified away, that is that part of the riskiness of cash flows which is associated with general movements in the economy (the market risk). That part of the total riskiness of cash flows which is unique to the individual company (the specific risk) is of no concern to the investor with a well-diversified portfolio. A comprehensive discussion of the evaluation of a firm's market risk is provided in chapter 4.

A firm can be regarded as a collection of individual projects, so the present value of the forecast cash flow profile relating to a *project* determines the profitability of the project and hence the contribution of the project to the profitability of the company. The chosen discount rate (or cost of capital) must reflect the riskiness of the individual project, and the identification of required rates of return on projects is discussed in detail in chapter 4.

The efficient market hypothesis suggests that at any point in time share prices fully reflect all information available to stock exchange participants, and most of the published research findings support the hypothesis. (The efficient market hypothesis is considered in more detail in chapter 4.) One of the implications of capital market efficiency is that the value of a quoted company is the market value of its shares on the stock exchange. Hence, the firm's objective of maximizing shareholder wealth is achieved by maximizing the current *market value* of the firm.

Investment decisions relate to the acquisition of assets. These may be *real assets*, such as land, buildings, plant, equipment, stocks, patents and trade-marks, or *financial assets*, such as shares and government securities. Financial management is concerned with how much the firm should invest and in which projects. *Financing decisions* mainly relate to the best mix of financing to fund the firm's operations.

It is important for the firm to evaluate investment opportunities correctly. However, successful investment programmes are more dependent on the ability of the firm to *create* profitable investment opportunities than on its investment *appraisal* ability.

Decisions regarding investment in projects and products fall within the field of *capital budgeting*, which is the art of investing in assets which are worth more than they cost (Myers, 1976). The objective of the firm is the maximization of shareholder wealth, but an investment is only wealth-creating if the present value of all forecast cash inflows (from customers) associated with the project exceeds the present value of all forecast cash outflows (to suppliers of labour, goods, etc.) relating to the project. Investment decisions usually involve an initial capital expenditure followed by a stream of cash receipts and disbursements in subsequent periods. The following net present value (*NPV*) formula may be used to evaluate the desirability of investment opportunities:

$$NPV = \sum_{t=1}^{n} \frac{x_t}{(1+k)^t} - I \tag{1.1}$$

where

NPV = the net present value of the project

$\sum_{t=1}^{n}$ = summation over years, 1,2, . . . , n

x_t = the forecast net cash flow arising at the end of year t, that is the difference between operational cash receipts and operational cash expenditures (including additional investment)

k = the required rate of return (or discount rate)

n = the life of the project in years

I = the initial cost of the investment

Thus, the net present value of a project is obtained by summing the forecast net cash flows over the project's life, discounted at a rate which reflects the cost of a loan of equivalent risk on the capital market, and deducting the initial investment outlay. Hence, an investment is wealth-creating if its NPV is positive, so *all projects that offer a positive net present value when discounted at the required rate of return for the investment should be accepted* in order to maximize the wealth of shareholders.

For example, suppose that a project requires an initial investment of £1,000 and that the forecast net cash inflows are £620 receivable after one year and £580 receivable after two years. The firm operates in a low risk industry and divides its various projects into three categories: class A where the risk is below average and the required rate of return is 10 per cent; class

B where the risk is average for the industry and the required rate of return is 13 per cent; class C where the risk is above average and the required rate of return is 16 per cent. The project may be evaluated from the NPV viewpoint by substituting into equation (1.1) as follows:

If the project falls in class A

$$NPV = \frac{620}{1+0.1} + \frac{580}{(1+0.1)^2} - 1,000$$

$$= £40$$

If the project falls in class B

$$NPV = \frac{620}{1+0.13} + \frac{580}{(1+0.13)^2} - 1,000$$

$$= £0$$

If the project falls in class C

$$NPV = \frac{620}{1+0.16} + \frac{580}{(1+0.16)^2} - 1,000$$

$$= -£30$$

Thus if the project is classified as below average risk for the firm, then it has a net present value of £40; as the NPV is positive the project should be accepted – given the forecast cash flows the market value of the firm should rise by £40 as a result. If the project is classified as average risk, it has a net present value of £0; the project is barely acceptable in this case. If the project is regarded as being of above average risk, then the NPV is – £30; as the NPV is negative the project is unacceptable and should be rejected.

Investors do not like risk, and the greater the riskiness of returns on an investment, the greater will be the return expected by investors. Accordingly, there is a trade-off between market risk and expected return which must be reflected in the required rates of return on investment opportunities. Figure 1.1 shows the risk-return relationships of seven projects. The dotted line indicates the trade-off between expected return and market risk for *securities* if the efficient market hypothesis holds. Projects 3, 6 and 7 fall on the line and thus their expected returns just compensate for their riskiness, that is they have net present values of zero. Projects 2 and 5 lie above the

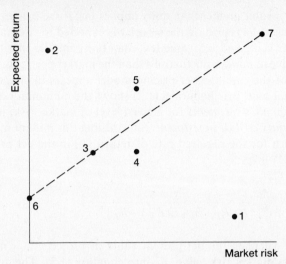

Figure 1.1   Risk-return relationships for alternative projects

line and thus their expected returns are higher than those required for the corresponding risk levels, that is they have positive net present values. Projects 1 and 4, which lie below the line, have negative net present values. The efficient market hypothesis implies that the risk-return combinations of all securities fall on the line. Product markets, however, are not perfectly efficient, and it is a manager's task to locate projects (such as 2 and 5) which lie above the line. These projects have positive net present values and therefore offer wealth-creating opportunities.

The precise form of the relationship between risk and return for a *security* is given by the capital-asset pricing model:

$$E(R_i) = R_F + \beta_i [E(R_M) - R_F] \qquad (1.2)$$

where $E(R_i)$ is the expected rate of return on any individual security (or portfolio of securities)
R_F is the risk-free rate of interest,
$E(R_M)$ is the expected rate of return on the market portfolio,
and
β_i is the market sensitivity index of the individual security (or portfolio of securities).

The market portfolio contains all risky securities in proportions reflecting the total equity values of the companies they represent. The β value of a security is a measure of the market risk of the security; a β value of unity implies that the market risk of the security is equal to that of the market portfolio, a β value greater than unity implies that if the market rises (falls) by one per cent the return on the security is expected to rise (fall) by more than one per cent, and a β value less than unity implies that the security is less sensitive to market fluctuations than the market portfolio. (A detailed discussion of the capital-asset pricing model appears in chapter 4.)

The capital-asset pricing model (1.2) shows the minimum rate of return acceptable on *all investments* for a given level of market risk; it represents the *opportunity cost of investment*. Substituting this minimum acceptable rate of return for the required rate of return (k) in the net present value formula (1.1) gives:

$$NPV = \sum_{t=1}^{n} \frac{x_t}{\{1 + R_F + \beta_i \, [E(R_M) - R_F]\}^t} - I \qquad (1.3)$$

In order to calculate the net present value of project i it is necessary to substitute its market risk value, β_i, into equation (1.3). The derivation of project β values is outlined in chapter 4.

In our example, we have a firm operating in a low risk industry where average risk projects have a required rate of return (k) of 13 per cent, below average risk projects have a required rate of return of 10 per cent and above average risk projects have a discount rate of 16 per cent. These rates are calculated from the capital-asset pricing model as follows. Suppose that the risk-free rate of interest is 9 per cent and the expected rate of return on the market portfolio is 16 per cent. The β value for the firm's securities is 0.57. Substituting into equation (1.2) gives

$$k = R_F + \beta_i \, [E(R_M) - R_F]$$

$$= 0.09 + 0.57 \times 0.07$$

$$= 13 \text{ per cent}$$

The method for obtaining the discount rates for below average and above average risk projects is described in chapter 4.

Practical Project and Product Decisions

The net present value rule offers a theoretically correct answer as to whether an investment opportunity should be accepted or rejected, but in practice many other techniques are employed in investment appraisal. Some alternatives to NPV are now considered.

Internal Rate of Return

The internal rate of return (IRR), or yield, on a project is the rate of return which equates the present value of anticipated net cash flows with the initial outlay. To calculate the internal rate of return it is necessary to solve the following formula for r:

$$0 = \sum_{t=1}^{n} \frac{x_t}{(1+r)^t} - I \tag{1.4}$$

where

x_t = the net cash flow arising at the end of year t

n = the life of the project in years

I = the initial cost of the investment

r is thus the rate of return which gives a zero NPV. A project is acceptable if its yield or internal rate of return is greater than the required rate of return on the project (k). This method of project appraisal usually gives the same accept/reject decision as NPV. Projects with positive NPVs will have values of r greater than k. In the case of the example used to illustrate the NPV rule, the internal rate of return on the project is 13 per cent, that is

$$0 = \frac{620}{1+0.13} + \frac{580}{(1+0.13)^2} - 1,000$$

Hence, in our previous example, if the project is in class A then it is acceptable as the yield of 13 per cent is greater than the required rate of return of 10 per cent. If the project is classified as B, it is just about acceptable, but it would be rejected as a class C project.

Managers are recommended to use the NPV method to assess capital projects because it is easier to handle than IRR. In addition, there are several problems associated with internal rate of return. For example, the size of a project needs to be borne in mind. Suppose there are two mutually exclusive investment opportunities, project (i) involving a £20,000 initial outlay and offering an internal rate of return of 30 per cent, and project (ii) involving a £10,000 initial outlay and offering an internal rate of return of 40 per cent. In this case project (i) may well have a higher NPV than project (ii). Thus the smaller project has a higher IRR and the larger project a higher NPV. If an investor has £20,000 to invest, then he can either select project (i), or alternatively invest £10,000 in project (ii) and £10,000 elsewhere. The NPVs of the two £20,000 investment schedules may then be compared and that with the higher NPV selected. NPV is a direct measure of wealth creation and therefore is the relevant criterion upon which project acceptance or rejection should be based.

A second problem associated with internal rate of return is that multiple solutions may exist to the IRR equation (1.4). Multiple solutions occur when the net cash flow changes sign, for example a negative initial outlay may be followed by a positive net cash flow at the end of the first year, a negative flow at the end of the second year, and a positive flow at the end of the third year. When several internal rates of return satisfy equation (1.4), it is difficult to use this method to assess projects, whereas the NPV rule presents no such problems.

Other complications occur with the IRR rule when it is necessary to make decisions between mutually exclusive projects with different lives or with different patterns of cash flows.

Profitability Index (Cost-Benefit Ratio)

The profitability index (PI), or cost-benefit ratio, on a project is the present value of the forecast net cash flows divided by the initial outlay. The only difference between the NPV and PI methods is that when using the NPV technique the initial outlay is deducted from the present value of anticipated cash flows, whereas with the PI approach the initial outlay is used as a divisor.

$$PI = \sum_{t=1}^{n} \frac{x_t}{(1+k)^t} \Big/ I \tag{1.5}$$

where x_t, k, n and I are as defined in equation (1.1). A project is acceptable if the profitability index exceeds unity. Clearly, if the $NPV > 0$, then the $PI > 1$.

If we return to our previous example where the NPV of the project was £40 as a class A project, £0 as a class B project, and − £30 as a class C project, we can see that the corresponding PI values are 1.04 for class A, 1.00 for class B, and 0.97 for class C.

The PI method gives exactly the same accept/reject indication as that offered by NPV. As with internal rate of return, however, complications occur with the PI rule when it is necessary to make decisions between mutually exclusive projects.

Payback Period

The payback period is the length of time required to recover the initial investment. It is generally assumed that the shorter the payback period, the better is the investment. In our example, the payback period is two years if the cash flows are received at the end of the first year and the end of the second year. By the end of the second year the sum of £1,200 is expected to be received, which more than recovers the initial outlay of £1,000. If the cash flows are receivable on a monthly basis, the payback period is approximately one and two-thirds years. Given the estimated payback period, it is necessary to decide whether the project is acceptable. Clearly, however, we do not have enough information to make a decision because we do not know whether or not the project is wealth-creating. The payback method involves the subjective establishment of an acceptable payback period (frequently cited as two and a half years), and ignores possible big returns beyond the payback point. Most managers, however, are eminently sensible people who in practice do not ignore big payoffs beyond the cut-off point. The main advantage with the payback period criterion is its simplicity. Payback period is used to test a manager's gut reaction to a project; it gives the manager a feel as to the length of time cash is at risk. However, it does not indicate whether a project is wealth-creating.

Discounted Payback Period

The discounted payback period differs from the payback period in that the payback period is calculated after discounting the cash flows, so in general it is longer than the payback period. In our example, the NPV for a class A project is £40 over two years on an initial outlay of £1,000. The discounted payback period is therefore just under two years. For a class B project the NPV is £0 over two years, so the discounted payback period is two years. For an above-average risk project (class C) payback is never achieved.

Discounted payback period represents a considerable improvement over payback period in that it allows for the riskiness of the project to be taken into account. As with payback period, we cannot decide on an appropriate given period for discounted payback which would show whether a project is wealth-creating, but once discounted payback is achieved any further discounted net cash flows would result in the creation of wealth. This method of investment appraisal does not give an indication of the magnitude of wealth-creation, however.

Return on Capital Employed

Return on capital employed (ROCE), or accounting rate of return, is widely used as an indicator of performance. It is generally assumed that the greater the ROCE, the better is the investment. ROCE is simply accounting profit measured as a percentage of capital employed, but this ratio ignores the size of cash flows, the timing of cash flows and risk.

In our example, the cash flows are £620 at the end of year 1 and £580 at the end of year 2. If the initial investment is written off on a straight-line basis, then depreciation would be £500 in year 1 and £500 in year 2. Accounting profit is therefore £120 in a year 1 and £80 in year 2. The capital employed of £1,000 falls to £500 at the end of year 1 and zero at the end of year 2. The average capital employed is therefore £750 in year 1 and £250 in year 2. Hence, the project offers a return on capital employed of 16 per cent in the first year and 32 per cent in the second year. We now have to decide if the project is acceptable, but we cannot make a decision on the basis of this information. ROCE does not indicate whether the project is wealth-creating. It is also clear that ROCE depends to some extent on the firm's depreciation policy.

Effect on Earnings per Share

Earnings per share (EPS) is calculated by dividing accounting profit by the number of shares in issue. It is generally assumed that the higher the EPS, the better. This ratio ignores the size and timing of cash flows, and risk, and thus is inappropriate. It is, however, another widely used indicator of performance, showing the amount of accounting profit a company has earned in one year for each share issued by the company.

In our example, suppose that the company issues 100 shares of £10 each to finance the project. In year 1 accounting profit is £120, and thus EPS amount to £1.20. In year 2 accounting profit is £80 and so EPS amount to £0.80. We now have to decide if the project is acceptable, but cannot do so on the basis of this information. EPS does not show whether the present value of the forecast net cash flows generated by the project exceeds the initial cost of the investment.

Using NPV in Practice: Example

Evets Snibbod plc is an all-equity financed company, undertaking high risk maintenance contracts for the UK oil industry. Its historic β coefficient has been estimated at 1.4. The directors are considering tendering for a maintenance contract worth about £1.2m gross for each of the next five years. The directors believe that this contract will be about twice as risky as the company's average project. The financial director estimates that the constant after tax risk-free rate of interest will be 9 per cent and that the overall after tax return on the market portfolio will be 16 per cent. Equipment costing £0.8m will be required immediately, to which the usual tax benefit (a 25 per cent writing-down allowance calculated on a reducing balance basis) applies. It is anticipated that the equipment can be sold at the end of the contract for £200,000. The incremental costs associated with the contract are £300,000 each year, excluding depreciation charges, and the company expects to pay corporation tax throughout the period at the rate of 52 per cent.

The calculations are shown in table 1.1. The required rate of return is given by substituting into equation (1.2):

$$k = R_F + \beta_i \, [\, E(R_M) - R_F \,]$$

$$= 0.09 + 2.8(0.16 - 0.09)$$

$$= 29 \text{ per cent}$$

The β value of 2.8 is double the company's average β, since the project is twice as risky as the company's average project. Applying the corresponding discount factors to the net cash flows gives a net present value for the project of £728,000. The contract is clearly acceptable since it offers a wealth-creating opportunity after allowing for risk.

Summary

The objective of the firm is to maximize the wealth of its shareholders, that is to maximize the current market value of the firm. An investment is wealth-creating if its net present value is positive, so *all projects that offer a positive net present value when discounted at the required rate of return for the investment should be accepted* in order to maximize the wealth of shareholders. Uncertainty surrounds the future returns from any capital investment, and *the discount rate must reflect the riskiness of the project.*

Although NPV is the theoretically correct approach to project appraisal, in practice simple models such as payback period are still popular, and have the merit of being easy to understand and calculate. One reason given for the use of payback analysis is that its strong emphasis on the early years of a project's life is appropriate to recent economic conditions under which medium and long-term forecasting have been extremely difficult and hazardous. The major problem with the NPV approach is the difficulty associated with forecasting cash flows. On balance, then, the *NPV rule is a practical and rational approach to project evaluation.* Notwithstanding its intrinsic faults, however, *payback analysis is the most popular technique used by managers.* (Support for payback has been given by Boardman et al. (1982) and Pike (1986).) Perhaps, then, *both techniques should be used*; NPV because it gives a guide to the amount of wealth being created, and payback because it tests a manager's instinctive reaction to cash at risk and because it is very easy to calculate. We leave managers to decide whether the calculated payback periods are acceptable.

Table 1.1 Calculation of net present value

Period	Incremental income (£000s)	Incremental expenditure (£000s)	Operational cash flow (£000s)	Taxation (£000s)	Tax allowance (£000s)	Residual value (£000s)	Balancing allowance (£000s)	Net cash flow (£000s)	Discount factor (29% interest)	Present value (£000s)
1	1,200	(300)	900					900	0.775	698
2	1,200	(300)	900	(468)	104			536	0.601	322
3	1,200	(300)	900	(468)	78			510	0.466	238
4	1,200	(300)	900	(468)	59			491	0.361	177
5	1,200	(300)	900	(468)	44	200		676	0.280	189
6				(468)			27	(441)	0.217	(96)

Total present value	1,528
Initial capital outlay	800
Net present value	728

Study Questions

1.1 A project is expected to generate the following cash flows:

Year	1	2	3
Expected cash flow	£4,000	£4,000	£6,000

An immediate investment in plant is required amounting to £9,000. Accounting policy stipulates that plant is written off on a straight-line basis. The required rate of return on the project is 20 per cent.

Calculate:

1 Net present value.
2 Cost-benefit ratio/profitability index.
3 Accounting profit: average capital employed.
4 Payback period.
5 Discounted payback period.
6 The EPS effect (assuming the project is financed by the issue of 9,000 ordinary £1 shares and that the firm has only one project).
7 Internal rate of return/yield.

1.2 The directors of Bradley plc are considering the acquisition of a new machine. The initial cost and setting-up expenses will amount to about £160,000. Its estimated life is about four years, and estimated annual accounting profit is as follows:

Year	1	2	3	4
Operational cash flow (£)	90,000	80,000	40,000	30,000
Depreciation (£)	80,000	30,000	30,000	20,000
Accounting profit (£)	10,000	50,000	10,000	10,000

At the end of its four-year life, the installation will yield only a few pounds in scrap value. The company classifies its projects as follows:

	Required rate of return
Low risk	10 per cent
Average risk	14 per cent
High risk	20 per cent

1 List some of the popular techniques for assessing capital projects.
2 Should the new machine be acquired? Ignore taxation.

1.3 The directors of Yorkshire Autopoints are considering the acquisition of an automatic car washing installation. The initial cost and setting up expenses will amount to about £140,000. Its estimated life is about seven years, and estimated annual accounting profit is as follows:

Year	1	2	3	4	5	6	7
Operational cash flow (£)	30,000	50,000	60,000	60,000	30,000	20,000	20,000
Depreciation (£)	20,000	20,000	20,000	20,000	20,000	20,000	20,000
Accounting profit (£)	10,000	30,000	40,000	40,000	10,000	—	—

At the end of its seven year life, the installation will yield only a few pounds in scrap value. The company classifies its projects as follows:

	Required rate of return
Low risk	20 per cent
Average risk	30 per cent
High risk	40 per cent

Car washing projects are estimated to be of average risk.

1 Should the car wash be installed?
2 List some of the popular errors made in assessing capital projects. Ignore taxation.

1.4 In December you are considering the replacement of a machine purchased two years ago for £70,000. Its replacement cost is £84,000. The old machine had an estimated life of six years and an estimated residual value of £14,000. A trade-in allowance of £25,000 has been offered against the new machine. The company's year end is 31 December and the machine could be purchased immediately and be operating in a few days. The firm depreciates plant on a straight-line basis. The new machine will produce incremental output generating sales income of £65,000 per annum for four years, after which time it is expected to realize about £15,000. Increased running and maintenance costs will be £36,000 per annum. The firm claims a 25 per cent annual allowance on plant and machinery. Assume that corporation tax is 30 per cent, and that tax is payable about one year after the company generates its cash flow. The after-tax required rate of return on plant replacement decisions is 10 per cent.

1 If the new machine is acquired, what will be the book profit or loss on disposal?
2 Should the new machine be acquired?
3 As Financial Director draft a report to your board outlining the theory of wealth creation, and comment on the methods firms use to evaluate investment proposals.

Further Reading

Brigham, Eugene F. *Financial Management: Theory and Practice*. New York: Dryden Press, 1985, chapters 8–10.
Franks, Julian R., Broyles, John E. and Carleton, Willard T. *Corporate Finance: Concepts and Applications*. Boston, Mass.: Kent Publishing, 1985, chapters 4–7.

2
Merger Decisions

The Theory of Merger Decisions

When companies formally combine into new corporate organizations this is termed a merger or acquisition. Mergers can be classified as horizontal, vertical or conglomerate. A *horizontal* merger occurs between two firms with similar business interests. A *vertical* merger occurs when a firm buys forwards towards the final consumer or backwards towards the source of raw materials. A *conglomerate* merger occurs between two firms with unrelated business interests.

The *merger* (or *acquisition) decision* is an *investment decision* and therefore the usual principles of capital investment decisions apply; hence the merger decision may be evaluated in terms of the *net present value* (NPV) rule. The objective of the firm is to maximize the wealth of its owners, that is the firm's shareholders. The firm should therefore go ahead with the merger if it makes a net contribution to shareholder wealth.

The principle of *value additivity* indicates that present values can be added, so in general if two firms A and B combine to form a new firm AB, the present value of the combined firm is simply the sum of the present values of the constituent parts:

$$V_{AB} = V_A + V_B \tag{2.1}$$

where V_{AB} is the value of the combined enterprise
V_A is the value of the acquiring firm
V_B is the value of the target company.

The present value of the sum of two cash flows is equal to the sum of the present values of the individual cash flows. Hence, in general, shareholder wealth is not increased by merging two companies; the particular merger policy adopted by a firm is irrelevant to the current wealth of shareholders.

18

It is *possible*, however, for a merger to give rise to a positive NPV. Wealth can be created by combining two companies if the *total* cash flow increases as a result. Mergers make *economic sense* when the combined enterprise has a higher market value than the sum of the market values of the two independent enterprises. The economic gain is the present value of the anticipated cash benefit resulting from the merger (*X*):

$$V_{AB} = V_A + V_B + X \tag{2.2}$$

Where the *X* factor is positive, there is economic justification for the merger, since wealth is created by bringing the two companies together.

Mergers can result in *genuine economic benefits* for various reasons. *Economies of scale* may arise; here the average unit cost of production decreases as production increases. These economies can result from spreading fixed costs over a larger volume of production, from sharing one research and development team, from sharing one marketing department, and so on. Clearly, economies of scale are an obvious reason for horizontal mergers. *Economies of vertical integration* may result when vertical mergers occur, since co-ordination and administration are often greatly simplified. A merger may also result in the acquired company receiving the benefit of *superior managerial skills*, whereby more cash flow is generated from the company's existing business. It may even be that the new management might *strip the company of its assets* when the market value of the acquired company is less than the disposal value of its investments. A further possible reason for mergers is to exploit the acquired company's *unused debt capacity*, when the managers of the acquired firm have failed to take advantage of the tax savings on borrowings. However, Franks and Pringle (1982) point out that in practice unused debt capacity provides little incentive for merger activity. Mergers also make economic sense when *synergy* is present, that is when firms have *complementary resources* which result in the two firms being worth more combined than apart; it may be more cost-effective for firms to merge than acquire a missing ingredient (for example, a well-developed sales organization) by acting alone. Also if a firm is exploiting a new product it may need to increase its production facilities, say, in a very short time which may best be achieved by merging. Similarly, it may be worthwhile to acquire another company's established brand name.

The division of any economic gains resulting from the merger of two companies – the *X* factor – between the two companies is crucial to the attractiveness of the merger to each company. For example, even when there are potential gains, if the entire *X* factor were to go to the shareholders in the target company, then there would be no incentive for the acquiring firm to go ahead with the merger. The NPV of a merger to a firm is given by the difference between shareholders' wealth if the merger goes ahead and shareholders' wealth if it does not proceed. Studies by Newbould (1970) and Franks et al. (1977) suggest that the major portion of the net merger benefit accrues to the shareholders in the acquired company.

In order to decide whether a merger should go ahead managers should:

1 Forecast the post-merger cash flows and required rates of return.
2 Use net present value to estimate the value of the enterprise after the merger.
3 Not proceed with the merger if the X factor is negative.
4 Split the X factor between the shareholders of the two companies if it is positive, and negotiate the merger.

Now when the two companies are quoted companies, the efficient market hypothesis suggests that share prices reflect all information. If the share prices of the two companies do *not* reflect the possibility of merger, the intrinsic values of the companies are given by their market values. If the share prices *do* reflect an anticipated merger, the companies should be valued independently of existing market values; the intrinsic values of the companies should be calculated without regard to the anticipated merger. The computation of the X factor is thus based on intrinsic values.

Practical Merger Decisions

Invalid Reasons for Mergers

In practice, many mergers are justified in terms that do *not* make *economic sense*. The reasons for such mergers are invalid as the mergers do not make a net contribution to shareholder wealth.

Diversification   A common reason for merger activity is diversification, but such conglomerate mergers are pointless from the shareholder's point of view. Investors can and do achieve diversification by spreading their holdings across a number of companies and so do not require assistance from corporate managers. Hence – as the value additivity concept implies – diversification does not add to a firm's value. Mergers which do not result in a positive X factor should not go ahead.

However, survival of the company is a top managerial priority, and it should be possible to *reduce the probability of liquidation* by corporate diversification. Individual companies can face financial distress not only because of movements in the economy as a whole, but also because of factors specific to the individual company, and hence the temptation for managers to diversify is understandable. Corporate diversification does achieve employment diversification for management and employees.

Managers also often claim that they can purchase companies at less than their intrinsic values, but in an efficient capital market there are no bargains. In fact, it is commonplace for the market value of a target company to increase when a takeover bid is made for its shares. The benefits of any increase in the value of the company on the announcement of a formal offer generally accrue to existing shareholders in the target company. If there is no positive X factor, as in the case of merger for pure diversification, the market value of the acquisitive company must suffer an offsetting fall, as shareholders realise that too high a price is being offered for the target company.

Earnings per share   A popular objective of industrial organizations is to increase earnings per share (EPS), and many mergers have been justified in terms of the effect on EPS. However, the measurement of corporate performance on the basis of EPS is unsatisfactory. The concept of earnings per share ignores cash flow and risk. It is an historic number based on accounting profit, which is subject to accounting policies on stock valuation, asset depreciation, bad debts, profit on long-term contracts, provisions for accrued income and expenditure, and so on. Now the price–earnings (P/E) ratio is equal to the share price divided by earnings per share, and is often regarded in essence as a payback period. However, accounting profit is usually taken from last year's profit and loss account, whereas share prices reflect anticipated cash flows, taking into account risk. Thus P/E ratios cannot be used as a basis for decision making. The numerator is the share price which reflects anticipated cash flows, whereas the denominator is last year's earnings per share. If the company broke even last year, then the price–earnings ratio is infinite. If the company made a loss last year, then the price–earnings ratio is negative. It does not make economic sense to use EPS or the P/E ratio as a basis for merger evaluation, but for many years mergers have been justified on the basis of such effects.

Consider the following example. Firm A is considering the acquisition of firm B. It is assumed that there are no merger benefits, that is the X factor is zero. A intends to acquire B by offering shares for shares; two shares in A will be given for five shares in B. Table 2.1 gives figures for firms A and B; the corresponding figures for the combined enterprise A + B are calculated as follows. Now the total market value of A + B is £20,000,000 since the X factor is zero. Total historic earnings are £700,000 for the merged firm, and there are now 200,000 A shares priced at £100. Earnings per share are £3.50 and thus the price–earnings ratio becomes 28.57. The figures for the merged firm are shown in table 2.2. If decisions are made on the basis of increasing earnings per share, this is an extremely profitable merger, since EPS have increased by 75 per cent for the combined company compared with each of the constituent companies. However, this is a *financial illusion*.

Table 2.1 Individual firm figures: zero X factor

	Firm A	Firm B
EPS (£)	2	2
PPS (£)	100	40
P/E ratio	50	20
Number of shares	100,000	250,000
Total earnings (historic) (£)	200,000	500,000
Total market value (£)	10,000,000	10,000,000

Table 2.2 Merged firm figures: zero X factor

	Firm A	Firm B	Firm A + B
EPS (£)	2	2	3.50
PPS (£)	100	40	100
P/E ratio	50	20	28.57
Number of shares	100,000	250,000	200,000
Total earnings (historic) (£)	200,000	500,000	700,000
Total market value (£)	10,000,000	10,000,000	20,000,000

Wealth has not been created, because the market value of A + B is equal to the sum of the market value of A and the market value of B. Furthermore, the wealth of each shareholder remains unchanged.

Consider a further example. Firm A is considering the acquisition of firm B, but in this case it is estimated that the X factor is £12,000. Initially, A offers B shares in A at 14 times B's historic earnings. Alternatively, a *reverse takeover* could be arranged whereby B offers A shares in B at 22 times A's historic earnings. Table 2.3 gives figures for firms A and B; the corresponding figures for the combined enterprises A + B and B + A are calculated as follows: now, if A acquires B, then the X factor is split on the basis of £4,000 for A shareholders and £8,000 for B shareholders. After

Table 2.3 Individual firm figures: positive X factor

	Firm A	Firm B
EPS (£)	2	2
PPS (£)	40	20
P/E ratio	20	10
Number of shares	1,000	1,000
Total earnings (historic) (£)	2,000	2,000
Total market value (£)	40,000	20,000

the merger the value of the combined firm to the original shareholders in A will be £44,000 and the price per share £44. The shareholders in B will receive shares in the new company, A + B, valued at £28,000. It will therefore be necessary to issue 636 shares at £44 per share. Clearly, the merger makes economic sense since the shareholders in both firms A and B are better off after the merger. Furthermore, earnings per share increase by 22 per cent for both companies to £2.44. If the reverse takeover is organized, then the total market value of B + A will also be £72,000. The split of the X factor remains exactly as before. Company A shareholders will receive £4,000, and company B shareholders will receive £8,000. After the merger the 1,000 shares owned by the B shareholders will be worth £28 each. At £28 it will be necessary to issue 1,571 shares to the shareholders in firm A. As a consequence, earnings per share in the combined enterprise fall to £1.56, a decrease of 22 per cent. The figures for the merged firms are shown in table 2.4.

If economic decisions are made on the basis of the EPS effect, then the merger B + A appears not to make economic sense, but this is obviously wrong. Shareholders in firms A and B are wealthier. The fact that earnings per share have fallen is of no consequence. If we did base our decisions on the EPS effect, then we would have to argue that A + B is a good idea, whereas B + A is a bad idea, and clearly such an argument is untenable.

The Method and Extent of Acquisition

An offer for the shares of the target company may come in the form of cash, or in the form of shares or other securities of the acquiring company. Generally gains arising on disposals for cash attract capital gains tax, whereas gains arising on shares exchanged for shares are not subject to capital gains tax until the shares exchanged are eventually sold for cash, so an offer in the form of shares in the acquiring company is likely to be more attractive to the shareholders in the target company if they have made capital gains, although in practice shareholders generally prefer the certainty of a cash offer.

Table 2.4 Merged firm figures: positive X factor

	Firm A	Firm B	Firm A + B	Firm B + A
EPS (£)	2	2	2.44	1.56
PPS (£)	40	20	44	28
P/E ratio	20	10	18	18
Number of shares	1,000	1,000	1,636	2,571
Total earnings (historic) (£)	2,000	2,000	4,000	4,000
Total market value (£)	40,000	20,000	72,000	72,000

An acquiring company may wish to completely take over a target company by making an offer for the shares of that company. In this case ownership of the shares in the target company changes hands, but the company's assets and liabilities remain unchanged. There are some circumstances in which the acquiring company may not wish to acquire control of all the assets in the target company, or accept responsibility for all its liabilities. For example, the target company may face considerable legal problems, its stock valuation may be suspect, bad debts may be understated, or the actual amount of creditors may be uncertain. The directors of the acquiring company may decide to make an offer for some of the assets of the target company, rather than purchase shares in the company. It may be considered desirable to purchase the target company's brand names and fixed assets, but allow the existing shareholders to collect cash from debtors, dispose of certain items of stock, settle the creditors and outstanding taxation liabilities, and wind up the company.

Merger Tactics

Merger negotiations and disputes can be very complex, so before entering merger negotiations managers should have a very clear plan. They should acquire an analysis of existing shareholders, set a price limit, decide on a package, make enquiries, enter into talks, and then make an offer. If the acquisition is opposed, then managers must decide whether to continue or withdraw. Speed is important, and an increased offer must only be made on the basis of new information. Increasing the offer without new information will be interpreted as an indication that an even better offer will follow.

If directors wish to protect themselves against takeover bids, then they should seek to maintain good shareholder relations. This can be achieved by maximizing the market value of the company by developing a successful investment schedule. Directors should also monitor share price movements, keep files on potential aggressors, consider long-term contracts with the company for themselves and suppliers, be prepared to appeal to government agencies, consider sale and lease back arrangements to discourage asset strippers, and avoid spare debt capacity.

During the period of an offer, directors should defend against the takeover by causing delays. They should find reasons for additional talking, emphasize the weaknesses of the bidder, set a non-rejectable share-price, justify rejection of the existing offer, attack the bidder's record, and continue to provide new information relating to future cash flows, dividends and investment opportunities. This could provide reason for the attacker to increase the offer price, as well as encourage existing shareholders to expect an increased offer.

Summary

The merger decision should be taken on the basis of *potential economic benefits*. As it is an investment decision it may be evaluated in terms of the NPV rule. An alternative strategy, such as direct investment in real assets, may well yield greater economic benefits, and so *alternatives to mergers* should be considered.

Mergers make economic sense if the two firms are worth more together than apart, but empirical evidence suggests that *target firms* generally *benefit substantially* whereas *acquiring firms* tend to make at most a *small gain* but more often just *break even* or make a *loss*. Hence most mergers do *not* make a net contribution to the wealth of shareholders in the acquiring company, and thus must occur to satisfy *other managerial objectives*. There have been four periods of merger waves this century – the early 1900s (mainly horizontal mergers), the 1920s (mainly vertical mergers), the 1960s (mainly conglomerate mergers), and the 1980s (mainly strategic or defensive mergers, that is where the objective is to acquire key personnel and technology to avoid takeover by a rival company). These merger cycles have all taken place during periods of buoyant stock market prices, so it appears that during bull markets the good prospects for existing shareholders and capital gains for shareholders in target companies enable managers to put together acceptable merger packages. Managers pursue objectives such as increasing sales, increasing the quantity of the firm's assets, increasing diversification, and avoiding acquisition, which may best be served by mergers.

Study Questions

2.1 Ray is chief executive of the Keighley Emporium Ltd. He believes in growth in earnings per share as the best corporate objective. Indeed, since joining the Emporium as a lad, he has seen the firm expand its sales, profit and earnings per share, largely by the acquisition of other stores in the Keighley area, financed almost always by cash generated from successful trading at the Emporium. Ray is about to pull off the greatest coup of his career by taking over Haworth Carding Ltd. Use of only one computer centre, head office, credit control and buying department will reduce the joint corporate costs by a considerable amount which should result in an immediate benefit of about £10m to the market value of the combined enterprise.

	Keighley	Haworth
Earnings per share (£)	1	1
Price per share (£)	20	10
P/E ratio	20	10
Number of shares	4,000,000	4,000,000
Historic earnings (£m)	4	4
Total market value (£m)	80	40

Ray's Financial Director suggests that Keighley could make Haworth an offer for shares at 11 times Haworth's historic earnings. Alternatively, a reverse takeover could be considered whereby Haworth could offer to buy Keighley shares at 21.5 times Keighley's historic earnings. Ray is anxious to examine the EPS effect.

1 Present data and a report on both proposals.
2 When do mergers make economic sense?
3 Why do most mergers fail?

2.2 Ruth is chief executive of the Thornton Dyers Ltd. She believes in growth in earnings per share as the best corporate objective. She has seen the firm expand its sales, profit and earnings per share, largely by the acquisition of other stores in the surrounding area, financed almost always by cash generated from successful trading. Ruth is about to pull off the greatest coup of her career by taking over Manningham Dyers Ltd. Use of only one computer centre, head office, credit control and buying department will reduce the joint corporate fixed costs by a considerable amount which should result in an immediate benefit of about £8m to the market value of the combined enterprise.

	Thornton	Manningham
Earnings per share (£)	2	1
Price per share (£)	10	10
P/E ratio	5	10
Number of shares	2,000,000	1,000,000
Historic earnings (£m)	4	1
Total market value (£m)	20	10

Ruth suggests that Thornton could make Manningham an offer for shares at 12 times Manningham's historic earnings. Alternatively, a reverse takeover could be considered whereby Manningham could offer to buy Thornton shares at 6.5 times Thornton's historic earnings. Ruth is anxious to examine the EPS effect.

1 Present data and a report on both proposals.
2 When do mergers make economic sense?
3 Why do most mergers fail?

2.3 Knotty Knowsley (NN) is considering a merger with High Huyton (II). Both companies pursue the objective of maximizing earnings per share, and both companies have expanded their sales, profits, and earnings per share to some extent by the acquisition of other companies in the Merseyside area. Many acquisitions have been financed by cash. Directors of NN estimate that the merger will add £40m to the value of the combined enterprise. The following data are available.

	NN	II
Earnings per share (£)	4	10
Price per share (£)	40	30
P/E ratio	10	3
Number of shares	5,000,000	1,000,000
Historic earnings (£m)	20	10
Total market value (£m)	200	30

The NN directors are considering making an offer for II at five times II's historic earnings. Alternatively, they could arrange a reverse takeover whereby II could make an offer for NN at 11 times NN's historic earnings. Both offers would be for shares, not cash.

As Financial Director draft a report to your board outlining the problems and prospects.

Further Reading

Franks, Julian R., Broyles, John E. and Carleton, Willard, T. *Corporate Finance: Concepts and Applications*. Boston, Mass.: Kent Publishing, 1985, chapter 14.
Schall, Lawrence D. and Haley, Charles W. *Introduction to Financial Management*. New York: McGraw-Hill, 1986, chapter 23.

3
Working Capital Management

The Theory of Working Capital Management

The working capital problem is an investment problem which can be solved within the framework of the net present value calculation.

$$\text{NPV} = \sum_{t=1}^{n} \frac{1}{(1+k)^t}(R-W-I)_t \text{ where,}$$

R = operational receipts from customers,
W = wages and other operational expenses,
I = new investment in working capital or fixed assets,
k = the required rate of return.

This is exactly the same NPV formula as introduced in chapter 1. Net operational cash flows are discounted at a rate which reflects the risk of the project. The present value of the project is compared with its cost or initial outlay. Projects with positive net present values are acceptable because they are wealth-creating opportunities. From the above equation we can see that if we increase operational cash flows $(R-W)$, then we increase net present value. If we reduce the level of investment (I) for any given set of operational cash flows, then we increase net present value. An increase in working capital penalises a project's net present value, and can be regarded as either an increase in W or an increase in I.

Working capital management is often completely ignored in the theory of financial management. Investment decisions are based on NPV calculations, and therefore the investment in working capital is subsumed into the cash flow forecasts of individual projects. This approach is inadequate since two projects with positive net present values may have similar or very different

28

cash flows. Where the cash flow profiles are similar, the firm will experience occasional cash surpluses which can be invested. The firm will also experience occasional cash deficits which must be financed. Even when firms do base all their decisions on net present value calculations, additional investment and financing decisions will therefore have to be made as the firm experiences cash surpluses and cash deficits.

When working capital management is not completely ignored, it is sometimes suggested that working capital decisions can be made on the same basis as any other investment decision.

Question   Your company is considering an increased investment in working capital of £70,000 which is expected to increase net operational cash flows from incremental sales of £10,000 per annum in perpetuity. The required rate of return on the investment is 10 per cent. Is the increased investment in working capital a wealth-creating opportunity?

Answer   The present value of the investment is $\dfrac{£10,000}{0.1} = £100,000$, or £10,000(9.999) = £100,000.

Since the cost or initial outlay is £70,000 and the project has a positive present value of £100,000, then the net present value is £30,000, and the increase in working capital is worthwhile. We ignore the residual value of the working capital because it is such a long way into the future that it has a zero present value. Clearly, if reduction in working capital will take place in two or three year's time, then we shall need to discount the expected value and take it into account in the NPV calculation.

Project Cash Flow Profiles

Figure 3.1 presents cash flow profiles on investments 1 and 2, and A and B. Cash balances are measured on the vertical axis, and time is measured along the horizontal axis. Projects 1 and 2 offer negative cash flows in the early stages, then positive cash flows, followed by negative cash flows. If we add investments 1 and 2 together, then we have a financing need in the early and later stages, and an opportunity to invest surplus funds in the intervening period. Projects A and B have positive cash flows in the early stages, cash deficits in the middle stages, followed by further cash surpluses. If projects A and B are the only two projects taken on by a firm, then the firm will have the opportunity to invest surplus funds in the early and late stages, and a need to raise finance during the intervening period. Clearly, even if all our projects have positive net present values then we cannot ignore cash surpluses and cash deficits as they arise. If all four projects are accepted by the same firm then the cash deficits and surpluses will to a great extent

Project cash flow profiles

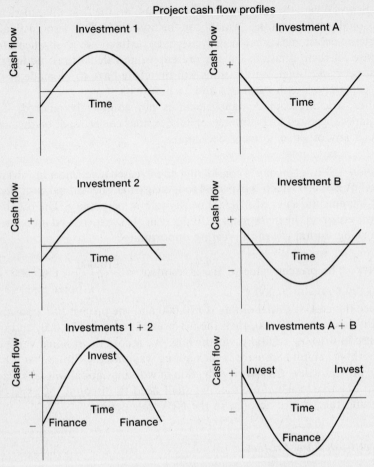

Figure 3.1 How working capital investment and financing decisions arise

cancel each other out, and fewer opportunities will arise to invest surpluses and fewer needs will arise to finance the deficits.

Practical Working Capital Management

In practice, if we ask any financial manager to list his or her biggest headaches, then working capital management is usually near the top of the list. Also, in practice, managers use ratio analysis to control working capital, rather than net present value calculations. The effect is similar. For any level of cash flows we require the minimum investment to maximize net present value. Several rules of thumb have been developed by managers to achieve the same effect. For example, for any level of sales (rather than operational cash flow) managers are encouraged to carry the minimum level of raw materials, work in progress, and finished goods (investment outlay). For any level of sales (rather than operational cash flow) managers are encouraged to carry the minimum level of debtors (investment outlay). Managers are also encouraged to use the maximum amount of interest-free and discount-free credit from suppliers (delaying the investment outlay). Surplus cash flows should be invested (to increase total cash flow) and cash deficits must be financed (to avoid the costs of financial distress). Business ratios are therefore used as rules of thumb to help managers make money satisfying consumer wants thereby increasing the return on capital employed (a surrogate for maximization of shareholder wealth). The net present value approach and the use of financial ratios should give the same indicators to managers to help manage resources efficiently with a view to creating wealth. Increases in working capital must be justified in terms of increasing net operational cash flows from additional sales. We prefer a minimum level of investment for any given set of cash flows. We prefer to maximize the level of sales for any given level of working capital, and minimize the level of investment in working capital for any given level of sales. A reduced investment in stock for any level of net operational cash flows should increase net present value. A reduced investment in debtors for any level of net operational cash flows should increase net present value. An increase in trade creditors (delaying cash payments) should also result in an increase in net present value for a given set of operational cash flows.

The Financing of a Business

Figure 3.2 shows the flow of cash through a business. All firms use cash. Cash is used to buy materials and pay wages, salaries, administrative, selling and distribution expenses. Materials, labour and other operational expenditures create work in progress which eventually is turned into finished goods which are sold to customers. Accountants usually refer to customers as debtors because they owe the firm cash. Eventually our debtors pay us in cash and this completes the working capital cycle. Cash flows into finished goods, finished goods are sold to our customers, then our customers pay us in cash. We do not pay all our expenses in cash but in fact receive credit from our suppliers. Firms do not only push cash into the working capital cycle, but cash is also used to acquire the fixed or permanent assets. These assets are also acquired to generate cash by satisfying consumer wants, but they are charged in the profit and loss account as an expense over their estimated useful lives. The annual expense is called depreciation. This is an important and unusual business expense in that it is a non-cash expense. We spend the cash as we acquire assets, but we then write them off as a

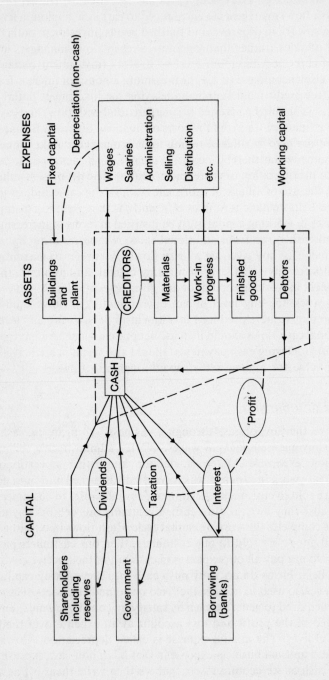

Figure 3.2 The financing of a business

business expense over their estimated useful lives. If our invoiced sales are greater than the cost of sales including depreciation, then the firm makes a profit. Accounting profit is therefore based on invoices, not cash. The profit at the bottom of the profit and loss account is invoiced sales less the invoiced cost of sales less estimated depreciation. Clearly, profit flow and cash flow are very different. The purchase of fixed assets reduces cash but does not affect profit until we charge depreciation. If we push cash into stock, this does affect cash but has no effect on profit until the stock is sold. If we delay collection of cash from our customers, then this does affect cash but has no effect on profit since the sales figure in the profit and loss account is based on invoices. Depreciation charges reduce the profit figure in the profit and loss account but have no effect on the cash balance. (It is a popular economic myth that depreciation is a source of funds).

Successful trading is not the only source of cash for our business. Banks lend us funds, but they require payment of interest. Interest is allowed as a charge against profit before we are charged corporation tax. Sometimes the government will provide funds for industry. Finally, after payment of taxation and interest we may pay a dividend to our shareholders. If we still have a positive number for profit after deducting interest, taxation, and dividends, then that positive number is added to the shareholders' funds and is usually described as 'reserves'. It may also be described as balance on profit and loss account, retained earnings, ploughed-back profits etc. 'Reserves' is a most misunderstood word in finance because there is no money in a financial reserve. There is definitely petrol in a reserve petrol tank, but there is definitely no money in a financial reserve. This number is simply a note that over the years the company has traded successfully, and that the dividends paid in cash are less than the reported earnings. We can now see several other reasons why profit flow and cash flow are different. If the shareholders put new cash into the business, this has no effect on profit but does increase the cash balance. If we borrow funds from the bank, this increases the cash balance but has no effect on profit. Figure 3.2 shows how cash flows through a business. We shall return at a later stage to the differences between profit flow and cash flow.

The Working Capital Cycle

We usually define working capital as stock, debtors and cash. These are the firm's current assets. Net working capital is usually defined as current assets less current liabilities. The working capital cycle appears again in figure 3.3. Cash is pushed into stock, stock is sold to our customers, then finally our debtors pay us in cash. This brief description of the working capital cycle appears in Section A, whereas Section B includes creditors, raw materials, and work in progress. Again, we do not pay for all our

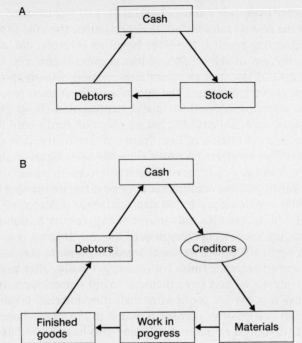

Figure 3.3 The working capital cycle

supplies immediately, but do in fact take advantage of trade credit. Management of trade creditors will be discussed later. Materials are processed to become work in progress, which finally is converted into finished goods. Finished goods are sold to our customers, who we hope eventually pay us in cash. This same cash then enters the working capital cycle to create further finished goods, new debtors, and additional cash receipts.

There is considerable risk to the company if working capital is mismanaged.

1 Too little trade credit taken will result in cash deficits.
2 High levels of raw material stock will result in high levels of creditors and then possibly cash deficits.
3 If production levels are higher than required then this will result in high work in progress figures needing finance from creditors or some other source.
4 If we carry too great a quantity or variety of finished goods, then these too must be financed.
5 If we slow down the collection of cash from our customers, then this too can result in cash shortages.

It may well be the case that we are trading very profitably, but a cash crisis can arise through the mismanagement of working capital. We emphasize that the level of profit may be unaffected. It is possible to cause the company financial distress by mismanagement of working capital, even though profit levels are perfectly adequate. Mismanagement of working capital may lead to the raising of expensive loans, higher interest payments, greater restrictive covenants applied by banks, and other costs of financial distress usually associated with excess gearing.

Generating Profit Flows and Cash Flows

The firm to which the information in tables 3.1 and 3.2 relates is concerned that it does not achieve a profit. A local management consultant is engaged to manage the company for Period 2. Remuneration is agreed at 50 per cent of the profits (if any). In Period 2 the consultant increases production to capacity but only manages to sell the same quantity as in Period 1. The firm values stock on a proportion of total cost basis. How much does the consultant earn? How is the firm affected by the fixing of its overdraft facility at £100,000? In the 2(a) case, assume that the firm values stock at variable cost only. What is the effect on profit flow and cash flow?

Table 3.1   Generating profit flows and cash flows (1)

	Period	1
(1)	Capacity (units)	300,000
(2)	Production (units)	100,000
(3)	Sales @ £1 per unit	100,000
(4)	Add closing stock (line 12)	—
(5)		100,000
(6)	Variable cost @ £0.70 per unit	70,000
(7)	Contribution	30,000
(8)	Fixed costs	45,000
(9)	Profit (Loss)	(15,000)
(10)	Closing stock – variable cost	—
(11)	— fixed cost	—
(12)	Stock at 'cost'	—
	Cash:	
(13)	Income	100,000
(14)	Expenditure	115,000
(15)	Cash (deficit)	(15,000)

Table 3.2 Generating profit flows and cash flows (2)

	Period	1	2	2(a)
(1)	Capacity (units)	300,000	300,000	300,000
(2)	Production (units)	100,000	300,000	300,000
(3)	Sales @ £1 per unit	100,000	100,000	100,000
(4)	Add closing stock (line 12)	—	170,000	140,000
(5)		100,000	270,000	240,000
(6)	Variable cost @ £0.70 per unit	70,000	210,000	210,000
(7)	Contribution	30,000	60,000	70,000
(8)	Fixed costs	45,000	45,000	45,000
(9)	Profit (loss)	(15,000)	15,000	(15,000)
(10)	Closing stock – variable cost	—	140,000	140,000
(11)	– fixed cost	—	30,000	
(12)	Stock at 'cost'	—	170,000	
	Cash:			
(13)	Income	100,000	100,000	100,000
(14)	Expenditure	115,000	255,000	255,000
(15)	Cash (deficit)	(15,000)	(155,000)	(155,000)

In Period 2, our ambitious consultant increases production to capacity, but unfortunately he is let down by the sales forces, and the same number of units are sold in Period 2 as in Period 1. The sales income is therefore £100,000, and we must now look to lines 10, 11 and 12, to value the closing stock as a proportion of total costs. Since the variable costs are 70 pence per unit, then the cost of 200,000 units in stock is £140,000. Our fixed costs are £45,000 for 300,000 units. For 200,000 units, the fixed costs are therefore £30,000, giving a stock at 'cost' of £170,000. At line 5, our total output is £270,000 being sales and stock produced at cost. If we deduct the variable costs for 300,000 units at 70 pence, i.e. £210,000, then we arrive at a contribution of £60,000 towards fixed costs and profit. After deducting the fixed costs of £45,000, we are left with a profit of £15,000.

Turning now to the cash, we have the same income from customers as in Period 1, amounting to £100,000. Our total expenditure has increased dramatically. The variable costs of £210,000 added to the fixed costs of £45,000 gives a total of £255,000, leaving us with a cash deficit of £155,000 for Period 2. Clearly, profit flow and cash flow are very different. The profit is positive £15,000, the cash flow negative £155,000. What has happened to the difference of £170,000? Our consultant has pushed £140,000 into variable costs included in the cost of stock. Furthermore, our consultant has included £30,000 of the fixed costs in the stock valuation. This accounts for the difference in profit flow and cash flow of £170,000.

It appears that we must also investigate the difference between the profit in Period 1 and the profit in Period 2. In both periods we have produced and sold 100,000 units. However, the consultant has managed to turn a £15,000 loss into a £15,000 profit. This has been achieved by charging £30,000 of the fixed costs, not in the profit and loss account as an expense, but as an investment in an asset, i.e. stock at 'cost'. Stock valuation is clearly a major headache in the problem of measuring profit, and in the 2(a) case, we now value stock at only variable cost. The question is: what happens to profit and cash flow if we change the basis of stock valuation?

In the 2(a) case, the consultant still increases production to capacity, and sells 100,000 units at £1 per unit. We now have a different figure for stock valuation at £140,000 since the fixed costs are now ignored. Our total output is now measured at £240,000, and after deducting the variable costs we arrive at a contribution towards fixed costs and profit of £30,000. After deducting the fixed costs of £45,000, we have a trading loss of £15,000. An examination of the cash flow shows the same cash income at £100,000, and the same cash expenditure of £255,000. The cash deficit is unchanged at £155,000, and our conclusion must be that the basis of stock valuation will affect the level of profit, but the basis of stock valuation does not affect cash flow. There are several other problems in profit measurement which result in different reported profits, but we must emphasize that the accounting treatment of such items does not affect cash flow. To these we now turn our attention.

As a final note on the consultancy experience we should ask the question: does the consultant get paid for his or her contribution? The company has exceeded its overdraft facility and could even be forced into liquidation. An attempt has been made to expand the company's sales very quickly. This is known as 'overtrading'. When a company tries to expand rapidly a great deal of cash tends to be pushed into stock. If the goods are sold then there is a greatly increased investment in debtors (stock at selling prices). Many companies experience financial distress when they overtrade. We suggest that the bank should refuse to cash the consultant's £7,500 cheque.

Profit Flow is an Opinion, Cash Flow is a Fact

The major headaches in the measurement of accounting profit are listed below. Readers are asked to take special note that the accounting treatment of such items has no effect on cash flow.

Problem	Effect on profit flow	Effect on cash flow
Stock valuation	yes	no
Depreciation	yes	no
Inflation	yes	no
Research and development	yes	no
After-sales services	yes	no
Contingent liabilities (possible bad news)	yes	no
Hire purchase transactions	yes	no
Exceptional items (Rationalization)	yes	no

The higher the level of stock valuation, the greater will be the accounting profit. The greater the depreciation charge, the lower will be the level of accounting profit. There are several suggested methods for accounting for inflation which result in a variety of profit figures. Research and development may be written off over one year, or perhaps five or even ten years. The greater the charge in this year's profit and loss account, the lower will be the accounting profit. High levels of expected after-sales service will result in lower accounting profit. The charging of contingent liabilities (which depend on some future event) will reduce the level of accounting profit. There are various suggested methods for treating hire purchase and instalment credit transactions which result in different profit figures. Finally, many firms have major expenses described as 'rationalization', and where these are not charged in the profit and loss account, then the level of reported accounting profit is increased. One final very important note, is that the level of cash flow remains exactly the same, since cash flow is a fact, whereas profit is only an opinion.

Profit Does Not Mean More Money in the Bank: Example

Mac starts business with £50. During his first period of trading he sells 10 Dobbos at £10 each. They cost £5 each. Consider the following situations.

Period	Buy	Sell	Profit flow (£)	Cash flow (£)	Difference
1	10 (Cash)	10 (Cash)	50	+ 50	—
2	10 (Cash)	10 (Credit)	50	− 50	Debtors £100
3	10 (Credit)	10 (Cash)	50	+ 100	Creditors £50
4	12 (Cash)	10 (Cash)	50	+ 40	Stock £10

For each profit there are a variety of possible cash flows.

Profit = Sales − Total Costs = 100 − 50 = 50

Profit = Increase in Net Assets as follows:

	1	2	3	4
Assets at end of period: Cash	100	—	150	90
Debtors	—	100	—	—
Stock	—	—	—	10
	100	100	150	100
Less: creditors	—	—	50	—
Net assets	100	100	100	100
Assets at start of period: Cash	50	50	50	50
Profit	50	50	50	50

The management of working capital can have a major effect on cash flow, although there may be no effect on the level of accounting profit. Mac has a level of invoiced sales at £100, his cost of sales being £50. His accounting profit is therefore £50. He may sell for cash, he may sell for credit, he may buy for cash, he may buy on credit, he may or may not carry stocks. His management of working capital does have an effect on cash flow, but his profit remains at £50.

Some Reasons why Profit and Cash are Different

We can now summarize our conclusions from figure 3.1 which illustrates the flow of cash through the business.

1 Depreciation is charged in the profit and loss account as an expense but does not affect the cash balance.
2 Stock is created by cash payments for material, labour etc. Stock is not charged as an expense in the profit and loss account until it is sold.
3 Debtors and Creditors; invoiced sales appear in the profit and loss account as turnover. Incurred expenses appear in the profit and loss account as costs. It may be several months before cash changes hands.
4 Stock Valuation may be arrived at in many different ways. The valuation will affect the reported profit but not affect the cash balance.
5 New Capital introduces cash into the firm when issued but never appears in the profit and loss account.
6 New Fixed Assets are paid for in cash as acquired but charged in the profit and loss account over their estimated lives.
7 Research and Development affects the cash balance when paid for but may be charged in the profit and loss account over several years.

Conclusion: Profit flow is a *concept*, an *opinion*.
Cash flow is a *fact*.

The Effect of Inflation on Profit Flow and Cash Flow

Accountants have not been able to agree on a sensible basis for adjusting accounting profits for inflation. This is not particularly important. Many parts of the world have prospered over long periods without inflation accounting. We usually give a very short lecture on inflation accounting along the following lines: 'There are 57 ways of adjusting accounts for inflation and none of them puts money in the bank'. This immediately leads us to one important problem which does arise for businesses through inflation. Inflation causes working capital problems for companies. Additional cash is required to finance the same level of physical stock. Additional cash is required to finance the same physical level of debtors. Additional cash is required to buy plant and equipment, which may replace similar equipment which was acquired for fewer pounds. New fixed assets are generally purchased out of funds generated from successful trading. The level of funds generated from successful trading may prove inadequate because fewer pounds were generated historically before inflation. It should not surprise us that the firms which suffered the most during periods of high inflation were those companies with long production cycles, and therefore very high levels of working capital. During periods of high inflation we should expect particularly severe cash flow problems for ship building, engineering and construction companies. We were once asked by a company to solve its 95 million pound cash shortfall which had arisen during a period of high inflation.

How can a Firm Cope with an Additional Cash Requirement of £95m Arising Through Inflation?

Solution	Comment
1 Borrow £95m	Yes, but annual interest £16m
2 Increase prices	Price Commission – customer resistance – competitor reaction
3 Reduce costs	Yes, but rising costs are creating the problem
4 Extend supplier credit	Yes, but difficult as they face same problems
5 Reduce level of investment in stock	i.e. more efficient use of capital employed
6 Collect debts more quickly	Yes, but difficult as they face same problems
7 Dispose of plant and equipment	Yes, but danger to earning ability
8 Property – sale and lease back – mortgage	Yes, but once only
9 Postpone new investment	Yes, but government wants *more* investment
10 Issue more shares	Difficult when dividend is threatened
11 Refuse to pay a dividend	Difficult when cost of living for shareholders is rising
12 Government subsidy	Unlikely until liquidation imminent, if at all

Measuring Changes in Working Capital

The statement of sources and applications of funds The change in a company's working capital position is published annually in the statement of sources and applications of funds which forms part of the company's published accounts. 'Funds' is a much misunderstood word. 'Funds' means cash or cash equivalent. An increase in trade credit, for example, is a source of funds. Although it is not a source of cash, it is a source of cash equivalent. Sources of funds and applications of funds are listed below.

Sources	*Applications*
Funds from operations (profit + non-cash expenses such as depreciation)	Losses from operations
Increase in trade credit	Reduction in trade credit
Reduction in stock	Increase in stock
Reduction in debtors	Increase in debtors
Sale of fixed assets	Purchase of fixed assets
Increase in instalment credit	Reduction in instalment credit
Increase in lease finance	Reduction in lease finance
Increase in loans	Repayment of loans
Increase in share capital	Reduction in share capital (most unusual)
Repayment of tax	Payment of tax
Dividends received	Dividends paid
Reduced investment in cash balances	Increased investment in cash balances
Increase in bank overdraft	Reduction in bank overdraft

Example

From the following balance sheets, prepare a statement of sources and applications of funds for the current year.

Toy Makers Ltd

	This year £000		Last year £000	
Sources of Capital:				
Share of capital		250		200
Profit and loss account		<u>356</u>		<u>330</u>
Shareholders' funds		606		530
Long-term loans		<u>30</u>		<u>80</u>
		636		610
Employment of Capital:				
Fixed assets:				
Freehold property at cost		380		320
Plant and equipment				
- Cost	275		240	
- Depreciation	<u>145</u>	130	<u>120</u>	120
Motor vehicles				
- Cost	135		120	
- Depreciation	<u>85</u>	<u>50</u>	<u>60</u>	<u>60</u>
		560		500

Toy Makers Ltd *(continued)*

	This year £000	Last year £000
Current Assets:		
Stock	160	70
Debtors	120	65
Cash at bank	—	125
	280	260
Less current liabilities		
Creditors	125	150
Bank overdraft	79	—
	204	150
Net current assets	76	110
	636	610

Answer

Toy Makers Ltd

Statement of Sources and Applications of Funds

		£000
Sources of Funds:		
Net profit for the year (356 – 330)		26
Add non-cash charges (depreciation)		
(145 – 120) + (85 – 60)		50
Funds from operations		76
Issue of shares (250 – 200)		50
		126
Applications of Funds:		
Increased investment in property (380 – 320)		60
Purchase of plant and equipment (275 – 240)		35
Purchase of motor vehicles (135 – 120)		15
Investment in fixed assets		110
Repayment of long-term loans (80 – 30)		50
Increased investment in stock	90	
Increased investment in debtors	55	
Reduction in creditors	25	
Increased investment in net working capital		170
		330
Reduction in balances at bank (125 + 79)		204

Although Toy Makers Ltd has positive retained earnings for the year amounting to £26,000, there has been a big reduction in the balance at the bank from £125,000 positive to £79,000 negative. Net working capital has required additional finance amounting to £170,000. Investment in additional fixed assets amounts to £110,000. Funds from successful trading amounting to £76,000 plus a new issue of shares amounting to £50,000 gives total new sources of funds amounting to £126,000. This is not enough to finance the additional requirement in net working capital and fixed assets together with the repayment of the long-term loan. Despite profitable trading, the company's cash balance has fallen by £204,000.

Practical Stock Management

Economic theory suggests that to maximize the market value of the firm we require the minimum cash outlay invested in raw materials, work in progress, and finished goods for any given set of operational cash flows. In practice, managers try to minimize the investment in raw materials, work in progress, and finished goods for any given level of sales with a view to maximizing return on capital employed. Ratio analysis is used to give indications of the success or failure of working capital management. With a view to measuring the effectiveness of inventory control, the following ratios are widely used.

$$\frac{\text{Annual sales}}{\text{Average stock at selling price}}$$

The number of times we have turned over the stock (at selling prices)

$$\frac{\text{Cost of annual sales}}{\text{Average stock at cost}}$$

The number of times we have turned over the stock (at cost)

$$\frac{\text{Stock}}{\text{Current assets}}$$

The proportion of current assets represented by stock (work in progress or finished goods)

$$\frac{\text{Stock}}{\text{Total assets}}$$

The proportion of total assets represented by stock (work in progress or finished goods)

Ratios can be used for four purposes.

1 *Trend Analysis*
Ratios can be plotted over time to indicate where we have been, and possibly indicate future problems.

2 *Inter-firm comparison*
We can compare our performance indicators with our competitors.
3 *Comparison of Actual with Target*
We can compare our actual statistics with targets set.
4 *Aid to Forecasting*
Once we have arrived at a target sales figure for future years, we can use historic ratios to estimate future costs and levels of investment.

For any level of sales or cash flow we prefer a minimum investment in inventory. The carrying of excessive stocks can result in the following:

1 Higher holding costs including storage, handling and inspection.
2 Higher insurance costs.
3 Pilferage.
4 Obsolescence.
5 Deterioration/evaporation.
6 Lost alternative investment opportunities.
7 Higher financing costs.

The carrying of higher levels of stock will tend to bring certain benefits:

1 Fewer lost immediate sales.
2 Less adverse customer reaction to stockouts.
3 Fewer production delays.
4 Less exposure to price increases.
5 Better discounts for large purchases.
6 Fewer orders and therefore lower ordering costs.
7 Lower manufacturing costs for large quantities.
8 Avoidance of the high cost of emergency suppliers.

Although financial and production managers may wish to operate on a zero level of investment in inventory, this can rarely be achieved. Raw material stock levels will be determined by seasonality, the reliability of supply, and the efficiency of production scheduling. The level of investment in work in progress will be largely determined by the length of the production cycle, the efficiency of production scheduling and production control. Investment in finished goods will be to a great extent determined by the co-ordination of production and marketing, fashion, and perishability. Nevertheless, we encourage financial and production managers to review on a regular basis the level of investment in raw materials, work in progress, and finished goods with a view to considering the following action.

1 Lowering the level of investment in stock, work in progress, and finished goods for any level of cash flow, output, or sales.
2 Elimination of certain sales items.
3 The sub-contraction of certain items or components.
4 A price reduction to clear low activity lines.
5 Availability of goods on sale or return and goods on consignment.
6 Immediate delivery for exclusive customers.
7 Establishment of optimal re-order levels for raw materials.

The establishment of approximate optimal ordering levels for raw materials is an important aspect of inventory control. For each manufacturing input we should establish a figure for base stock, and then determine an optimum purchase size called the economic order quantity (EOQ). The procedure necessitates the specification of costs which rise and fall with higher levels of inventory. Carrying costs rise with larger inventories – warehousing, interest on invested capital, insurance, obsolescence. Ordering costs and costs of stockouts fall with large inventories – loss of sales, cost of production delays, purchase-size discount. The next step is to locate the least cost order quantity. Theoretically the EOQ is found at the point where the curve of rising costs of carrying inventory intersects the curve of falling ordering and stockout costs. An optimal average inventory investment can be determined, where the average investment equals half the replenishment quantity (i.e. EOQ) plus the level of safety stock. The calculation of the point at which to order is an important aspect of inventory control procedure. It affects the level of investment in inventories and the firm's ability to satisfy consumer wants. The order point is equal to the expected usage during the lead-time (time between ordering and delivery).

Example
A kennel feeds 40 lbs of dog food to its 'guests' each week. This food is deep-frozen, and may be obtained upon demand from the supplier who sells it in 20 lbs lots at a price of £4.00 a lot. The kennel owner needs to drive to the supplier, some 20 miles away, to pick up the dog food and the van he must use consumes 1 gallon of petrol for each 20 miles travelled. If the cost of holding stock is assumed to be 26 per cent per annum of the purchase price, and there are ample refrigeration facilities at the kennels, what quantity of dog food would you recommend should be purchased at any one time?
   One gallon of petrol costs £1.56.

Answer

(Demand fixed and known, with no shortages)

$$EOQ = \sqrt{\frac{2 \times R \times C_S}{C_1 \times T}}$$

where R = total annual usage = 2,080
T = time = 52 weeks,
C_1 = holding cost per unit per unit of time, and
C_S = set-up cost.

Holding cost, C_1

Annual total purchase costs $= 40 \times 52 \times \frac{4}{20}$

Annual total holding cost $= \frac{26}{100} (40 \times 52 \times \frac{4}{20})$

Holding cost per unit per
week $= \dfrac{\frac{26}{100} (40 \times 52 \times \frac{4}{20})}{(40 \times 52) \times 52}$

$$= \frac{1}{1,000}$$

Set-up cost, C_S

Return journey $= 2$ gallons petrol

$= £3.12$

then $\qquad EOQ = \sqrt{\dfrac{2 \times 2080 \times 3.12}{\frac{1}{1,000} \times 52}}$

$\qquad\qquad\quad = \quad$ approx 500 lbs = 25 lots

If the delivery period is three weeks, then the re-order point is reached when stocks fall to 120 lbs, plus any safety stock arising owing to the variability of usage.

Inventory control models should be applied with caution. There are problems in determining ordering costs, carrying costs, stockout costs, and expected usage. A good management information system must be available before embarking on an elaborate inventory control programme. The key to good inventory management appears to rest on sufficient knowledge of the fundamental techniques to develop enough self-confidence to permit their practical application to the needs of the company, without regarding the techniques as a bag of tools expressed in the form of mysterious mathematical equations solving all problems without considering abnormal circumstances. The objective is to minimize the level of investment in stocks for a given level of cash flow or sales.

Practical Credit Management

The amount 'debtors' shown in a company's balance sheet relates to stock at selling prices with customers for which payment has not yet been received. Much of the preceding discussion relating to inventory management is therefore of relevance to the management of trade debtors, which is usually referred to as credit management. For any level of cash flow or sales, we prefer a minimum level of investment in debtors to maximize the market value of the firm or maximize return on capital employed. A generous credit policy towards our customers should increase sales, but it will also increase the level of investment in working capital which must be financed. Credit policy may not be restricted to allowing one or two month's credit to customers. It may include the granting of customer loans, organizing leases, financing customer stocks, provision of goods on consignment, and delivery of goods on sale or return.

A credit policy must be established for the company and for individual customers on the following lines.

1 A credit period for the vast majority of customers, with special provisions for some customers.
2 A total credit amount for the company with individual amounts for each customer.
3 A discount policy for the company with special provisions for individual customers.
4 The establishment of a credit rating system.
5 The establishment of a collection policy for insuring that invoices are paid.
6 Guidelines for monthly or weekly payments on long-term contracts.
7 The establishment of an accurate and reliable accounting system, together with monthly reports including an age analysis of debtors.
8 Consideration of a credit insurance policy against bad debts.

The Credit Rating System

For individual customers the credit period, the credit amount, discount policy, and collection policy will depend to a large extent on the credit rating. Several sources of information are available to help in setting a credit rating:

1 The experience of the sales force.
2 Trade references.
3 Reference from the firm's banker.
4 Reference from the firm's auditor.
5 Analysis of published accounts from Companies House.
6 Statistics provided by credit rating agencies such as Dun and Bradstreet.

Traditional financial management texts suggest that credit managers should take note of the five C's – character, capacity, capital, collateral and conditions. Character relates to the customer's willingness to pay, capacity to his or her ability to pay, capital to his or her financial position, collateral to any security available, and conditions to the effect of economic trends on the customer's position.

Collection Policy

When a customer fails to pay an invoice on the due date, it is often our natural reaction to think in terms of solicitors and legal action. It must be emphasized that this is a last resort, since we do not want to lose our customers. We recommend that companies should establish a procedure for late collections along the following lines:

1 A reminder.
2 Perhaps a personal letter.
3 Several telephone calls.
4 A personal visit.
5 A telegram.
6 A visit from the salesman responsible for that customer.
7 A reminder to the sales person that commission is based on cash received not invoiced sales.
8 Restriction of credit.
9 Use of collection agencies.
10 Legal action.

Ratio Analysis

In addition to the regular preparation of an age analysis of debtors, companies can use ratio analysis to analyse the success or failure of their credit policies.

$$\frac{\text{Debtors} \times 365}{\text{Sales}} \qquad = \quad \text{The average credit period in days}$$

$$\frac{\text{Debtors} \times 52}{\text{Sales}} \qquad = \quad \text{The average credit period in weeks}$$

$$\frac{\text{Debtors} \times 12}{\text{Sales}} \qquad = \quad \text{The average credit period in months}$$

$$\frac{\text{Debtors}}{\text{Current assets}} \qquad = \quad \text{The proportion of current assets accounted for by debtors}$$

$$\frac{\text{Debtors}}{\text{Total assets}} \qquad = \quad \text{The proportion of total assets represented by debtors}$$

$$\frac{\text{Bad debts}}{\text{Sales}} \qquad = \quad \text{The proportion of sales represented by bad debts}$$

$$\frac{\text{Bad debts}}{\text{Debtors}} \qquad = \quad \text{The proportion of debtors represented by bad debts}$$

These ratios can be plotted over time to demonstrate any trends. They can be compared with other firms in the same industry. The actuals achieved can be compared with targets or standards. In addition, financial ratios can be used as an aid to business forecasting.

Practical Cash Management

The objective of the firm is to create wealth. In operational terms this means generating positive cash flows from successful trading. Firms which do generate lots of cash from successful trading can finance new investment, and are usually able to raise additional finance as required. They generate their own cash surpluses which can be invested. Even companies which trade successfully may experience occasional cash deficits when projects generate occasional negative cash flows. These cash deficits must be financed. Cash shortages can result in the making of sub-optimal investment decisions and sub-optimal financing decisions. Sub-optimal investment decisions would include the disposal of profitable lines or divisions, inability to undertake profitable investment projects, and failure to maintain an adequate level of working capital. Sub-optimal financing decisions would include the taking out of very expensive loans, and being granted overdraft facilities subject to restrictive covenants which could include personal guarantees from directors, restrictions on investment, restrictions on additional finance, restrictions on directors' remuneration, and restrictions on dividend payments.

All companies use cash and bank balances. Cash is used to pay creditors for raw material and other inputs. It is used to pay wages and salaries. This cash expenditure results in the creation of finished goods which are sold to our customers who eventually pay us in cash. Cash is therefore essential to finance the working capital cycle. Cash is also used to acquire fixed assets which are written off over their estimated useful lives. Furthermore, cash is required to pay interest on loans, taxation, and dividends to shareholders.

Cash Balances

There are several reasons for holding cash balances.

1 *Transactions* As already stated, firms use cash to finance working capital and fixed assets.

2 *Interest earnings* On a short-term basis cash balances can be placed on bank deposits or invested in government securities to earn interest. Loans can be made to subsidiaries, associated companies, and other companies.

3 *Precaution* Some firms hold a safety stock of cash to provide against unanticipated fluctuations in their ability to generate cash. We would expect this to be less likely to occur in those firms which have easy access to additional finance.

4 *Speculation* Some firms hold very high cash balances with a view to taking advantage of speculative investment opportunities. Such cash balances are often justified in terms of their ability to finance mergers. On the other hand, many companies have been acquired because they have large cash balances.

5 *Investment* Firms with cash surpluses can give more credit to customers thereby generating additional sales. They can undertake promotional exercises to increase sales to utilize unabsorbed production capacity. Cash balances can be used to provide loans to customers, and make available lease finance to increase sales. Firms with surplus cash balances can undertake additional investment in fixed assets and working capital, and even acquire other companies for cash.

Cash Forecasting

We emphasize that all firms should generate cash flow forecasts for one month, three months, six months, one year, and five years. These cash flow forecasts are continuously updated, and action taken to invest surpluses and finance deficits. A target should be set for a minimum or safety stock of cash. Actual cash flows should be continuously measured against forecast cash flows, and action taken where appropriate to provide for forecast surpluses and shortfalls. Of course, all the forecasts will be incorrect, but this is not important. What is important is that we learn from experience in forecasting cash flows and measuring actual against target. Managers often argue that since the future cannot be predicted with certainty, then planning is not a good idea. We have to point out that the alternative to planning is not planning. Planning and learning from experience have to be better. As a practical fact of life, more and more firms are having to produce forecast cash flows on a regular basis for the attention of the bank.

The Choice of Bank

We suggest that most individuals choose their bank on the basis of location, cheque processing costs, and other bank charges. The managers of trading companies should also consider the following factors.

1 The policy of the bank towards risky debt.
2 The bank's policy on venture capital.
3 The bank's record on loyalty when companies face difficult situations. (Some banks are quicker to pull the rug than other banks)
4 The variety of loan schemes available.
5 The size of the local branch. Does every decision have to go to Head Office? How much information is required and how often is it required?
6 Other services. Can the branch handle letters of credit, bills of exchange, foreign exchange? Does the bank provide factoring, invoice discounting, leasing, stock finance, hire purchase finance, mortgages, sale and leaseback, debentures?
7 The security required. Will personal guarantees be required of directors?

We add as a final note on bank negotiation, that the overdraft or loan facility should be negotiated from a position of strength. Financial managers should negotiate the facility when they are very much in credit. We have experience of a small publishing company which prepares its account to a date when the company is in subst ntial credit at the bank. These accounts, showing a cash rich position, are always used for negotiating loans and overdrafts.

Practical Management of Trade Creditors

In economics it is taught that nothing is free. There is always an opportunity cost, i.e. the benefit foregone. In financial management the nearest we get to free money is trade credit. Trade credit is free until we start to lose discounts. Once we start to lose discounts, then trade credit is a very expensive source of finance. Remember that a 2 per cent discount for paying at 10 days is equivalent to a very high annual rate. We generally suggest that financial managers should pay late *and* take the discount if possible. We also recommend that suppliers should be rotated to obtain the best possible credit terms. The financial manager should regularly prepare an age list of creditors to ascertain a list of suppliers who take the maximum time to collect a debt. We all have experience of the tricks of paying late – forget to sign the cheque, put the wrong year on the cheque, refuse to pay other than on statements, refuse to pay other than on invoices, lose statements and invoices, insist that the only person who can sign cheques is 'away'. The most common lie in business is 'the cheque is in the post!'

There is another form of short-term credit usually referred to as 'accrued expenses'. This can be a substantial source of interest-free and discount-free credit. It includes outstanding PAYE and NIC, outstanding VAT, outstanding heat and light bills, outstanding telephone bills, and unpaid taxation. Financial managers should strive to balance accrued expenses and trade credit against debtors and investment in stock. A useful rule of thumb in the management of working capital is the acid test, sometimes called the quick ratio, the solvency test, or the liquidity ratio. It is traditionally suggested that cash plus debtors should equal current liabilities. Another traditional rule of thumb is that current assets should be double the amount of current liabilities. The current ratio is cash plus debtors plus stock, divided by the current liabilities. Again, the rule of thumb is that the current ratio should be 2:1. A final traditional rule of thumb is that short-term finance which includes creditors and overdrafts should only be used to finance short-term assets which includes stock and debtors. Furthermore, long-term finance which includes long-term loans and equity should be used to finance the fixed or permanent assets. These practical rules of thumb do not slot comfortably into the theory of finance, but they are widely used in practice as important indicators.

Estimating the Working Capital Requirements: Example

Dobrob Ltd is attempting to expand its product range to include Dicko. The product would be sold on an eight week credit policy. However, managers recognize that half the customers will take an extra four weeks credit even though they will lose their 2 per cent cash discount.

Dobrob pays for labour at the end of the week following and overheads after an average of four weeks. Materials are paid for at the end of the four week month following the four week month of delivery. Stocks which the company maintains are as follows:

Raw materials	8 weeks
Finished products	4 weeks

The production cycle is two weeks. Labour and expenses are accrued evenly through the production cycle, but all the material is imputed at the commencement of the process.

Statistics per ton of product are as follows:

Selling price	£60
Raw materials	£20
Labour	£15
Overheads	£10

The firm expects to sell 250 tons of Dicko per week.

Working Capital Budget – Dicko

Details	Cost/Week	Number of weeks		Amount (£)	
Stocks:					
Raw materials	5,000	8		40,000	
Work in progress					
R.M.	5,000	2	10,000		
Labour	3,750	1	3,750		
O/H	2,500	1	2,500	16,250	
Finished stock	11,250	4		45,000	101,250
Debtors	11,250	10			112,500
					213,750
Less: Creditors					
R.M.	5,000	6		30,000	
Labour	3,750	1		3,750	
O/H	2,500	4		10,000	43,750
	Working capital required				170,000

Study Questions

3.1 Sheila Lee Cooper is disturbed that her jean manufacturing outfit has made excellent accounting profit but is experiencing cash problems. From the following balance sheets, prepare a Statement of Sources and Applications of Funds for the year ended 31 December 1987.

Sheila Lee Cooper Ltd

		1987		1986
		£000		£000
Sources of Capital				
Share of capital		70		60
Profit and loss account		105		40
Shareholders' funds		175		100
Long-term loans		30		60
		205		160
Employment of Capital				
Fixed Assets:				
Freehold property at cost		120		90
Plant and equipment - Cost	84		60	
Depreciation	40	44	32	28
Motor vehicles - Cost	42		24	
Depreciation	22	20	12	12
		184		130
Current Assets:				
Stock	37		22	
Debtors	29		18	
Cash at bank	—		30	
	66		70	
Less Current Liabilities:				
Creditors	32		40	
Bank overdraft	13		—	
	45		40	
Net Current Assets:		21		30
		205		160

As management accountant explain to Sheila why the cash problem has arisen.

3.2 The following information relates to Stott Lawn Seed Inc.

    1 Sales and profits have increased rapidly.
    2 Generous credit facilities are offered to dealers.
    3 Salesmen are paid commissions on deliveries to dealers.
      (a) As Financial Director, draft a report to your board outlining the likely implications of the above information for the corporation.
      (b) Reconcile your theoretical understanding of 'working capital management' with 'modern financial theory'.

3.3 Silsden Manufacturing Limited is about to launch a new product, Kildo. Customers will be allowed eight weeks credit, although 75 per cent of them will take twelve weeks. Wages are paid at the end of the week following production, and overheads are paid at the end of each four week period. Materials are paid for at the end of the four week period following the four week production period. The company maintains eight weeks of raw materials and eight weeks of finished products. The production cycle is four weeks, and labour and other expenses accrue evenly during the production cycle. All materials are introduced at the beginning of the production process.

Statistics per ton of product are as follows:

Selling price	£100
Raw Materials	£25
Labour	£20
Variable overheads	£30

The company expects to sell 300 units of Kildo per week.

Estimate the additional working capital requirement for the production and marketing of Kildo.

Further Reading

Brealey, Richard and Myers, Stewart, *Principles of Corporate Finance*. New York: McGraw-Hill, 1984, chapters 25–30.
Schall, Lawrence D. and Haley, Charles W., *Introduction to Financial Management*. New York: McGraw-Hill, 1986, chapters 15–17.

4

Portfolio Management

Introduction

Portfolio theory has undergone a revolution in the last thirty years, and in this chapter the implications of modern portfolio theory for *pension fund investment management* and for the estimation of *required rates of return on projects exhibiting various levels of risk* are examined. Investment appraisal involves discounting forecast project cash flows at some rate which reflects the economic risk of the project, and hence selection of the appropriate discount rate is of prime importance.

The Markowitz Mean-Variance Model

Modern portfolio theory is concerned with the choice of efficient combinations of assets and its foundation lies in the work of Markowitz (1952, 1959). Although investors have long been aware, in a *qualitative* sense, of the benefits resulting from diversification of security holdings, the Markowitz model represented the first substantial *quantitative* analysis of these benefits. The assumptions underlying the model are as follows:

1 The return on an investment adequately summarizes the outcome of the investment, and investors visualize a probability distribution of rates of return.
2 Investors' risk estimates are proportional to the variance of return they perceive for a security or portfolio.
3 Investors are willing to base their decisions on just two parameters of the probability distribution function – the expected return and variance of return.

57

4 The investor exhibits risk aversion, so for a given expected return he
prefers minimum risk. Obviously, for a given level of risk the investor
prefers maximum expected return.

In general, diversification of asset holdings permits a reduction in the
variance of return, even for the same level of expected return.

Return on equities comes in two forms – dividends and capital gains. The
return on an individual security or portfolio can be measured as follows:

$$R_t = \frac{P_t - P_{t-1} + D_t}{P_{t-1}} \tag{4.1}$$

where R_t is the periodic return,

P_t is the price at the end of the period,

P_{t-1} is the price at the beginning of the period,

$P_t - P_{t-1}$ is the capital gain or loss, and

D_t is the dividend received at the end of the period.

For example, if the value of a portfolio is 100 at the beginning of a period,
and 120 at the end of the period after receiving a dividend of 10, then the
return on the portfolio is 30 per cent:

$$R_t = \frac{120 - 100 + 10}{100} = 30 \text{ per cent}$$

Risk is the one-in-six rule. Risk relates to the volatility of an expected
outcome, the dispersion or spread of likely returns around the expected
return. In figure 4.1, the expected return on a project is 16 per cent. If returns
are normally distributed, then we know that for 67 per cent of the time
the actual return will lie within one standard deviation of the expected return.
The standard deviation is a measure of dispersion or spread. Four out of
six actual outcomes should, on average, lie within one standard deviation
of the expected outcome, so in figure 4.1 four out of six outcomes should,
on average, lie between 10 per cent and 22 per cent, 6 per cent being the
standard deviation. However, two times in six the outcome can be expected
to lie outside one standard deviation. On average, one time in six the
outcome will be above 22 per cent, and this is generally referred to as upside
potential. On average, one time in six the actual return is likely to be less
than 10 per cent – this is the bad news, and is generally referred to as
downside risk. This is the one-in-six rule.

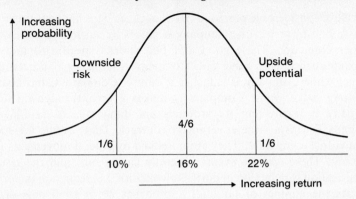

Figure 4.1 Risk is the one-in-six rule

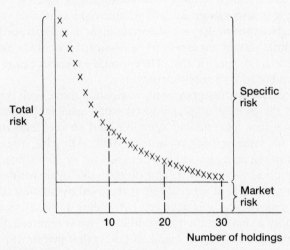

Figure 4.2 Risk reduction by diversification

Investors do not like risk, and the greater the riskiness of returns on an investment, the greater will be the return expected by investors. There is a trade-off between risk and return which must be reflected in the required rates of return on investment opportunities.

The standard deviation (or variance) of return measures the total risk of an investment. It is not necessary for an investor to accept the total risk of an individual security. Investors can and do diversify to reduce risk. Figure 4.2 shows how some of the total risk associated with individual securities can be avoided by diversification. We should not advise investors to put all their funds into a single investment as this exposes them to more risk than is necessary for the level of expected return. Figure 4.2 shows that if we increase the number of investment holdings from 1 to 2, 3, 4 etc., then we achieve considerable portfolio risk reduction. This happens because the surprise bad news for one company is offset by surprise good news for another company. These good and bad shocks specific to individual companies cancel each other out. Company A launches a successful new product while Company B launches a failure. Company C has a sudden damaging strike, while Company D makes a breakthrough on design. Company E learns that its products are dangerous to health, while Company F wins a large government contract. These events are specific to individual companies. They are unrelated to general movements in the economy. These specific events generally cancel out, and the result of diversification is reduction in portfolio volatility, i.e. reduction in portfolio risk. As the number of holdings approaches 20, a good deal of total risk is removed by diversification. This risk which can be removed by diversification is called specific risk because it is specific to individual companies; it is also known as diversifiable risk, avoidable risk, or non-market risk. Now one of the very important ideas in modern portfolio theory is that investors should not expect to be rewarded for taking on risk which can be avoided, i.e. specific risk. They should expect to be rewarded only for unavoidable or non-specific risk.

To some extent the fortunes of all companies move with the economy. Changes in the money supply, interest rates, exchange rates, taxation, commodity prices, government spending and so on, tend to affect all companies to some greater or lesser extent. The risk associated with movements in the economy cannot be removed by diversification, and is generally referred to as market, non-diversifiable or unavoidable risk. In figure 4.2 a great deal of specific risk is removed by holding 10 securities, some extra risk reduction is achieved by holding 11 to 20 securities, and thereafter only a small amount of additional risk is removed. (It has been shown empirically by Wagner and Lau (1971) that investment in 16 to 20 randomly selected securities removes 80 per cent of diversifiable risk.) Eventually, by holding a portfolio comprising all securities weighted in proportion to the market values of the underlying companies we could remove all specific risk. At this point we would hold M, the market portfolio which has no specific risk.

The expected return on a portfolio comprising n securities is simply the weighted average of the expected return on each security in the portfolio:

$$E(R) = \sum_{i=1}^{n} X_i \mu_i \tag{4.2}$$

where $E(R)$ is the expected return on the portfolio
X_i is the proportion of security i in the portfolio
μ_i is the expected return on security i.

Now the risk of a portfolio is measured by the variance of its return, and this is determined by the variance of return on each security and also by the correlation coefficient between the returns on each pair of securities:

$$V(R) = \sum_{i=1}^{n} X_i^2 \sigma_i^2 + 2 \sum_{i=1}^{n-1} \sum_{j=i+1}^{n} X_i X_j \varrho_{ij} \sigma_i \sigma_j \qquad (4.3)$$

where $V(R)$ is the variance of return on the portfolio
σ_i^2 is the variance of return on security i
ϱ_{ij} is the correlation coefficient between the returns on securities i and j. The latter component is a measure of the extent to which the returns move together.

It is important to note that the variance of return on a portfolio is determined by the correlation of returns between each pair of securities, as well as on the variance of return on each security. Low correlation of returns between the securities results in low variance of return on the portfolio, and, in particular, negatively correlated returns result in substantial risk reduction benefits. In practice, however, returns on securities tend to be highly positively correlated, as they are all influenced by the same economic and political factors. Hence, as discussed earlier, only a certain part of total risk may be eliminated by diversification.

The Markowitz formulation does not determine a single optimal portfolio. It provides a series of portfolios which are *efficient in terms of risk and return*, in that each portfolio offers the maximum expected return corresponding to a given level of risk, or the minimum risk corresponding to a given level of expected return. The problem can be formulated as the minimization of an objective function subject to constraints. The objective function f incorporates the concept of trading off risk against return and is given by:

$$f = -A(E(R)) + V(R), \ 0 \le A \le \infty \qquad (4.4)$$

where A is a risk aversion index. If $A = 0$, the portfolio with the lowest variance of return will be selected. As A increases the investor becomes more willing to accept risk in order to achieve a higher expected return, and if $A = \infty$ the portfolio with the highest expected return will be optimal. The first constraint is that negative investment (selling short) is not permitted:

$$X_i \ge 0 \qquad (4.5)$$

and the second is that the portfolio consists of n securities:

$$\sum_{i=1}^{n} X_i = 1 \qquad (4.6)$$

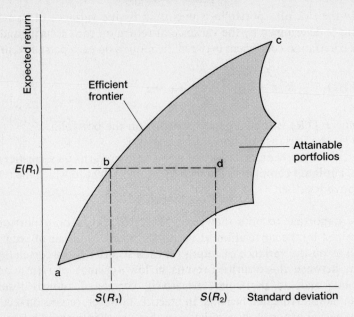

Figure 4.3   Markowitz efficient frontier

The minimization of equation (4.4) subject to constraints (4.5) and (4.6) may be carried out using the technique of quadratic programming, since the objective function is non-linear whilst the constraints are linear. A set of efficient portfolios results, each portfolio corresponding to a particular value of the risk aversion index. The solution is represented graphically in figure 4.3, where standard deviation of return is used as the measure of risk.

The shaded area represents all attainable portfolios, that is all the combinations of risk and expected return which may be achieved with the available securities. The *efficient frontier* denotes all possible efficient portfolios, and any point on the frontier dominates any point to the right of it. As an illustration, consider the portfolios represented by points b and d. Portfolios b and d promise the same expected return $E(R_1)$ but the risk associated with b is $S(R_1)$ whereas that associated with d is $S(R_2)$. Investors therefore prefer portfolios on the efficient frontier rather than interior portfolios given the assumption of risk aversion. Obviously, point a on the frontier represents the portfolio with the least possible risk, whilst c represents the portfolio with the highest possible rate of return.

The investor has to select a portfolio from amongst all those represented by the efficient frontier: this will depend upon his risk-return preference. As different individuals have different preferences with respect to expected return and risk, the optimal portfolio of securities will vary considerably among individuals.

The main objection to the Markowitz approach is its lack of practical application. In order to generate the efficient portfolios an enormous amount of data is required even if the number of available securities is relatively small. For example, if we wish to select the efficient portfolios from a universe of 100 securities, we need data on 100 expected returns, 100 standard deviations, and 4,950 pairs of correlation coefficients. (The number of correlation coefficients required may be calculated from the formula $n(n-1)/2$, where n is the size of the security universe.) In addition to the problem of data collection, the computations required for this approach are substantial.

The Capital-Asset Pricing Model

The major assumptions underlying the capital-asset pricing model (CAPM) are as follows:

1 Investors base their portfolio investment decisions on the Markowitz expected return and standard deviation criteria.
2 Investors may borrow and lend without limit at the risk-free rate of interest.
3 Investors have homogeneous expectations about future outcomes over a one-period time horizon.
4 Capital markets are in equilibrium.
5 There are no market imperfections; investments are infinitely divisible, information is costless, there are no taxes, transaction costs or interest rate changes, and there is no inflation.

Some of these assumptions are obviously unrealistic, but they greatly simplify the model-building process. Furthermore, even if assumptions are relaxed, it is likely that the CAPM may still hold approximately.

The Capital Market Line

The Markowitz mean-variance model may be modified by introducing into the analysis the concept of a risk-free asset. If it is assumed that the investor has access to risk-free securities (for example, Treasury bills) in addition to the universe of risky securities, then he can construct a new set of portfolios as depicted by the line $R_F M$ in figure 4.4. At point R_F the individual is investing all his wealth in risk-free securities, whilst at point M he is holding an all-equity portfolio. The combinations of risk-free asset and risky portfolio which may be achieved by points between these two limits are termed 'lending' portfolios.

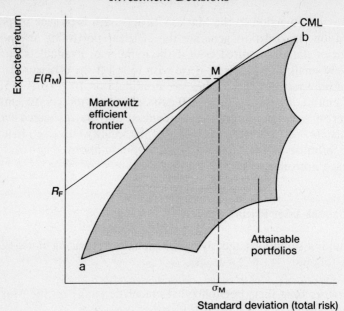

Figure 4.4 Capital market line

The risky portfolio chosen by an individual will always be at the point of contact between a straight line from the risk-free rate of interest R_F on the vertical axis drawn tangential to the efficient frontier, as illustrated by M in figure 4.4. Risky portfolio M will clearly be preferred to any other portfolio on the section of the efficient frontier between a and M. For the array of points between a and M, or any combination of these Markowitz efficient portfolios with the risk-free asset, there exists a corresponding portfolio on the line R_FM which has a higher expected return for the same level of risk. Hence, by introducing the concept of a risk-free asset into the analysis, a new set of portfolios depicted by the line R_FM may be derived, which dominates the section of the Markowitz efficient frontier between a and M.

If the investor is able to borrow money at the same risk-free rate of interest, R_F, at which he can invest, then he can supplement his available wealth and construct a 'borrowing' portfolio. If the straight line joining R_F and M is extended to the right of point M, this section of the line represents borrowing portfolios, that is portfolios in which the individual invests his available capital and an additional borrowed amount. As one moves further to the right of point M, an increasing amount of borrowed money is being invested. Clearly the borrowing portfolios dominate the section of the Markowitz efficient frontier between M and b.

The straight line from R_F passing through point M shows the range of all possible portfolios in which the individual can invest, by borrowing or lending at the risk-free rate of interest R_F and investing in the risky portfolio M. This line dominates the Markowitz efficient frontier, and is termed the *capital market line* (CML). The particular point chosen on the line will depend upon the individual's attitude towards risk and expected return.

All investors will hold a portfolio on the CML, that is a portfolio comprising some ratio of the risky portfolio M and the risk-free security. Hence portfolio M is the *universally desired optimal portfolio* which must therefore contain all risky securities in proportions reflecting the total equity values of the companies they represent, and is known as the 'market' portfolio. Every security must enter the market portfolio in order to be traded, since all investors hold combinations of the market portfolio and the risk-free asset. Tobin (1958) thus derived a *separation theorem* which states that an investor's choice of risk level is completely independent of the problem of deriving the optimal portfolio of risky securities. The market portfolio represents the optimal combination of risky securities. Therefore, in choosing an efficient portfolio, all investors are directed towards the market portfolio. The risk level associated with the market portfolio may be too high or too low for an individual investor, and so he may hold a lending portfolio if he prefers lower risk and expected return than the market, or a borrowing portfolio if he prefers higher risk and expected return than the market. The decision to hold a lending or borrowing portfolio is, however, purely a financial decision based upon the investor's risk preference, and is completely independent of the investment decision to construct an efficient portfolio, that is the market portfolio.

The equation of the capital market line is as follows:

$$E(R_P) = R_F + \frac{E(R_M) - R_F}{\sigma_M} S(R_P) \qquad (4.7)$$

where $E(R_P)$ is the expected rate of return on any portfolio on the CML,

R_F is the risk-free rate of interest,

$E(R_M)$ is the expected rate of return on the market portfolio,

σ_M is the risk (standard deviation of return) of the market portfolio, and

$S(R_P)$ is the total risk (standard deviation of return) of a portfolio on the CML.

The expected rate of return on a portfolio on the CML thus comprises the risk-free rate of interest plus a risk premium. This premium is given by the market price of risk, $(E(R_M) - R_F)/\sigma_M$, multiplied by the risk of the portfolio. The CML depicts the expected return from perfectly diversified portfolios as a function of portfolio total risk.

The Security Market Line

The CML equation (4.7) shows the return expected from any efficient portfolio. The problem now is to obtain the equation for the equilibrium expected return of an individual asset, that is the *security market line* (SML). The SML may be formally derived from the CML by analysing a portfolio comprising a risky security and the market portfolio in varying proportions. For a formal proof see, for example, Sharpe (1964). An alternative formal derivation of the SML from the CML is given by Jensen (1972).

The market portfolio is the sole example of a perfectly diversified risky portfolio. To hold individual risky securities or imperfectly diversified portfolios is inefficient because specific risk can be eliminated by further diversification. The prices of risky securities and their expected returns therefore compensate for market risk alone, since the market will not provide rewards for risk which can be eliminated. In an efficient market, securities with the same systematic risk should have the same expected rate of return, and those with higher systematic risk should have higher expected returns. The precise form of the relationship between risk and return is given by the *capital-asset pricing model* (CAPM):

$$E(R_i) = R_F + \beta_i [E(R_M) - R_F] \qquad (4.8)$$

where $E(R_i)$ is the expected rate of return on any individual security (or portfolio of securities)

R_F is the risk-free rate of interest

$E(R_M)$ is the expected rate of return on the market portfolio

β_i is the market sensitivity index of the individual security (or portfolio of securities).

Now, as discussed earlier, the risk of a security may be split into its specific risk and market risk components; the latter is given by

$$\text{market risk of security } i = \beta_i \sigma_M \qquad (4.9)$$

where σ_M is the standard deviation of return on the market portfolio. Since the term σ_M is common to all securities, it is often more convenient to think of the systematic risk of a security in relative terms, that is merely in terms of its β value. Equation (4.8) shows that there is a linear relationship between the expected return on a security (or portfolio) and its systematic risk (as measured by its β factor). When $\beta = 0$, the expected rate of return is equal to the risk-free rate of interest, but for risky investments ($\beta > 0$), the expected rate of return exceeds the risk-free rate of interest by an amount proportional to the market sensitivity (β) of the investment. The CAPM is depicted graphically by the security market line (SML) in figure 4.5. The intercept of the SML on the vertical axis is given by the risk-free rate of interest R_F, and the slope is given by $[E(R_M) - R_F]$ – the market risk premium, that is the expected excess return on the market portfolio. Point M denotes the market portfolio, and here the expected return is $E(R_M)$ and the β factor equals unity.

The CAPM may also be re-stated in 'risk-premium' form by subtracting the risk-free rate of interest from both sides of equation (4.8):

$$E(R_i) - R_F = \beta_i [E(R_M) - R_F] \tag{4.9}$$

In this form the CAPM states that the expected security (or portfolio) risk premium (or excess return over the risk-free rate of interest) is equal to its

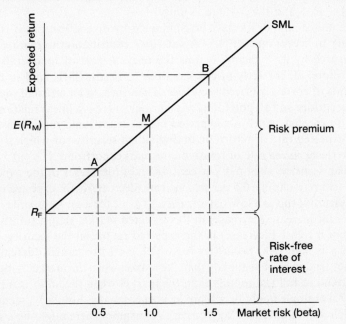

Figure 4.5   Security market line

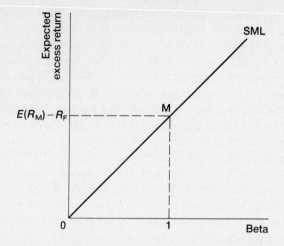

Figure 4.6 Security market line: risk-premium form

β factor multiplied by the expected market risk premium (or excess return over the risk-free rate of interest). The SML corresponding to equation (4.9) is shown graphically in figure 4.6. In this case the SML goes through the origin, but the slope again measures the market risk premium. Point M represents the market portfolio, and here the expected excess return is $[E(R_M) - R_F]$ and the β value is unity.

Since unsystematic risk may be eliminated by diversification, it is only necessary to accept market risk. A security's contribution to market risk, as measured by its β factor, is thus the relevant part of its overall risk. Furthermore, all correctly priced securities lie on the SML, and so do all portfolios of correctly priced securities. Therefore, in an efficient market, for all securities and all portfolios of securities, there is a linear relationship between expected return (or expected excess return) and market risk.

The expected rate of return on an individual security for which $\beta = 1$ is equal to the expected rate of return on the market portfolio. If $\beta = 0.5$ for a particular security, then a 1 per cent increase (decrease) in the expected market return results in a 0.5 per cent increase (decrease) in the expected return on the security; this is a low risk security. If $\beta = 2$ for a given security, then a 1 per cent increase (decrease) in the expected market return results in a 2 per cent increase (decrease) in the expected return on the security; such a security is high risk. Securities for which $\beta < 1$ are termed 'defensive', since they tend to rise less rapidly than the market when the market is moving up and tend to fall less rapidly than the market when the latter is moving down. An example might be a share in a tea company. Similarly, securities for which $\beta > 1$ are termed 'aggressive'. An example here might be a share in a hire-purchase company.

The CAPM may be illustrated numerically as follows. It is supposed that

R_F $= 8\%$ and

$E(R_M) = 14\%$

The CAPM equation (4.8) shows that

$E(R_i)$ $= 0.08 + \beta_i(0.14 - 0.08)$

therefore

$$E(R_i) = 0.08 + 0.06\, \beta_i \tag{4.10}$$

The expected market risk premium is therefore 6 per cent, that is investors holding the market portfolio should expect a return 6 per cent higher than they would if they invested in risk-free securities. Given the β value of an individual security or portfolio of securities, equation (4.10) may be used to calculate the corresponding expected return. For example, if we have a defensive security with $\beta = 0.5$, then the expected return on the security equals 11 per cent; the expected return on the security lies between the risk-free rate of interest and the expected return on the market portfolio. If we have an aggressive security with $\beta = 2$, then equation (4.10) shows that the expected return equals 20 per cent; the expected return on the security is higher than that on the market portfolio.

The Market Model

The β value for a security may be estimated using the market model developed by Sharpe (1963). This assumes that each security's price movement can be related to the price of the market portfolio. (Sharpe suggested that in practice, a popular average, such as the Financial Times All-Share Index, may be used as a surrogate for the market index.) The market model generates a characteristic line by assuming that the return on a security is determined merely by the market index and random factors.

$$R_i = \alpha_i + \beta_i R_M + U_i \tag{4.11}$$

where R_i is the return on the ith security

R_M is the return on the market portfolio

α_i and β_i are parameters

U_i is a random error term.

The error term is assumed to satisfy the usual properties required by the classical linear regression model: it has a mean of zero and finite variance; the error terms are independent of each other, that is covariance $(U_i, U_j) = 0$ for all i and j, $i \neq j$; R_M is independent of the error term, that is covariance $(R_M, U_i) = 0$ for all i. The return on a security is split into two parts, that which is perfectly correlated with the market return (the systematic return) and that which is independent of the market return (the specific return). Since the systematic return is perfectly correlated with the market return, it is expressed as a factor β times the market return, so the coefficient β_i indicates the expected responsiveness of security i's return to changes in the level of the market index. The intercept term α gives the expected return on the stock when the market return is zero, and represents the average value over time of the unsystematic returns on the security.

The market model equation (4.11) is illustrated graphically in figure 4.7. The intercept of the characteristic line on the vertical axis is given by α_i, and the slope is given by β_i. The points represent a set of observations over time on the return on the security and the market return, and the vertical distance from any observation to the characteristic line is given by the error term. The market model may be fitted to these points by least-squares regression techniques, giving estimates of the parameters α_i and β_i.

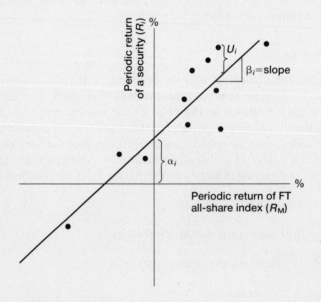

Figure 4.7 Characteristic line

A Comparison of the CAPM and the Market Model

The market model may be compared with the CAPM. For a portfolio of securities, the market model (4.11) may be rewritten as

$$R_p = [\alpha_p - R_F(1 - \beta_p)] + R_F + \beta_p(R_M - R_F) + U_p \tag{4.12}$$

where R_p is the return on the portfolio

R_M is the return on the market index

R_F is the risk-free rate of interest

α_p and β_p are parameters

U_p is a random error term.

If the expectations operator is applied to equation (4.12) this yields

$$E(R_p) = [\alpha_p - R_F(1 - \beta_p)] + R_F + \beta_p[E(R_M) - R_F] \tag{4.13}$$

The expectational market model (4.13) may be compared with the CAPM equation (4.8):

$$E(R_p) = R_F + \beta_p[E(R_M) - R_F]$$

Now the term $[\alpha_p - R_F(1 - \beta_p)]$ in equation (4.13) may be interpreted as the portfolio expected risk premium (or expected excess return over the risk-free rate of interest) when the market return is equal to the risk-free rate of interest, that is when the market risk premium (or excess return over the risk-free rate of interest) is zero, and is termed the 'risk-adjusted excess return'. It is clear that if a portfolio has a positive risk-adjusted excess return, that is $\alpha_p > R_F(1 - \beta_p)$, then its expected return is greater than that predicted by the CAPM; thus an investor holding a portfolio with a positive risk-adjusted excess return tends to beat the market. Similarly, if a portfolio has a negative risk-adjusted excess return, that is $\alpha_p < R_F(1 - \beta_p)$, then the expected return on the portfolio is less than that predicted by the CAPM; such a portfolio tends to underperform the market.

The market model (4.13) asserts that the risk-adjusted excess return may be positive, negative or zero. This model only reduces to the CAPM equation (4.8), however, when the risk-adjusted excess return is zero. It can be shown that in an efficient market all securities are priced so that the risk-adjusted excess return is zero, and thus the risk-adjusted excess return on any given portfolio must also be zero. The market model (4.13) therefore reduces to the CAPM equation (4.8) only in an efficient market.

Measurement of Portfolio Performance

The returns on managed portfolios, such as pension funds, may be judged relative to the returns on unmanaged portfolios at the same level of risk using the CAPM. If the return on a managed portfolio exceeds the corresponding return on an unmanaged portfolio (the 'performance standard'), then the portfolio manager has beaten the market – he has performed in a superior manner. Similarly, if the return on a managed portfolio is less than the return on the performance standard, then the portfolio manager has underperformed the market. The 'benchmark' portfolios against which the performance of managed portfolios may be evaluated are merely combinations of the risk-free asset and the market index. The CAPM equation (4.8) is stated in terms of investors' expectations rather than in terms of realized returns. If, however, realized returns are observed over a reasonably large number of periods and average realized returns calculated, then the following relationship holds approximately:

$$\bar{R} = \bar{R}_F + \beta_p(\bar{R}_M - \bar{R}_F) \tag{4.14}$$

where $\bar{R}$, $\bar{R}_M$ and $\bar{R}_F$ are the (arithmetic) average realized rates of return on the portfolio, the market and the risk-free asset. Thus the return on the performance standard for a managed portfolio with risk factor β_p is given by

$$\bar{R}_S = \bar{R}_F + \beta_p(\bar{R}_M - \bar{R}_F) \tag{4.15}$$

where $\bar{R}_S$ is the average realized rate of return on the performance standard. If $\bar{R}_p$ denotes the (arithmetic) average realized rate of return on the managed portfolio, then the portfolio manager's performance may be measured by

$$\bar{\alpha}^*_p = \bar{R}_p - \bar{R}_S \tag{4.16}$$

Managed portfolios for which $\bar{\alpha}^*_p$ is positive have outperformed the standard, and those for which $\bar{\alpha}^*_p$ is negative have underperformed the standard. Of course, the CAPM assumes that $E(\bar{R}_p) = E(\bar{R}_S)$, that is $E(\bar{\alpha}^*_p) = 0$.

The return on the managed portfolio is given by the market model (4.12):

$$R_p = [\alpha_p - R_F(1 - \beta_p)] + R_F + \beta_p(R_M - R_F) + U_p$$

If realized returns are observed over a reasonably large number of periods and average realized returns calculated, then the following market model relationship holds approximately:

$$\overline{R}_p = [\,\alpha_p - \overline{R}_F(1 - \beta_p)\,] + \overline{R}_F + \beta_p(\overline{R}_M - \overline{R}_F) \tag{4.17}$$

Subtracting equation (4.15) from equation (4.17) gives

$$\overline{R}_p - \overline{R}_S = \alpha_p - \overline{R}_F(1 - \beta_p) \tag{4.18}$$

Thus

$$\overline{\alpha}^*{}_p = \alpha_p - \overline{R}_F(1 - \beta_p) \tag{4.19}$$

or

$$\alpha^*{}_p = \alpha_p - R_F(1 - \beta_p) \tag{4.20}$$

Now $[\alpha_p - R_F(1 - \beta_p)]$ is the 'risk-adjusted excess return'. Hence, a managed portfolio with a positive estimated risk-adjusted excess return has beaten the performance standard, whereas one with a negative value has underperformed the standard.

Risk Measurement Services

In order to obtain risk and return measures for individual securities or portfolios, risk measurement services may be consulted. Organizations which provide such services on a regular basis exist in several countries. In the UK a major institution which provides risk measures is the London Business School (LBS) through its *Risk Measurement Service* (RMS). A more comprehensive description of the RMS is given in Dimson and Marsh (1979, 1982) and Marsh (1980). Each quarter the RMS publishes risk and return measures for approximately 2000 British shares. These measures are based on an analysis of share price movements over the previous five years, using data collected at monthly intervals. Thus, in general, each estimate is based on 60 observations. In order to estimate the market model (4.11) the monthly returns (dividend yield plus capital appreciation) are calculated for each share, and also the corresponding returns for the market index. The Financial Times All-Share Index, which accounts for approximately 90 per cent of the UK market by value, is used as an approximation for the market index. An ordinary least-squares regression of the return on the ith security on the market return yields estimates of the coefficients α and β for the ith security, which may be denoted by $\hat{\alpha}_i$ and $\hat{\beta}_i$, respectively. Several risk measures are tabulated: the *variability* of a share is measured by the standard deviation of the returns on the share, and indicates the total risk attaching to the share; *beta* represents the market risk component of total risk; the *specific risk* figure is calculated as the standard deviation of the error term in equation (4.11). In addition, the *quarterly* (and *annual*) *abnormal return* figures are tabulated; these measure the performance of the share over the previous quarter (year), relative to the market as a whole, and correspond to the concept of 'risk-adjusted excess return'. The abnormal return is thus equal to the difference between the actual return on a share and the return which could have been obtained over the same period from an investment in a perfectly diversified portfolio with the same beta.

Portfolio risk and return measures may be estimated from information on the constituent shares of the portfolio. The β *factor* of a portfolio is equal to a weighted average of those of the individual securities:

$$\beta_p = \sum_{i=1}^{n} X_i \beta_i \tag{4.21}$$

where β_p is the beta of the portfolio

β_i is the beta of security i

X_i is the proportion of the market value of the portfolio invested in security i

n is the number of securities in the portfolio.

The measurement of the *specific risk* of a portfolio is somewhat more complicated. However, if the portfolio is fairly well-diversified, so that it is reasonable to assume that the only link amongst the constituent shares is through their tendency to move with the market, then the specific risk of a portfolio may be calculated approximately from the specific risk figures for the individual shares as follows:

$$(\sigma_p^u)^2 = \sum_{i=1}^{n} X_i^2 (\sigma_i^u)^2 \tag{4.22}$$

where σ_p^u is portfolio unsystematic risk

σ_i^u is the unsystematic risk of security i

X_i and n are as defined in equation (4.21).

Portfolio *variability* may be calculated from a knowledge of the market risk and specific risk of the portfolio:

$$\left(\begin{matrix} \text{Portfolio} \\ \text{variability} \end{matrix} \right)^2 = \left(\begin{matrix} \text{Portfolio} \\ \text{market risk} \end{matrix} \right)^2 + \left(\begin{matrix} \text{Portfolio} \\ \text{specific risk} \end{matrix} \right)^2 \tag{4.23}$$

The variability of a portfolio may therefore be calculated once the beta value and specific risk of the portfolio are known. The only additional information required is the variability of the market index, σ_M.

The following example shows how the risk and return measures for individual securities given in the RMS may be used to calculate the corresponding measures for portfolios. It is supposed that a portfolio comprises holdings in the three companies listed in table 4.1 in the proportions given in table 4.2. The three risk measures, variability, beta and specific risk, are calculated as follows. The beta of the portfolio, β_p, is obtained by substituting into equation (4.21):

$$\beta_p = \sum_{i=1}^{n} X_i \beta_i$$

$$= (0.5)(1.03) + (0.4)(0.44) + (0.1)(1.18)$$

$$= 0.81$$

Thus the market risk of the portfolio is 0.81 times the risk of the Financial Times All-Share Index. Now the values for the risk measures tabulated in the RMS imply that the variability of the Index is 17 per cent, and so the market risk of the portfolio is $(0.81)(17) = 14$ per cent. The specific risk of the portfolio, $\sigma_p{}^u$, is given by substituting into equation (4.22):

$$(\sigma_p{}^u)^2 = \sum_{i=1}^{n} X_i^2 (\sigma_i{}^u)^2$$

$$= (0.5)^2(15)^2 + (0.4)^2(13)^2 + (0.1)^2(22)^2$$

$$= 88$$

$$\therefore \sigma_p{}^u = 9 \text{ per cent}$$

Finally, the variability of the portfolio, $S(R_p)$, may be calculated by substituting the appropriate values into equation (4.23):

$$[S(R_p)]^2 = \left(\begin{array}{c} \text{Portfolio} \\ \text{market risk} \end{array} \right)^2 + \left(\begin{array}{c} \text{Portfolio} \\ \text{specific risk} \end{array} \right)^2$$

$$= 190 + 88$$

$$= 278$$

$$\therefore S(R_p) = 17 \text{ per cent}$$

Table 4.1 Risk and return measures for selected companies

Company name	Stock Exchange industry classification	Variability (%)	Beta	Specific risk (%)	Annual actual return (%)	Quarterly abnormal return (%)	Annual abnormal return (%)
Hambros Investment Trust plc	Investment Trust	22	1.03	15	27	–7	–9
Hardys and Hansons	Brewery	15	0.44	13	43	8	21
Hepworth Ceramic	Building Materials	30	1.18	22	62	8	20

Source: Dimson, E. and Marsh, P. R. (eds), *Risk Measurement Service*, vol 8, No 2, April 1986, p. 48

Table 4.2 Portfolio composition (example)

Company name	Fraction of porfolio
Hambros Investment Trust plc	0.5
Hardys and Hansons	0.4
Hepworth Ceramic	0.1

The return measures for portfolios are simply the weighted averages of the corresponding returns on the constituent securities. Thus the annual actual return of the portfolio depicted in table 4.2 is calculated as follows, using information from tables 4.1 and 4.2:

Annual actual
return on portfolio $= (0.5)(27) + (0.4)(43) + (0.1)(62)$

$= 37$ per cent

The quarterly and annual abnormal returns may also be calculated from the data in tables 4.1 and 4.2:

Quarterly abnormal
return on portfolio $= (0.5)(-7) + (0.4)(8) + (0.1)(8)$
$= 1$ per cent

Annual abnormal
return on portfolio $= (0.5)(-9) + (0.4)(21) + (0.1)(20)$

$= 6$ per cent

The Efficient Market Hypothesis

The efficient market hypothesis (EMH) suggests that at any point in time share prices fully reflect all information, any new or shock information being immediately incorporated into the share price. In highly competitive markets such as the New York Stock Exchange or London Stock Exchange we should expect prices to fully reflect anticipations. A great many individuals and financial institutions participate in the market. They have access to a great deal of information such as economic forecasts, stockbrokers' reports, newspaper articles, investment advisory services, and company reports. They know the current market price of all quoted securities and have access to past price movements. Many have access to computers, and some use risk measurement services. In such highly competitive and well-informed markets, we should expect prices to fully reflect all available information, and we should expect prices to adjust very rapidly to any new or shock information.

This apparently simple hypothesis, to the extent that it holds in the real world, has very powerful implications for investment analysis and corporate management. The hypothesis is impossible to test directly, as we would need to know the market's anticipated net operational cash flows and anticipated required rates of return for all future periods. We would need to know all information relevant to security prices and the way this information is reflected in prices. It is therefore necessary to design tests of the hypothesis based on available information and available statistical techniques. Tests of the EMH are generally made under the assumptions of zero transaction costs, no taxation, free access to all available information for all traders, and agreement among them as to the implications of information for security prices. A great deal of evidence supports the hypothesis, such evidence appearing in three forms – the weak form, the semi-strong form and the strong form. Weak form tests of the EMH are concerned with the extent to which historic share prices can be used to predict future prices. A great deal of evidence suggests that such footsteps cannot predict the future. Semi-strong form tests attempt to measure the extent to which share prices fully reflect all publicly available information. Investors anticipate and react to publicly available information relating to stock splits, earnings announcements, dividend announcements, forecasts, and large block trades. Most of the research suggests that it is extremely difficult to earn excess returns using publicly available information. Finally, strong form tests are designed to discover whether share prices reflect all information, even information which is not available to the public. The studies are generally concerned with the stock market performance of professional investors and fund managers. Most of the evidence suggests that the professionals do not have access to techniques enabling them to earn returns greater than returns expected for the level of accepted market risk.

Some evidence against the EMH is available. Stock market specialists and corporate insiders have monopolistic access to information which, on occasions, enables them to earn superior returns. Furthermore, there is evidence that some people do have better forecasting ability than the rest of us. It is therefore possible to beat the EMH – but it is extremely difficult. Modern stock markets do appear to be efficient in that share prices do reflect all available information, any new information being very rapidly incorporated into the share price in an unbiased way by the competitive trading activities of many investors.

At first glance the EMH is readily acceptable to students, managers and even stock market professionals. Surely, in very competitive, open markets such as the New York and London Stock Exchanges, the activities of millions of market participants will generate the equilibrium price which reflects anticipations about cash flows and market risk. Surely in these competitive markets we would expect share prices to react immediately to new information affecting anticipations. The hypothesis of efficient capital markets seems reasonable and fairly harmless – until we examine its implications. Once we discuss the implications of the EMH many students, managers and particularly stock market professionals, become strongly opposed to the idea of market efficiency. We shall now discuss some of these implications.

The EMH suggests that the net present value of any security acquisition is zero, i.e. investors pay the market price for investments. Market prices are the best estimates of present value. It is therefore not necessary for the individual to take a view as to the appropriateness of the current share price, as he or she can accept the existing market price as the best estimate of intrinsic value. There are no bargains. A whole lifetime can be spent by investors studying the wealth of accounting data and press coverage relating to companies, industries and economies, but for the investor such study is almost certainly a waste of time as all the available information is already reflected in the share price. In an efficient market share prices reflect anticipations. Investors take a view about future net operational cash flow and risk. Therefore, when a company's earnings for the current year are announced as being a significant improvement on the preceding year we should not expect the share price to either rise or fall. On average the market gets it right. Only the shock announcements result in price changes, and share prices do change very rapidly on the announcement of new information relating to expected cash flow and risk. In a market in which share prices fully reflect all available information, and in which the net present value of all acquisitions is zero, there is little point in continuous switching from one security to another. Switching investments incurs transaction costs and the possibility of taxation. Modern portfolio theory suggests that investors should choose their preferred portfolio and then avoid transaction costs by pursuing buy-and-hold policies, revising the portfolio on occasion to maintain the preferred level of risk.

Pension Fund Management

Portfolio managers may adopt either an active or a passive management strategy. It is also possible to pursue a combination of active and passive policies.

Passive management accepts all forms of the efficient market hypotheses (EMH). In this case it is assumed that the stock market is so efficient that it is almost impossible to construct a portfolio which is superior to the market portfolio, and so the equity part of the investor's portfolio should merely comprise the market portfolio. The latter may then be combined with lending or borrowing at the risk-free rate of interest in order to yield, respectively, a (low-risk) lending or (high-risk) borrowing portfolio. Since the market portfolio represents the optimal combination of risky securities, the investor's choice of risk level is a purely financial decision – whether to hold a lending or borrowing portfolio. A passive investment strategy involves constructing and maintaining a portfolio that always lies on the capital market line. The portfolio under management should only be reorganized when there is a change in either the investor's risk-return preference or the market portfolio. A portfolio manager pursuing a passive strategy accepts that it is impossible to beat the market, and thus attempts to minimize transactions and research costs. In practice, the market portfolio may be approximated by index funds. These funds are widely diversified portfolios of securities which attempt to match the performance of broad stock market averages such as the FT All-Share Index. The cost of pension fund portfolio management can be very low if a fund's trustees use a professional service offering the required level of risk, rather than employing investment analysts with their associated office, information, and computing costs.

If the EMH is not accepted, a portfolio manager may engage in active management. This is an attempt to profit from stock selection and/or market timing. A manager who rejects the semi-strong form of the EMH believes that it is possible to use superior analytical skills to construct a portfolio which, if properly managed, will consistently outperform the market portfolio. Such a portfolio manager uses fundamental analysis to identify undervalued securities which are then used to construct a portfolio with the desired risk level. As the portfolio comprises undervalued securities, it should perform consistently better than the market portfolio. An investment manager who rejects the weak form of the EMH believes that it is possible to beat the market by identifying when a given security or the market is overbought or oversold. This type of portfolio manager uses technical analysis to predict the level of security prices in the immediate future. A comparison of the predicted with the actual price level indicates whether the security (or the market) is currently priced too high or too low. Consistent above-average returns have not generally been associated with individual professional managers, other than those having access to inside information – corporate insiders and specialists. Excess returns can be made where the investor has access to non-public information as well as all other information available to other investors. Unfortunately, inside information is very difficult to obtain and even when such information is available there are legal pitfalls should the user of the information be discovered.

Furthermore, the receiver of inside information must forecast correctly the effect of such information on share prices when the information becomes public.

Combined active-passive management strategies may be used for big portfolios if the EMH is largely, but not entirely, accepted. A proportion of an investment fund, say 90 per cent, may be indexed to the market, and the remainder controlled by active portfolio managers. The higher the degree of confidence in benefiting from active management strategies, the greater the proportion of total assets which will be allocated to active managers.

Risk measurement services can assist active portfolio managers in their attempts to outperform the market. With regard to correct market timing, if the investment manager expects the market to move up then the correct strategy would be to move into high β shares. Similarly, if the investment manager expects the market to fall he should move into low β shares or go liquid. If the market movement is forecast correctly, the chosen portfolio should outperform the market index. With regard to share selection, the greatest scope for finding undervalued securities occurs amongst those with the highest specific risk, and thus the RMS gives an indication as to where analytical effort should be concentrated. The abnormal return figures for a security show whether it appears to have been undervalued or overvalued in the recent past. If securities are selected which turn out to be undervalued, then the chosen portfolio will outperform the market index.

Implications of Modern Portfolio Theory for Capital Budgeting

The linear trade-off between risk and return embodied in the capital-asset pricing model can help to identify the required rates of return on industrial and commercial projects. To plot the security market line it is necessary to identify the risk-free rate of interest (where the β coefficient is zero) and the return on the market portfolio (where the β coefficient is one). The firm's beta can be calculated by regressing its periodic returns on the periodic returns of the market index, or alternatively, it may be located in, say, the London Business School's *Risk Measurement Service*. The firm's beta identifies the average required rate of return from the security market line. However, this average cost of capital cannot be used for individual projects. There is a trade-off between risk and return and theoretically we should estimate a beta coefficient for each individual project within the firm.

The corporate β for a company financed entirely by equity is the weighted average beta of all projects. For example, suppose a company has two projects. Project A is a low risk investment with a required rate of return of 10 per cent, while project B is a higher risk project with a required rate

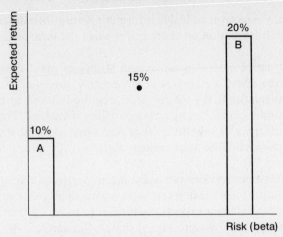

Figure 4.8   Weighted average required rate of return

of return of 20 per cent. Both projects are of equal value, having a present value of £1,000. Figure 4.8 shows both projects and the weighted average required rate of return for the portfolio at 15 per cent. Project A is expected to earn £100 on the £1,000 investment, and project B is expected to earn £200 on the £1,000 investment. The expected weighted average is £300 on a £2,000 investment, i.e. 15 per cent. If the company invests only in projects similar to A and B, then the weighted average required rate of return of 15 per cent is arithmetically interesting but cannot be used as the discount rate on the company's projects. It is simply the weighted average. Each individual project must be assessed by its market risk, i.e. by its own beta, not the corporate weighted average. In our example, 15 per cent is not the required rate of return on any of the company's projects. If a financial manager uses the weighted average cost of capital to assess individual projects, then that manager is ignoring risk.

Figure 4.9 illustrates the errors which could be made if risk is ignored. The security market line (SML) is our best estimate of the trade-off between risk and return. The financial manager discounts the anticipated cash flows on all projects at 15 per cent. Project A would be rejected because it earns less than 15 per cent. However, if the SML illustrates the true trade-off between risk and return, then project A should be accepted because it earns a higher rate of return than the required rate of return. It has a positive net present value. Project B earns more than 15 per cent. The financial manager might accept it. However, it is expected to earn a lower rate of return than the required rate of return for a project with its individual level of risk. It should be rejected. If we ignore risk in the capital budgeting process, then there will be a tendency to reject low risk profitable projects such as project A, and a tendency to accept high risk unprofitable projects

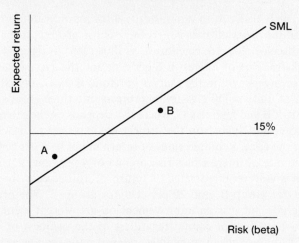

Figure 4.9 Trade-off between risk and return

such as project B. It is therefore essential to discount the anticipated cash flows on individual projects at different discount rates. The discount rate or required rate of return depends on individual project risk.

A *firm* can be viewed as a *collection* or *portfolio* of *individual projects*. Now diversification removes specific risk and therefore the inclusion of one more investment in a well diversified portfolio implies only a change in the portfolio's market risk. Thus a *project's value* is *its anticipated cash flows discounted at a rate which reflects its economic or market risk*. In figure 4.8 our two projects are discounted at 10 per cent and 20 per cent respectively.

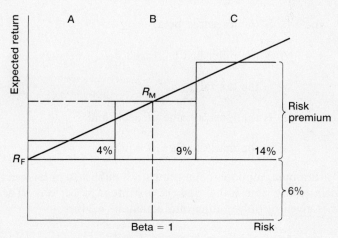

Figure 4.10 Assessing individual project risk

It is extremely difficult to establish the β for an individual project, but for practical purposes all that is necessary is for projects to be classified into, say, three or five risk categories, as illustrated in figure 4.10. If the historic risk-free rate of interest is 6 per cent and the average historic risk premium for investment in the market portfolio is 9 per cent, then a firm with a beta of unity might classify its projects into three groups – low risk A, average risk B and high risk C, where risk depends on the extent to which the cash flows anticipated on the project are expected to move with the average for the firm. Required rates of return might be 6 per cent to cover the risk-free rate of interest plus risk premia of 4 per cent, 9 per cent and 14 per cent giving required rates of return of 10 per cent for group A, 15 per cent for group B, and 20 per cent for group C. The procedure is obviously crude but it is an improvement on net present value using the estimated overall cost of capital regardless of the riskiness of individual projects. For divisionalized companies, rates of return can be generated for each division by identifying the betas of independent quoted companies in the same business or risk class.

A firm's β is influenced by economic risk and financial risk. Financial risk arises on the introduction of debt into a firm's capital structure. Projects should offer returns commensurate with their economic risk, and it is therefore necessary to reduce the reported corporate beta to an unlevered corporate beta for the purposes of capital expenditure analysis. A published beta can be reduced to an ungeared beta as follows:

$$\beta_u = \frac{\beta_\ell}{1 + [1 - t]\frac{D}{E}} \tag{4.24}$$

where β_u is the ungeared beta,

β_ℓ is the published leveraged beta,

t is the tax rate,

D is the market value of debt, and

E is the market value of equity.

For example, suppose that a company's published or levered beta is 1.5, its debt-equity ratio is 0.4, and the tax rate is 52 per cent. The unlevered beta is given by substituting into equation (4.24):

$$\frac{5}{1 + (0.48)(0.4)} = 1.26$$

If the after-tax risk-free rate of interest is 6 per cent, and the after-tax required rate of return on the market portfolio is 15 per cent, then the weighted average expected rate of return on company i's investments is given by the CAPM (4.8):

$$E(R_i) = R_F + \beta_i [E(R_M) - R_F]$$

$$= 7\% + 1.26(15\% - 7\%) = 17 \text{ per cent.}$$

The required rate of return on an individual investment is then obtained by classifying the project as low risk, average risk or high risk; the required rate of return on average risk projects is 17 per cent, on low risk projects $17 - 5$ (say) $= 12$ per cent, and on high risk projects $17 + 5$ (say) $= 22$ per cent.

Summary

Modern investment management is based on *risk management*, and various risk measurement services offer the necessary data. If an investor accepts the efficient market hypothesis and the capital-asset pricing model then there is no point in trying to achieve security returns in excess of those offered for accepting market risk as measured by beta. The investor must *decide* on the *level of market risk* he or she is prepared to accept, bearing in mind that, on average, rewards are related to market risk. Diversification removes specific risk, so the *market portfolio*, or a *reasonable approximation*, should be held by all investors. Risk can be reduced or increased by the use of *leverage*.

Investors can make excess return by luck, use of inside information, or by demonstrating forecasting ability. If investors pursue *active management*, the *performance* of the portfolio can be measured to see whether *positive risk adjusted excess returns* are consistently achieved.

The capital-asset pricing model may also be used to identify the *required rates of return* on *industrial* and *commercial projects*. It is essential to discount forecast project cash flows at a rate which reflects the economic risk of the project.

Appendix: Options

An alternative to purchasing a share is to purchase an option on a share. Pension fund managers who wish to diversify their asset holdings may make use of this additional form of investment.

An option is a contract between two investors A and B in which A pays B a sum of money, and in exchange B grants A the right to buy from or sell to B, at A's discretion, a share at a fixed price until a pre-determined date after which any rights or obligations expire. Investor A, who possesses the discretionary right to buy or sell, is known as the buyer of the option or the giver of option money. If he or she uses his right, investor A is said to exercise or declare the option. Investor B, who grants the right to buy or sell, is called the seller or writer of the option, or the taker of option money. An option to buy is termed a call option, and an option to sell is termed a put option. The sum of money paid for the right of the option is known as the premium or option money. The fixed price specified in the option contract is called the exercise, striking or contract price. The future fixed date is known as the expiration, maturity or last declaration date; a European option may only be exercised on the date when the option expires, whereas an American option may be exercised at any time until the expiration date.

A call option gives the buyer the right to purchase from the writer, for a specified length of time, a given number of shares in a company at a price fixed by the contract. The benefit to the seller of a call option is that whilst he or she typically forgoes the opportunity for further appreciation in the value of a stock which he or she owns, the option premium is gained in the event that the value of the asset drops. *The buyer of a call option benefits from being able to control a larger quantity of stock through the payment of option premiums than would be the case if he or she purchased the stock outright.* The buyer gains from any increase in the value of the stock although his or her only expenditure is the option premium. Potential loss is limited to the amount of the option money, but this loss will be total unless the share price rises above the exercise price of the option. The option writer has a limited possible gain and potentially unlimited loss. The option buyer has limited possible loss and potentially unlimited gain.

The profit or loss arising from the option contract is illustrated for both seller and buyer in figure 4.11. It is supposed that the exercise price is 100 pence and the option premium is 10 pence. It can be seen that the break-even point is the exercise price plus the option premium; here the option seller and buyer are neither better nor worse off than they would have been if the contract had not been agreed. If the share price at the expiration date is 100 pence or less the owner of the share gains 10 pence by having written the option, and the option buyer loses 10 pence. As the share price increases from 100 to 110 pence, there is a steady reduction in the option seller's gain and the option buyer's loss. For share prices which exceed 110 pence at the expiration date, the option buyer makes a profit which rises in line with the share price. Similarly, the option writer makes an economic loss for stock prices in excess of 110 pence, since he or she would have fared better had they not written the option.

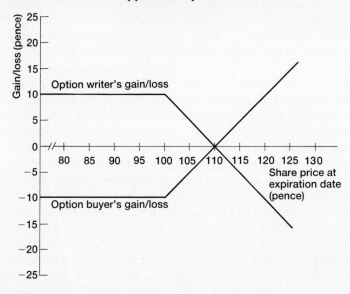

Figure 4.11 Gain/loss arising from call option contract (Example)

A put option gives the buyer the right of delivering to the writer, for a specified length of time, a given number of shares in a company at a price fixed by the contract. The positions of the option buyer and option writer in the case of the put contract are reversed compared with the call contract; for a put option the writer gains from any increase in the value of the stock and the buyer benefits if the share price falls.

The most popular type of option contract is the call option, and so for illustrative purposes we shall concentrate on this type of contract. To aid simplification we assume that no cash payments are made by the underlying asset, and we restrict our attention to European options.

The market price of an option (or option premium) is determined by the following set of factors:

1 the current price of the underlying share;
2 the exercise price;
3 the length of time to expiration;
4 the risk attaching to the underlying share;
5 the risk-free rate of interest.

Obviously, we should expect that the higher the current market value of a share, the greater the value of an option written on it, *ceteris paribus*. Similarly, the lower the exercise price, the higher the value of the option. Now the minimum possible level of the option premium is termed the intrinsic value of the option. If the current price of the underlying share exceeds the exercise price, that is the option is 'in the money', then the intrinsic value of the option is the difference between the share price and exercise price. If the exercise price exceeds the current share price, that is the option is 'out of the money', then the intrinsic value of the option is zero. The intrinsic value thus depends merely on the share price and exercise price.

The excess of the option premium over its intrinsic value is known as the time value of the option. For example, even if the share price is less than the exercise price, the option will still be valuable provided that investors believe that there is a chance that the share price will exceed the exercise price before the option expires. On account of the possibility that the share price may be at a higher level in the future than now, investors are generally prepared to pay more for an option than its intrinsic value, that is the time value of an option is positive. The greater the length of time to maturity, the higher the time value of the option, since there is increasing opportunity for the price of the underlying share to rise. Thus the value of an option increases with the length of time to expiration.

The price of an option varies with the risk of the underlying share. Clearly if there were no risk, that is the variance of the return on the share were zero, then the price of the share would remain constant into the future, and the time value of the option would be zero. The more risky the underlying share, the more valuable the option, as there is a higher probability that the share price will exceed the exercise price, and the option holder only benefits if this latter condition holds at the expiration date. For a given expected return, the investor prefers to hold shares with minimum risk but options on shares which have maximum risk.

The risk-free rate of interest also affects the value of an option. By purchasing an option, the holder is provided with a form of gearing. If an investor expects the price of a share to rise in the future, he or she may either purchase that share or alternatively an option on that share in order to realize the expected capital gain. If the current price of the underlying share is 200 pence and the option price is 20 pence, then the holder spends 180 pence less by buying the option rather than the share itself. An option thus provides a substitute for borrowing. The higher the risk-free rate of interest, the greater the amount of interest saved by purchasing the option rather than the share, and therefore the higher the value of the option.

The market value of an option is given by the following relationship:

$$P_o = f(P_s, E, \sigma, T, R_F) \qquad (4.25)$$

where P_o is the current value of the option,

P_s is the current price of the share,

E is the exercise price of the option,

σ is the standard deviation of the return on the share,

T is the length of time to expiration of the option,

R_F is the risk-free rate of interest, and

f is some function.

The partial derivatives of the option price with respect to the various arguments are

$$\frac{\delta P_o}{\delta P_s} > 0, \frac{\delta P_o}{\delta E} < 0, \frac{\delta P_o}{\delta \sigma} > 0, \frac{\delta P_o}{\delta T} > 0, \frac{\delta P_o}{\delta R_F} > 0 \qquad (4.26)$$

Black and Scholes (1973) have derived a precise mathematical formula for the valuation of European call options, which incorporates the variables specified in equation (4.25). Now, share price information is readily available, and the exercise price and time to maturity are given for each option. The risk-free rate of interest may easily be approximated. The riskiness of the underlying share is usually obtained from historical data; for example, the London Business School's *Risk Measurement Service* provides estimates of the variabilities (or standard deviations) of return for all tabulated shares. Empirical evidence from the USA reported by Black and Scholes (1972) and Galai (1977) implies that the Black-Scholes option pricing model predicts prices so well that it is possible to earn excess returns in the absence of transactions costs. These excess returns disappear, however, once transactions costs are introduced, so prices are determined efficiently down to the level of transactions costs.

The London Traded Option Market was established in 1978. Share options are therefore relatively new to the UK, but represent an alternative investment channel for pension fund managers who seek to diversify their asset holdings.

Study Questions

4.1   The directors of Crosshills Engineering are considering the acquisition of a new machine. The initial cost and setting-up expenses will amount to about £150,000. Its estimated life is about three years, and estimated annual accounting profit is as follows:

Year	1	2	3
Operational cash flow (£)	60,000	100,000	30,000
Depreciation (£)	50,000	50,000	50,000
Accounting profit (£)	10,000	50,000	(20,000)

At the end of its three year life, the installation will yield only a few pounds in scrap value. The company classifies its projects as follows:

Required rate of return

Low risk	14 per cent
Average risk	22 per cent
High risk	30 per cent

1 Should the machine in installed?
2 Discuss the techniques available for assessing capital projects.

4.2 The directors of Kildwick Engineering Ltd are considering the acquisition of a new CNC machine which could generate incremental cash inflows and outflows as follows:

Year	1	2	3	4	5
Income (£)	80,000	90,000	60,000	50,000	30,000
Expenditure (£)	30,000	50,000	20,000	30,000	20,000
Incremental cash flow before tax (£)	50,000	40,000	40,000	20,000	10,000

The immediate initial outlay to acquire the CNC machine and set it up for operations is estimated at £80,000. (For financial accounting purposes, new machinery is depreciated on a straight-line basis.) The corporate planning team has categorized all projects as follows:

	Risk	After tax required rate of return (%)
A	Low	15
B	Average	25
C	High	30

The facility under consideration is expected to be of interest to existing customers and the riskiness of the project no greater than average. The company pays tax at 30 per cent about one year after earning its cash flow, and the residual value of the CNC machine after five years is estimated at £18,000. An annual allowance of 25 per cent is available.

1 Present data showing whether or not the acquisition is wealth-creating.
2 List the techniques for assessing capital projects. Why is NPV generally recommended?

4.3 The directors of Kenley & Co usually undertake high-risk contracts (beta = 2.0) in the demolition industry. They have been offered a housing clearance contract which they consider to be about 50 per cent as risky as the company's other contracts. The contract under consideration offers about £800,000 per annum for two years, incremental costs associated with the project being about £400,000 per annum. An initial outlay for plant and setting-up costs will be required amounting to £100,000 which qualifies for a 25 per cent annual allowance. The directors expect the company to be paying corporation tax at 30 per cent for the foreseeable future, about 1 year after earning its cash flows. In the financial accounts depreciation at 40 per cent straight-line will be charged on the new plant. The project will be charged with a proportion of the firm's fixed costs. At the end of the contract the acquired plant will probably be sold for about £20,000. After-tax interest rates stand at 6 per cent and the after-tax return on the market is estimated at 15 per cent.

As financial director, draft a report to your board outlining the theory of wealth creation and make a recommendation on the above project using traditional and modern techniques of investment appraisal.

4.4 The directors of Ultracrux Inc usually undertake high risk contracts (beta = 2.5) in the publishing industry. They have been offered a local authority print contract which they consider to be about 30 per cent as risky as the company's other contracts. The contract under consideration offers about £50,000 per annum for 3 years, incremental costs associated with the project being about £20,000 per annum. An initial outlay for plant and setting-up costs will be required amounting to £15,000 (which we shall assume will qualify for a 25 per cent annual allowance). The directors expect the company to be paying corporation tax at 30 per cent for the foreseeable future, about one year after earning its cash flows. (Depreciation at 30 per cent straight-line will be charged on the new plant and the project will be charged with a proportion of the firm's fixed costs.) At the end of the contract the acquired plant will probably be sold for about £6,000. After-tax interest rates stand at 7 per cent and the after-tax return on the market is estimated at 15 per cent.

As Financial Director, draft a report to your board covering the following:

1 How can firms make sensible wealth-creating investment decisions?
2 Should the above print contract be accepted?
3 The Marketing Director of Ultracrux suggests that the above project could be financed partly by debt. Comment briefly.

4.5 The securities of companies A and B have the following expected returns and standard deviations of return:

Company	Expected return (%)	Standard deviation of return (%)
A	13	18
B	8	12

In addition the expected correlation of returns between the two stocks is 0.5.

1 Calculate the expected return and risk for the following portfolios:
   (a) 100% in A
   (b) 100% in B
   (c) 75% in A, 25% in B
   (d) 25% in A, 75% in B
   (e) 50% in A, 50% in B.
2 How much of the portfolio should be invested in company A in order to minimize risk?
3 Plot the results.
4 Which of the portfolios described in 1 and 2 are optimal?
5 Repeat 1, 2, 3 and 4 for expected correlations of:
      (i)   − 0.5
      (ii)   1.0
      (iii) − 1.0
      (iv)   0.0.

4.6 Suppose that, over a five-year period, the average risk-free rate of interest was 7 per cent, the average market return was 12 per cent and the performances of four portfolio managers were as follows:

Portfolio manager	Average return (%)	Beta
A	10	0.70
B	12	0.95
C	13	1.20
D	16	1.35

1 Calculate the expected return for each portfolio manager.
2 Calculate the risk-adjusted excess return for each portfolio manager.
2 Rank the portfolio managers in terms of risk-adjusted performance.

Further Reading

Brealey, Richard and Myers, Stewart. *Principles of Corporate Finance*. New York: McGraw-Hill, 1984, chapters 7, 8, 9, 13.

Dobbins, Richard and Witt, Stephen F. *Portfolio Theory and Investment Management*. Oxford: Basil Blackwell, 1983.

Franks, Julian R., Broyles, John E. and Carleton, Willard T. *Corporate Finance: Concepts and Applications*. Boston, Mass.: Kent Publishing, 1985, chapter 8.

Part II
Financing Decisions

5

Capital Structure Decisions

The Theory of Capital Structure Decisions

The objective of the firm is to maximize its current market value, that is to maximize shareholder wealth. Firms create wealth by making successful investment decisions which generate positive net cash flows. Now, the *capital structure decision* determines the balance of debt and equity in the firm, and is a *financing decision*. Investment decisions are far more important than financing decisions, but it is still necessary to make sensible financing decisions. Thus if corporate managers can maximize the market value of the firm by manipulating the debt–equity ratio, then they should do so. The optimal capital structure policy, if there is one, is the policy which maximizes shareholder wealth.

Leverage, or gearing, is the extent to which the firm is financed by borrowing. As equity is more risky than debt, rational risk-averse investors will expect a higher rate of return on equity. Leverage can therefore also be defined as *the use of low cost debt*, although there is a compensating increased required rate of return on equity – the hidden cost of debt. A salient problem with increasing total borrowing is that it increases the volatility of residual cash flows for shareholders; it adds *financial risk* to *business risk*. Shareholders do not like risk, and will expect higher returns for taking on this financial risk in addition to the business risk they have accepted by purchasing a stake in the firm's future volatile operational cash flows. Now if taxation and costs of financial distress are ignored, it is unlikely that there is an optimal capital structure. However, as interest is tax deductible, firms can increase after-tax cash flows by borrowing, that is corporate taxation favours the use of low cost debt, but there is a risk of the firm being forced into liquidation should the investment schedule not produce adequate cash flows to pay interest on debt, and make the necessary debt repayments. There are considerable costs associated with

financial distress, and if the company is eventually forced into liquidation
then heavy transaction costs and delays will be borne by shareholders. There
is therefore a trade-off between the tax benefit of borrowing and the costs
of financial distress or bankruptcy; *firms should borrow to get the tax
benefit on interest paid but not so much as to incur the costs of financial
distress.*

At the optimal level of borrowing – if such a level exists – the firm's
weighted average cost of capital is minimized, and the market value of any
given level of cash flows is maximized, assuming that cash flows are
capitalized at the firm's weighted average cost of capital. For example, a
constant £10,000 per annum in perpetuity discounted at a weighted average
cost of capital of 25 per cent has a present value of £10,000/0.25 = £40,000.
If the discount rate is reduced to 20 per cent the same constant level of
cash flows has a present value of £50,000. Hence, lowering the required
rate of return increases the present value of anticipated cash flows. Now,
is it possible for firms to lower the average required rate of return by varying
the mix of debt and equity?

The market value of a firm is its discounted net anticipated operational
cash flows:

$$V = \sum_{t=1}^{n} \frac{1}{(1+r)^t}(R - W - I)_t \tag{5.1}$$

where

V = the value of the firm

r = the required rate of return

R = operational cash receipts

W = operational cash expenditures

I = new investment

This present value formula does not make any reference to the financing
of projects; the value of the firm is not determined by leverage policies.
In an efficient market, two companies with identical investment schedules
promising the same cash flows at the same level of risk must have exactly
the same market value, regardless of the method of financing (ignoring
taxation, and transaction and bankruptcy costs). Consider two companies
with anticipated cash flows of £6,000 per annum in perpetuity in an industry
risk class where anticipated cash flows are capitalized at 20 per cent:

$$V = \frac{\bar{X}}{r} = \frac{\pounds6,000}{0.2} = \frac{\text{net operational cash flows}}{\text{capitalization rate}} \qquad (5.2)$$

Value = £30,000

Company A
Financing decision
(%)

Debt	40
Equity	60
	100

Company B
Financing decision
(%)

	60
	40
	100

The market value of the investment schedules must be identical at £30,000. Company A is financed by 40 per cent debt and 60 per cent equity while Company B is financed by 60 per cent debt and 40 per cent equity. The financing decision must be distinguished from the investment decision. Investment schedules are valued on the basis of operational cash flows and operational risk. Financing decisions in a world without taxation, transaction and bankruptcy costs do not influence the value of the investment schedule.

The *traditional view* of capital structure policy is that the market value of the firm's investment schedule can be increased by the judicious use of debt finance. Table 5.1 illustrates an extreme view of the traditional approach in that the cost of equity remains constant for all levels of leverage at 15 per cent. If this is the case, then it is possible for managers to manipulate the market value of the company by manipulating the capital structure. In company B, the market value of equity is £2.4m and the total market value of the firm is increased from £2.667m for the all-equity financed company (C), to £2.8m by borrowing £400,000. Company A, by borrowing £1.6m, has increased the market value of the firm's investment schedule to £3.2m. This is, however, not feasible because rational investors will expect higher rewards for the increased financial risk they must bear as leverage is increased.

Although this extreme approach is rejected, a less extreme interpretation of the traditional view demands closer examination. Figure 5.1 shows that the cost of debt (K_i) is lower than the cost of equity (K_e). Firms can borrow at some low rate of interest until lenders begin to worry about the

Table 5.1 Traditional view – no change in cost of equity with increasing leverage

	Company A £000	B £000	C £000
Equity (£1 shares)	400	1,600	2,000
Debt (10% interest payable)	1,600	400	—
	2,000	2,000	2,000
Cash flow from trading	400	400	400
Less interest on debt	160	40	—
Cash flow for equity	240	360	400
Equity market capitalization rate 15%			
Market value of shares	1,600	2,400	2,667
Market value of debt (par)	1,600	400	—
Market values	3,200	2,800	2,667

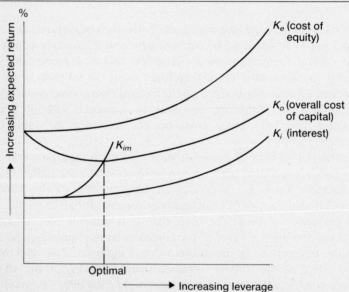

Figure 5.1 The traditional view of capital structure policy

security of interest payments and repayment of loans. The interest rate will be higher on additional loans. Therefore, K_i, the average cost of all loans, will begin to rise. The ordinary shareholders will ignore small amounts of debt completely but will eventually become concerned about the level of interest payments affecting the volatility of the cash flow for equity, and so demand higher rates of return for taking on additional risk. A combination of both sources of finance, K_o, the weighted average cost of capital, will therefore start at K_e with no borrowings, fall initially as low-cost debt is introduced into the capital structure, and then at some stage rise with increasing leverage as both K_i and K_e are rising. The optimal level of borrowing is the lowest point on K_o, the point where the marginal cost of borrowing, K_{im}, equals K_o. If the traditionalists are right, then there is an optimal capital structure which financial managers should seek. If we believe this less extreme version of the traditional view, then we probably feel that the required rate of a project depends mainly upon its economic risk, but that there is also a little bit of extra wealth to be created by finding the optimal capital structure.

This traditional view of capital structure policy is rejected by proponents of the *modern view*, which was originally expounded by Modigliani and Miller (1958). They assert that in a rational world, the traditional view must be rejected because ordinary shareholders will not ignore small amounts of debt, but rather demand increasing expected returns for every incremental increase in financial risk. The Modigliani-Miller (MM) approach is illustrated in figure 5.2. As in figure 5.1, debt is less expensive than equity but has a hidden cost which is the increasing required rate of return on equity as borrowing is increased. The increase in K_e is just enough to offset the benefit of low-cost debt, and consequently K_o, the overall cost of capital, is constant for all levels of leverage. The value of the firm depends upon anticipated net operational cash flows, new investment and risk, that is the

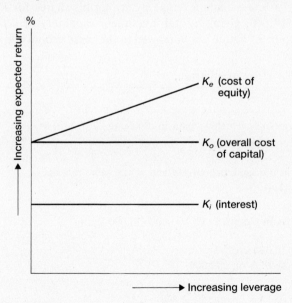

Figure 5.2 The modern view of capital structure policy

firm's investment schedule, and is independent of the method of financing. Leverage determines the split of cash flows between the providers of debt and the providers of equity. It does not determine the level of cash flows arising from successful trading, or the volatility of total operational cash flows.

The basic MM proposition is that in a rational world identical commodities – the cash flows generated by the investment schedules of companies A, B and C in table 5.1 – cannot sell in highly competitive and efficient markets at different prices; should any such tendency occur, it will be eliminated by a process akin to arbitrage (buying and selling the same commodity in different markets).

Table 5.1 shows how companies A and B are overvalued compared with company C if the extreme traditional view is maintained – that the cost of equity does not change with increasing leverage. On this assumption, the market value of company A would be £3.2m, company B £2.8m, and company C £2.667m. In a rational world the shares of companies A and B are clearly overvalued. The income streams of £0.4m, being of the equivalent risk class, must have the same market value if taxation and the cost of financial distress are ignored. In a rational world the cash flows of companies A, B and C cannot be valued at £3.2m, £2.8m, and £2.667m, respectively. If such irrationality were to occur, investors could indulge in home-made leverage and restore equilibrium. This arbitrage process is illustrated in table 5.2. Suppose a shareholder owns 2,000 shares in company A. His present income is £1,200. He can indulge in home-made leverage by selling his shares for £8,000 and borrowing £32,000, giving a total investment capability of £40,000. The important point is that he has borrowed in the same proportion and at the

Table 5.2   The effect of arbitrage

	£
Present income (all cash flows paid in dividends) $2,000 \times 0.6$	1,200
He can sell for $2,000 \left(\dfrac{1,600}{400} \right)$	8,000
and borrow in the same proportion and at the same rate as Company A (1:4)	32,000
	40,000
He buys shares in Company C: $\dfrac{40,000}{1,333} = 30,000$ shares	
New income $30,000 \times 0.2$	6,000
Less interest at 10% on £32,000	3,200
	2,800
He has increased his income by $2,800 - 1,200$	1,600

Table 5.3 The leverage (gearing) effect

		Company		
		A	B	C
	Equity (£1 shares)	£0.4m	1.6m	2m
	Debt (10% interest payable)	£1.6m	0.4m	—
	Total financing (and total investment)	£2m	2m	2m
I	Cash flow from trading	£0.4m	0.4m	0.4m
	Less interest on debt	£0.16m	0.04m	—
	Cash flow for equity	£0.24m	0.36m	0.4m
	Return on equity (%)	60	22.5	20
	Cash flow per share	£0.60	0.225	0.20
	Cash flow on total investment (%)	20	20	20
II	Assume fall in cash flow on total investment of 20 per cent			
	Cash flow from trading	£0.32m	0.32m	0.32m
	Less interest on debt	£0.16m	0.04m	—
	Cash flow for equity	£0.16m	0.28m	0.32m
	Return on equity (%)	40	17.5	16
	Cash flow per share	£0.40	0.175	0.16
	Cash flow on total investment (%)	16	16	16
	Fall in cash flow per share (%)	33.3	22.2	20

same rate as company A. He can now buy 30,000 shares in company C, giving a new income of £2,800. Thus, by investing in company C he increases his income by £1,600. In effect, the shareholder has turned himself into the equivalent of company A, and increased his income. The modern view of capital structure policy is that a sufficient number of investors would exploit such wealth-creating opportunities until market equilibrium is restored and the market values of companies A, B and C are equated.

The impact of leverage on financial risk is now considered in detail. Table 5.3 shows the volatility of cash flow per share for companies A, B and C which all have the same investment schedule (generating the same level of cash flow from trading) but differing capital structures. A is highly geared, B is low-geared and C is all-equity financed. All three companies are initially assumed to generate £400,000 from successful trading. A has to pay interest at 10 per cent on £1.6m and B 10 per cent on £400,000. Cash flow for equity is therefore £240,000 for company A, £360,000 for company B, and £400,000 for company C, and the corresponding returns on equity are 60 per cent, 22.5 per cent and 20 per cent. The cash flows per share are therefore £0.6, £0.225 and £0.2, respectively. Section II of table 5.3 illustrates the consequences of a fall in cash flow of 20 per cent from £400,000 to £320,000 for all three companies. It should be noted that interest has to be paid exactly as before. The return on equity falls to 40 per cent for company A, 17.5 per cent for B, and 16 per cent for C, and as a result the fall in cash flow per share is 33.3 per cent for the highly geared company A, 22.2 per cent for company B, and only 20 per cent for company C, the company with no borrowings. It is apparent that the greater the gearing, the greater is the volatility of cash flow per share, but the greater the risk, the greater the reward expected by share-holders. This is the hidden cost of debt. As companies add financial risk to business risk, the rate of return required by shareholders increases. The trade-off between risk and expected return ensures that three companies with the same investment schedule must have the same market value regardless of differing capital structures if taxation and costs of financial distress are ignored. All three firms exist in the same economic environment – their business risks are the same. Only the financial risk changes with leverage, increasing leverage increasing the financial risk of cash flow per share. Investors do not like risk and they require increasing returns with increasing leverage.

Table 5.3 shows that cash flows from trading amount to £400,000 for companies A, B and C. Assuming that the market risk associated with each firm's investment schedule dictates that the cash flows are capitalized at 15 per cent for a perpetual income stream, then the value of each firm is

$$V = \frac{£400,000}{0.15} = £2.667\text{m}$$

If the firm's investment schedule is valued at £2.667m and the debt is valued at par, then the market value of the equity must be the balancing figure, i.e. £1.067m for A, £2.267m for B, and £2.667m for C. For this to happen, the cost of equity, K_e, must increase with the increased financial risk associated with increased leverage by just enough to offset the increased expected return generated by increased leverage. The calculations appear in table 5.4. The market value of shares and the market value of debt are added to give the market value of the firm's investment schedule. As company C has no debt the cost of equity (= cash flow for equity/market value of equity) reflects only business risk at 15 per cent. Company B has some financial risk as well as business risk, and the cost of equity therefore rises to 15.9 per cent. In company A, the cost of equity rises to 22.5 per cent. Ignoring taxation and the cost of financial distress, the market value of each company is the same, and is determined by anticipated net operational cash flows and market risk. The value of the firm is clearly determined by the value of the firm's investment schedule, and not by the

Table 5.4 Modern view – increasing cost of equity with increasing leverage

		Company	
	A	B	C
Market value of debt	£1.6m	0.4m	—
Market value of equity	£1.067m	2.267m	2.667m
Value of investment schedule	£2.667m	2.667m	2.667m
Cost of equity (K_e)	$\dfrac{0.24}{1.067} = 22.5\%$	$\dfrac{0.36}{2.267} = 15.9\%$	$\dfrac{0.4}{2.667} = 15\%$

capital structure. The weighted average cost of capital, K_o, is the same for all three firms at 15 per cent. Interest payable on debt is 10 per cent and hence for company A:

$$K_o = \frac{1.6}{2.667} \times 0.1 + \frac{1.067}{2.667} \times 0.225 = 0.06 + 0.09 = 0.15 \qquad (5.3)$$

For company B:

$$K_o = \frac{0.4}{2.667} \times 0.1 + \frac{2.267}{2.667} \times 0.159 = 0.015 + 0.135 = 0.15 \qquad (5.4)$$

Underlying the modern view of capital structure policy is the following set of assumptions:

1 Transaction costs and the costs of financial distress can be ignored.
2 The firm's investment schedule is held constant.
3 Taxes are ignored.
4 Stock markets are perfectly competitive.
5 Investors are rational and expect other investors to behave rationally.
6 Firms can be classified into equivalent risk categories.
7 Individuals can borrow at the same rate as companies.

Practical Capital Structure Decisions

In practice, not all of the assumptions underlying the modern view of capital structure policy may hold. For example, interest payments are allowed as a tax deduction whereas dividends are not. Secondly, when firms have very high levels of borrowing they are more likely to run into the costs of financial distress.

Table 5.5 The gain from taxation by using debt

	Company A £000	B £000	C £000
Cash flow from trading	800	800	800
Less interest on debt	160	40	—
Cash flow after interest	640	760	800
Taxation at 50%	320	380	400
Cash flow from trading after tax	320	380	400
Market value of debt	1,600	400	—
Market value of equity			
$A \dfrac{320}{0.225}$	1,422		
$B \dfrac{380}{0.159}$		2,390	
$C \dfrac{400}{0.15}$			2,667
Market value of firm	3,022	2,790	2,667
Less:			
Value of firm without tax shield	2,667	2,667	2,667
Market value of tax shield	355	123	—

The Tax Shield on Interest Payments

The impact of taking corporation tax into account is shown in table 5.5. If the corporation tax rate is assumed to be 50 per cent, the benefits from gearing are quite apparent. Cash flows from successful trading are £800,000, with companies A and B deducting interest to arrive at taxable profits. After-tax cash flows from successful trading for equity amount to £320,000 for A, £380,000 for B, and £400,000 for C. If debt is valued at par and after-tax cash flows capitalized at 22.5 per cent for company A, 15.9 per cent for company B, and 15 per cent for company C, then the market values of the companies are £3.022m, £2.790m and £2.667m, respectively. Company C, with no tax shield, is valued exactly as before. Companies A and B have increased their market values by the capitalized value of the tax savings. We have used the same capitalization rate for tax savings as that used for cash flows for shareholders, but it is maintained by many authors (see, for example, Myers, 1974), that the tax savings should be capitalized at K_i (the cost of debt) rather than K_e (the cost of equity) because the tax savings are based entirely on the interest payments and must therefore be of the same risk. Now the tax savings are worth $\dfrac{80,000}{0.1} = £800,000$ for A, and $\dfrac{20,000}{0.1}$ = £200,000 for B, and the market values of companies A and B become £3.467m and £2.867m, respectively. In this case, the value (V) of the leveraged firm is its capitalized after-tax operational cash flows plus the present value of the tax savings (which is the market value of debt multiplied by the tax rate for a company with tax savings on interest in perpetuity):

$$V = \frac{\overline{X}}{r} + DT \qquad\qquad (5.5)$$

where $\overline{X}$ = anticipated net operational cash flows

$\quad r$ = capitalization rate

$\quad D$ = market value of debt

$\quad T$ = the corporation tax rate

Thus for company A, $V = \dfrac{400,000}{0.15} + 1,600,000\ (0.5) = \underline{£3.467\text{m}}$

and

for company B, $V = \dfrac{400,000}{0.15} + 400,000\ (0.5)\quad = \underline{£2.867\text{m}}$

The tax benefit derived from borrowing is an incentive to use debt, and this point is acknowledged by Modigliani and Miller (1963). However, equation (5.5) probably overstates the benefit for the following reasons:

1 The firm may not pay corporation tax at the present time or perhaps even for the foreseeable future. The tax benefit may therefore be delayed for several years or lost completely.
2 If the tax benefit from debt is real, then the strong demand for borrowed funds may push up interest rates, thereby reducing, to some extent, the benefit of low-cost debt. It is argued by Miller (1977) that the tax benefit of debt has been overstated generally. He affirms that the cost of debt after taxes is the same as the cost of equity (if risk differences are assumed away). The Miller argument has attracted a good deal of attention in recent years, as researchers have had considerable difficulty trying to explain why higher rates of corporation tax have not been accompanied by higher levels of borrowing, and why firms in the same industry with similar risk characteristics have a wide range of debt-equity ratios.

3 Even if equation (5.5) holds for moderate levels of debt, it cannot hold
for high levels of debt because it ignores the costs of financial distress.
An increase in debt is associated with increased tax savings but also an
increased probability of running into the costs of financial distress.
Equation (5.5) must therefore be modified to incorporate the anticipated
costs of bankruptcy (BC) or other financial distress, giving

$$V = \frac{\bar{X}}{r} + DT - BC \qquad\qquad (5.6)$$

where V, $\bar{X}$, r and DT are as defined in equation (5.5).

Hence, the optimal capital structure exists where the marginal benefit of
increased tax savings is matched by the marginal cost of anticipated financial
distress, that is where $(DT - BC)$ is maximized.

The Costs of Bankruptcy or other Financial Distress

An increase in the debt–equity ratio results in tax savings but an increased
probability of bankruptcy. If firms finance their investment schedules by
very high levels of borrowing (for example, 99 per cent), then it is very likely
that at some stage they will not be able to make annual interest payments
and loan repayments. The debt holders would then take control of the firm
as shareholders. In practice, companies pursue target debt–equity ratios
much lower than 99 per cent as they wish to avoid the costs of financial
distress and ultimately the costs and delays of liquidation. Dividends for
shareholders can be bypassed but failure to pay interest on loans often gives
the lender the right to claim the company's operating assets thereby
preventing the continuation of trading. It makes sense to try and avoid this –
both for managers and employees who wish to protect their employment,
and for investors who wish to avoid the costs and delays of liquidation.
It should be noted that managers and employees are concerned with total
risk, not simply market risk. Shareholders can and do diversify, and are
therefore concerned only with the market risk of their investment. The
financial well-being of the company, however, is endangered by total risk,
that is by market risk and specific risk. Directors in private companies are
particularly concerned with the well-being of the firm since it is very common
for loan creditors to lift the veil of incorporation and demand that directors
personally guarantee loans made to the company. The costs of financial
distress can therefore be very high for managers as well as shareholders.
These costs comprise not only the costs and delays of liquidation, but may
also include making sub-optimal investment and financing decisions as the
company experiences financial distress.

Possible sub-optimal investment decisions resulting from financial distress include the sale of successful investments and products at bargain prices, disinvestment in successful areas, abandonment of promising new projects, emphasis on short-term projects to generate cash, avoidance of highly profitable projects which do not promise immediate positive cash flows, reduced investment in training, promotion, research and development, reductions in stock levels (which may lose sales), reduction in credit periods (which may lose customers), damage to corporate image by publicity and price reductions, and the go-ahead of an unprofitable merger simply to acquire cash. Possible sub-optimal financing decisions resulting from financial distress include borrowing beyond the level of the company's target debt–equity ratio, acceptance of higher interest rates, leasing rather than borrowing and buying, a cut in dividend (thereby giving a false signal to the market which depresses share prices and makes a new issue difficult), and the loss of credit availability from suppliers making it necessary to borrow even more. The considerable costs associated with financial distress imply that efficient capital markets may penalize firms which are perceived as being overlevered. Hence, two firms with exactly the same investment schedule, in a rational world, may be priced differently where one firm is running a higher risk of incurring the costs of financial distress. These costs are reflected in market values when firms face an increased probability of financial distress or even eventual liquidation.

The existence of the tax benefit for modest amounts of debt, and the need to avoid the costs of financial distress, suggest that there is an optimal capital structure as illustrated in figure 5.3. Equation (5.6) shows that the value of the firm with debt is equal to the value of the firm without debt plus the present value of the tax savings (DT) minus the present value of the costs of anticipated financial distress (BC). Figure 5.3 indicates that there is an optimal capital structure at the point where the market value of the firm is maximized, that is where ($DT - BC$) is maximized.

The following points should be noted in selecting the debt–equity ratio for a firm:

1 There is an optimal capital structure where the marginal tax benefit is equal to the marginal costs of anticipated financial distress. The optimal capital structure for the individual firm will change to reflect the changing volatility of cash flows – the more stable a company's cash flow, the greater the level of interest (and hence debt) it can sustain.
2 The optimal capital structure depends on both the level and volatility of cash flows. Financial managers should therefore examine the capital structures, levels of cash flows, and volatility of cash flows for other firms in the same industry in order to help in determining the firm's optimal debt–equity ratio.

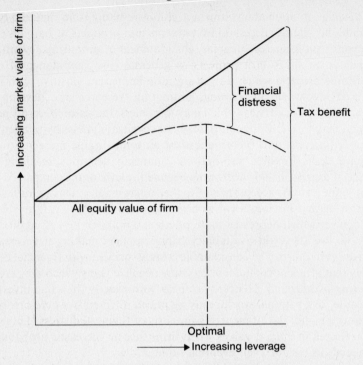

Figure 5.3   Leverage with corporation tax and liquidation costs

3 Survival of the firm is a top priority for corporate managers, but they should also strive to get the benefit of the tax deductibility of interest payments. Target debt–equity ratios of 30–40 per cent would appear to be appropriate for higher risk companies, although low risk companies might be expected to have as much as 70 per cent debt in their capital structures.

4 Corporate managers should recognize that in some years the investment schedule will fail to generate adequate cash. As suggested by Donaldson (1969), firms should have a strategy for financial emergencies and opportunity exploitation. With the possibility of a cash shortage always in mind, managers should be able to reorganize the firm's asset structure and financial structure to generate cash.

5 At each decision point, the debt or equity decision is part of a sequential financing decision. As the firm trades successfully it generates cash flows, of which some are paid in dividends and the remainder reinvested in the company. Increasing equity can be used as the base to justify and sustain more debt.

6 At any decision point, if in doubt, we recommend that companies should issue equity. An increase in equity can always be used as the basis for increasing debt in the future. An increase in debt beyond the optimal

debt–equity ratio implies that more equity will *have to* be raised in the future. Issuing more equity gives more future financing flexibility. (However, *too* much equity can also have negative signalling value, see Jensen and Meckling, 1976.)

Implications for Capital Structure from Option Pricing Theory

Considerable advances in option pricing theory have been made since the introduction of the Black-Scholes (1973) option pricing model, and the theory has yielded new insights into corporate financial policy.

Suppose a company is financed entirely by equity and its investment schedule collapses. In this case the total loss is borne by shareholders. If, on the other hand, the company is financed partly by equity and partly by debt and the investment schedule collapses, then part of the loss may be borne by debtholders. For example, if the company has an investment schedule worth £1,000 financed £400 by equity and £600 by debt and its investment schedule collapses to £300, then shareholders lose their £400 and debtholders the remaining £300. Shareholders declare bankruptcy and allow the debtholders to inherit the corporate collapse.

In option pricing theory terminology, the equity in a levered firm may be viewed as a call option on the value of a firm's assets. Now a call option is a contract between two investors A and B in which A pays B a sum of money, and in exchange B grants A the right to buy from B, at A's discretion, a given asset at a fixed price until a predetermined date after which any rights or obligations expire. The fixed price specified in the option contract is the exercise price. Thus when shareholders issue bonds, this is equivalent to selling the firm's assets to the bondholders in exchange for cash and a call option. The exercise price is the set of payments promised to the debtholders. If the value of the firm is less than the exercise price (that is, in the event of bankruptcy), shareholders will not exercise their option and the firm's assets will be retained by the bondholders. If the value of the firm exceeds the exercise price, shareholders will exercise their option by making the payments promised to the bondholders and thus re-acquire the firm's assets. It is the shareholders' ability to declare bankruptcy which gives a share the attributes of a call option, and the importance of these characteristics will depend upon the degree to which the firm is levered and the probability of bankruptcy. Clearly, this option is of value to shareholders.

Debtholders can reduce the possibility of default by imposing financial and operational constraints in their loan agreements with borrowing firms. The purpose of restrictive covenants is to protect debtholders against the owners of equity. These restrictive covenants come in many forms such as the ability to appoint a receiver on the failure of a company to make repayments of capital or pay interest, insistence on personal guarantees by officers of the company for corporate loans, restrictions on dividend payments, restrictions on additional borrowings which increase the risk to the original debtholders, restrictions on leases (which are, in effect, additional debt), agreement that interest payments must be covered some number of times by earnings or cash flows, maintenance of working capital at agreed levels, and restrictions on new investment in fixed assets. Managers should enter into loan agreements which involve restrictive covenants with great caution, as it is usually the breaking of the terms of loan agreements which results in bankruptcy proceedings.

Summary

When it is assumed that there are no taxes or costs of financial distress the financing decision is irrelevant to firm valuation. The value of the firm depends on its investment schedule. However, when the 'no corporation tax' assumption is relaxed, it appears that firms should borrow a lot on account of the tax deductibility of interest. The optimal capital structure stops short of 99 per cent debt, though, as managers seek to avoid liquidation costs and the other costs of financial distress. The capital

Table 5.6 Debt versus equity checklist

Debt	Equity
Capital repayable	Capital not repayable
Interest compulsory	Dividends not compulsory
Interest tax deductible	Dividends not tax deductible
Increases financial risk	No increase in financial risk
Increases probability of financial distress	No increase in probability of financial distress
Possible option value to shareholders	No option value
Restrictive covenants	No restrictive covenants
No control dilution, until terms of restrictive covenant broken	New issue may lead to control dilution
Cheaper issuing costs	Higher issuing costs
Often easier to issue to financial institutions	More complex rights issues, or new issue
Less future financing flexibility	Greater future financing flexibility
Earnings per share and return on equity higher, but higher risk	Earnings per share and return on equity lower, but lower risk
Possible adverse effect on supplier credit rating	No adverse effect on supplier credit rating
Possible conventional constraints such as book asset cover, income cover etc	No corresponding constraints

structure policy which maximizes shareholder wealth is still something of a puzzle, as pointed out by Myers (1984). Although there is some evidence that high risk companies have debt ratios lower than low risk companies, there is still a wide disparity amongst the debt–equity ratios of firms in the same industry. Furthermore, higher rates of taxation are not necessarily associated with higher levels of borrowing. *Our conclusion on the capital structure decision is that firms should borrow the amount of debt which they can sustain. Firms should borrow to finance their investment schedules because interest payable on borrowings is tax deductible, but they should not borrow beyond the point where bankruptcy becomes a distinct possibility.* To ensure the survival of the firm, even during periods of financial distress, corporate managers should have a strategy for financial emergencies. The traditional rules of thumb of 30–40 per cent debt for high risk companies (for example, manufacturing companies) and 70 per cent debt for low risk companies (for example, property companies) appear to make good sense. Table 5.6 provides a debt versus equity checklist for financial managers making capital structure decisions.

Study Questions

5.1   Malham Processing Ltd

Capital structure	A	B	C
Equity	700	300	1,000
Long-term debt (15%)	300	700	—
	1,000	1,000	1,000
Operational cash flows	200	200	200

As Financial Director of Malham Processing Ltd, you are considering the financing arrangements for a new subsidiary company. Any long-term debt introduced into the subsidiary's capital structure will have to pay interest at 15 per cent. The total financing requirement is 1,000, and expected operational cash flows are 200.

Demonstrate the effects on return to equity of the different capital structures. Operational cash flows may increase to 300, or even fall to 100. Demonstrate the effects on cash flow for equity.

5.2   The Carlton Manufacturing Co Ltd has to raise £3m immediately as part of its five-year expansion programme. The company can raise the £3m by issuing either debt or equity.

As Financial Director, draft a report to your board outlining the factors to be considered in identifying an optimal capital structure, and making a firm recommendation for the current year.

5.3 The Krown Corporation must raise £30m during the coming year by issuing either debt or equity. The company recently made a large loan and plans to raise further additional capital in the next 2–5 years. The company's balance sheet debt–equity ratio is 34 per cent which is less than the 40–60 per cent ratio of other firms in the same industry. However, both the company's earnings and share price are more volatile than the industry averages. As Financial Director draft a report to your co-directors:

1 outlining the factors for consideration in making this decision;
2 summarizing the theory of optimal capital structure;
3 suggesting the best course of action for the coming year.

Further Reading

Brigham, Eugene F. *Financial Management: Theory and Practice*. New York: Dryden Press, 1985, chapters 11–12.
Jensen, Michael C. and Smith, Jr, Clifford W. (eds) *The Modern Theory of Corporate Finance*. New York: McGraw-Hill, 1986, chapters 2–3.

6

Dividend Decisions

The Theory of Dividend Decisions

The objective of the firm is to maximize the wealth of its owners, that is the firm's shareholders. Successful investment decisions generate positive net cash flows which may be used to make dividend or interest payments, or can be retained within the company to finance new investment thereby generating higher positive net cash flows in the future. The *dividend decision* is regarded as a *financing decision* since any cash dividend paid reduces the amount of cash available for investment by the firm and therefore may have to be replaced either by a new issue of shares or an issue of debt. Now although investment decisions are far more important than financing decisions, it is still important to make good financing decisions. Thus if corporate managers can maximize the market value of the firm by manipulating dividend payments, then they should do so. The optimal dividend policy, if there is one, is the policy which maximizes shareholder wealth. As the value of the firm depends upon expected net operational cash flows, new investment, and risk, it is not clear that managers can create wealth by distributing net cash flows generated by successful trading between dividend payments and retentions within the company.

Graham, Dodd and Cottle (1962) state that one dollar of dividends is worth approximately three dollars of retained cash flows. This view that dividends are worth more to investors than retained earnings intuitively sounds reasonable since it is assumed that the purchaser of a share buys the expectation of future dividends. However, it is necessary to consider what happens to the cash flows generated from trading which are not paid out in dividends – they are reinvested in the company. Which, then, is preferable: £1 in the bank or £1 reinvested in the company? Once we take into account the fact that funds not paid in dividends are reinvested in the company on the shareholder's behalf to create higher dividends or retentions in the future, the assumed preference for dividends is not at all obvious. When we also take into account the taxation of dividends and the costs incurred by shareholders reinvesting cash dividends, it appears that shareholders should in general prefer retentions. The question then arises as to why companies pay dividends at all; an investigation of this becomes something of a puzzle. Shareholders who want cash can sell their shares. If a shareholder has a need for cash, he can devise his own dividend policy. If the company has a very low payout ratio, then its increased investment schedule should generate higher cash expectations in the future, resulting in increased share prices. The shareholder can sell shares to obtain cash and have the same level of investment as before. An advantage is that capital gains are taxed at a maximum of 30 per cent. The fact that dividend yields are around 5 per cent suggests that investors are looking for and anticipating substantial capital gains in addition to dividends.

Dividend policy determines the distribution of net cash flows generated from successful trading between dividend payments and corporate retentions. Shareholders are interested in dividends because they receive their returns in two forms – dividends and changes in the value of shares. The return for a period on an equity investment is:

$$R = \frac{D + P_2 - P_1}{P_1} \tag{6.1}$$

where

R = the return

D = the dividend

P_2 = the end of period price, and

P_1 = the beginning of period price

For example, if a shareholder buys a share for 100 which has a price of 110 at the end of the period, and receives a dividend of 5, then

$$R = \frac{5 + 110 - 100}{100} = 15 \text{ per cent}$$

The question now is whether corporate managers can increase total returns to shareholders by manipulating dividend policy.

The value of the firm depends on its investment schedule

$$V = \sum_{t=1}^{n} \frac{1}{(1+r)^t}(R - W - I)_t \tag{6.2}$$

where

V = the value of the firm

r = the required rate of return

R = operational cash receipts

W = operational cash expenditures

I = new investment

Having generated positive net operational cash flows from trading, these may be termed dividends, retentions, depreciation, transfer to capital reserve, revenue reserve, plant replacement reserve, or deferred taxation. Now is it necessary to value differently the various streams into which the cash flows are divided by devising weighting factors for each stream? If we accept the present value formula, this is not the case; hence the dividend decision, given the firm's investment decision, is irrelevant to shareholder returns (ignoring taxation and transaction costs). From the valuation formula it is clear that the various streams into which net operational cash flows are divided all have the same capitalization rate and are therefore valued equally. For example, a company which is expected to generate net cash flows of £6,000 per annum in perpetuity in an industry which capitalizes those cash flows at 20 per cent will be valued at £30,000. This is indicated below.

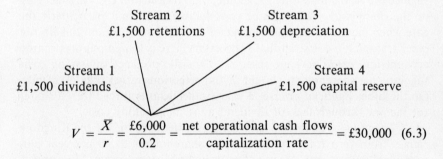

$$V = \frac{\overline{X}}{r} = \frac{\text{£6,000}}{0.2} = \frac{\text{net operational cash flows}}{\text{capitalization rate}} = \text{£30,000} \quad (6.3)$$

Those who believe that dividends are worth more than retentions do not accept that the net present value (NPV) of a project is its cash flows discounted at some rate reflecting the project's economic risk. They maintain that different capitalization rates should be used to reflect the intended allocation of future cash flows amongst dividends, retentions, depreciation, and so on.

It can be proved both mathematically and graphically that the particular dividend policy adopted by a firm is irrelevant to the current wealth of shareholders, given the following set of assumptions:

1 Transaction costs can be ignored.
2 Capital gains and dividends are taxed at the same rate.
3 The firm's investment schedule is held constant.
4 Dividends convey no information to the stock market.
5 Stock markets are perfectly efficient.
6 Investors are rational and expect other investors to behave rationally.

Miller and Modigliani (1961) offer a mathematical proof of dividend irrelevance, and this is shown in appendix 1. Fama and Miller (1972) present a graphical proof of dividend irrelevance, and this is given in appendix 2. Empirical support for the dividend irrelevance argument is provided by Black and Scholes (1974) who conclude that generous dividend payments do not result in increased shareholder returns.

Practical Dividend Decisions

For and Against Dividend Payments

1 *Transaction costs* In practice, the assumptions underlying the dividend irrelevance arguments may not hold. For example, transaction costs may be substantial. If companies pay dividends and issue new shares to finance the firm's investment schedule, then transaction costs are incurred on the share issue. These can be considerable and this is particularly the case when measured as a percentage of smaller issues. Retentions do not incur transaction costs; all that is necessary here is to *debit* appropriation account and *credit* revenue reserves. Thus the presence of issuing costs suggests that shareholders should favour retentions rather than dividends. On the other hand, of course, a shareholder who is forced to sell shares for income through lack of dividend must incur selling costs.

2 *Taxation* The rate of taxation on dividends in the United Kingdom ranges from zero for very low income shareholders to 60 per cent plus occasional investment surcharges for the highest income group. Most private shareholders are liable to pay income tax, and the starting rate is 27 per cent (1987/88). By contrast, taxation on realized (i.e. converted into cash) capital gains is at a maximum of 30 per cent and the first £6,600 of net capital gains are tax-free in the UK (1987/88). Now, when dividends are paid the amount must be grossed up at the standard rate of taxation and the company must pay tax to the collector of taxes in the next quarter. This

advance corporation tax is deemed to cover the shareholders' basic rate of tax, and may be set off against the company's mainstream corporation tax liability on its taxable trading income – if there is any. Excesses of advance corporation tax over the mainstream liability cannot be reclaimed but may be carried forward and used against future mainstream taxation. The time-lag between the payment of advance corporation tax and mainstream corporation tax can result in considerable cashflow costs. Taxation considerations do not clearly favour dividends or retentions in every case; in determining its dividend policy the firm needs to take into account its tax-paying position and that of its investors. For example, £100 paid to a shareholder in dividends is worth the same as £100 in capital gains if he is paying basic rate income tax and not paying capital gains tax. The encouragement not to pay dividends was greater under the 'classical' system of taxation before the introduction of the imputation system in April 1973. Under the earlier system, tax deducted from dividends could not be set off against mainstream corporation tax. Corporate profits were taxed, and dividends paid out of after-tax cash flows were subject to income tax in the hands of shareholders. The tax system has therefore tended to favour retentions, and hence low dividend yield shares have been likely to be in great demand by high rate taxpayers. On the other hand, many institutional investors such as pension funds do not pay tax at all and thus generally express a preference for dividends.

Plant and equipment allowances work in favour of retentions rather than dividend payments. The 100 per cent first year plant and equipment allowance (phased out following the 1984 budget) was a deliberate government incentive for firms to reinvest rather than pay dividends.

3 *Investment schedule* Although issuing costs and taxation consider-ations have generally favoured retentions rather than dividend payments, it may be the case that shareholders prefer dividends if companies use retained cash flows inefficiently. Directors may use these sums generated by successful trading to finance new projects which do not generate cash. They may build monuments in the centres of major cities to enhance their own status. They may regard retained cash flows as 'free' money, available for indulgence in excessive diversification to provide job security for management and employees. Under these circumstances shareholders may well prefer dividends rather than retentions. However, this is a criticism of the investment policies of the firm, rather than a criticism of its dividend policy.

4 *Stability/information content of dividends* In practice, firms appear to place great emphasis on last year's dividend when deciding this year's dividend. Dividends tend to be more stable than earnings; companies appear to pursue some long-term payout ratio (i.e. ratio of dividends to earnings), and dividends are changed in line with expected future net cash flows. Lintner (1956) shows that companies do have target payout ratios and that

dividend payments are related to long-term earnings. Managers seek stability of dividends and try to avoid making changes which might later have to be reversed. Lintner found that managers place great emphasis on the change in dividend from the previous period. This suggests that directors use dividends as a signal relating to long run expectations, and hence that they stress the role of the information content of dividends.

Changes in dividend policy may convey information to the stock market. An increase in dividends is likely to be interpreted as good news and a cut as bad news. The complete bypassing of a dividend is likely to be regarded as very bad news indeed. Managers can use this information channel to inform investors. Many tests of the efficient market hypothesis suggest that stock markets are efficient to the extent that share prices fully reflect all *available* information, but not to the extent that they reflect *all information*. Shareholders do not have access to all information relating to a company's future cash flows and risk. Corporate managers should be better informed about cash flow expectations than the market, and thus the efficiency of the stock market in generating best estimates of intrinsic values depends to some extent on the ability of management to communicate economic information to the market place. Dividend policy is a vehicle for conveying such information to shareholders; the common practice of declaring quarterly dividends provides a regular indicator. This is probably the major role of dividend policy. An increase in dividend is an announcement by the directors that higher average cash flows are expected in the future than in the past. If this information has not already been anticipated by the stock market, then the 'shock' will result in higher share prices. However, it is not the change in dividend which has changed the share price but *new information relating to the firm's investment schedule*. Figure 6.1 shows three possible effects of the dividend announcement on share price. In a perfectly efficient market shareholders anticipate the dividend announcement. On average they get it right and nothing happens to the share price at the date of the announcement. Sometimes, shareholders get a pleasant surprise in that the dividend declared is greater than expected. This raises their hopes relating to future cash flows (bearing in mind that the firm pursues a target payout ratio) and the share price immediately reflects the shock good news. Alternatively, if the dividend is not increased to the anticipated level then the shock will result in a fall in share price. The target payout ratio is important because directors only increase dividends when they are fairly certain that the new dividend can be maintained. A study by Pettit (1972) suggests that it is possible to fool shareholders for a short period of time by increasing the dividend capriciously. However, the share price soon reflects the subsequent disappointment. Directors are very reluctant to cut dividends until they feel certain that the present dividend cannot be maintained. A cut in dividend is interpreted by shareholders as being very bad news.

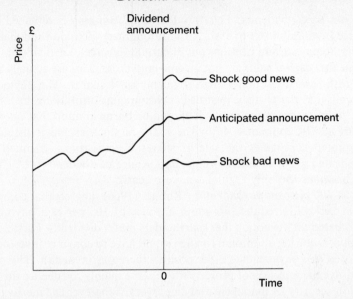

Figure 6.1 The possible effects of dividend announcement on share price

5 *Investor rationality* Shefrin and Statman (1984) provide an innovative psychological explanation of individual investor preference for cash dividends. Various reasons are suggested. For example, because of an individual's lack of 'self-control' (or 'will-power'), he or she may find it difficult to delay consumption, and thus wish to impose constraints on his or her actions in the form of a *rule*. An investor who wishes to conserve his or her long-run wealth could stipulate that portfolio capital should not be consumed, only dividends. He or she can then select a dividend payout ratio that conforms to his or her desired consumption level. Thus, even though taxes and transaction costs may favour capital gains, an investor may find cash dividends attractive and therefore be willing to pay the appropriate premium.

Another reason for dividend payments is that they can reduce 'regret'. If a rule is established which permits the consumption of dividends but not capital, then consuming dividends becomes standard procedure. Selling shares to permit consumption involves a positive decision to break the rule, and therefore the investor feels 'responsible' for his action if it turns out badly – for example, the share price subsequently rises – and experiences regret. If he or she spends dividends instead – and the share price subsequently rises – this is standard procedure and regret is avoided or diminished.

6 *Institutional investors* Many charities, pension funds, insurance companies and banks have not been allowed to invest in companies which

have not paid dividends. This 'prudent man' thinking is reflected in the Trustee Investment Act of 1961. In addition, many pension fund managers attempt to pay current pensions out of current 'income', i.e. dividends. They assume that capital gains are not income until those gains are actually turned into cash, and thus prefer high dividend yield shares. The payment of dividends may therefore be regarded as encouraging institutional investment.

7 *Non-quoted companies* It should be borne in mind that only 2 per cent of all UK companies enjoy the status of stock exchange listing. For non-quoted companies the sale of shares by investors is a much more complicated process, and hence the importance of dividends is heightened as it becomes the only regular source of cash.

8 *A 100 per cent payout ratio* Rubner (1966) suggests that companies should be legally required to adopt a policy of 100 per cent payout. His idea is based on the notion that shareholders prefer dividends. Furthermore, directors requiring additional finance would have to convince investors that proposed new investments offer positive increases in wealth. This would encourage the rejection of projects which serve mainly to enhance the status and job security of managers and employees. Whatever the merits of this proposal, companies do not generally pursue a target payout ratio of 100 per cent.

9 *A 100 per cent retention ratio* The position of Clarkson and Elliot (1969) is at the opposite end of the spectrum from Rubner. They argue that given taxation and transaction costs, dividends are a luxury that neither shareholders nor companies can afford. Again, whatever the merits of the proposal, firms very rarely pursue a dividend policy of 100 per cent retentions. Where they do, they generally claim that successful investment opportunities are open to the firm and that there is no point in paying dividends and then raising additional capital.

10 *Dividends as a residual* The suggestion here is that firms should proceed with all investments which increase the wealth of shareholders, i.e. all projects with positive net present values. Any excess cash should be used to pay dividends to shareholders, or make repayments of capital if this is possible. Clearly such a policy is not pursued by companies. Dividends appear to be the active decision variable with retentions being the residual. Figure 6.2 shows a typical firm's dividend policy. Earnings per share (EPS) increase over time but are very volatile. Dividends per share (DPS) are far less volatile than earnings; they increase with a lag after earnings, and appear to signal the directors' expectations of higher future earnings. The company pursues a long-term payout ratio of approximately 50 per cent. Even in a period when EPS falls below DPS, the directors maintain the dividend in line with long-term expectations. The dividend appears to be the active decision variable, with retentions (EPS – DPS) the residual. The dotted line represents the dividend that would be paid if the company pursued a policy

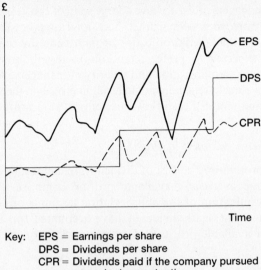

Key: EPS = Earnings per share
DPS = Dividends per share
CPR = Dividends paid if the company pursued
a constant payout ratio

Figure 6.2   A firm's typical dividend policy

of constant payout ratio (CPR), but in practice it is very rare for a company to pursue such a policy.

A further argument against the residual theory is that many firms increase their borrowings (or even make new issues of shares) and at the same time continue to pay dividends. This contradicts the assumption that directors take on all projects with positive net present values and then repay any surplus cash to shareholders. The residual theory is interesting from a theoretical viewpoint, because it suggests that directors should take on all projects with positive net present values, but no others. They should not use shareholders' funds to turn the company into a unit trust by indulging in pure diversification in the form of mergers/takeovers without synergy or economies of scale resulting from the investment. Such activities remove companies from the stock market, thereby restricting investor choice, and turn the company into a well-diversified conglomerate which gives job security to directors and employees but does not create wealth. Shareholders should criticize directors to the extent that they are doing what shareholders are perfectly competent to do without managerial assistance; shareholders can achieve diversification by purchasing shares in a variety of companies. Directors should be required to pay higher dividends or make repayments of capital rather than indulge in pure diversification. Again, it is the investment policies of directors that we are criticizing rather than their dividend policies.

11 *Span of control* Managers see the cash flows generated from successful trading as an important and convenient source of new capital.

Professional managers prefer to have a large span of control as measured by the number of employees, sales, market share, total assets or total expenditure. In pursuit of the managerial objective of increasing the span of control, directors are expected to prefer retentions to distributions. Retentions increase the status, remuneration and security of managers. Also, increases in the firm's investment schedule should result in growth in the value of shares to the extent that retained cash flows are reinvested in profitable projects.

Dividend Policies Adopted in Practice

Corporate appropriations consist of dividends, retentions, interest, taxation and profits due overseas. 'Available profits' comprise dividends plus retentions. Examination of the appropriation accounts of UK companies shows that in recent years dividends have accounted for approximately 15 per cent of available profits and retentions 85 per cent.

A Summary of Dividend Policy Considerations

1 The most important determinants of this year's dividend appear to be last year's dividend, recent earnings and expected earnings.
2 Dividend payments must be legal. The general rule is that the cash dividend payment is restricted to the amount of accounting profit. The rules are devised for the protection of creditors, and prevent directors making over-generous dividend payments to shareholders and possibly bankrupting the company.
3 Dividends are paid 'out of cash' and not 'out of profits'. The measurement of accounting profit is extremely difficult and the bottom line figure is subject to accounting policies relating to stock valuation, depreciation, treatment of bad debts, treatment of goodwill, and the view taken of accrued income and expenditures.
4 Corporate treasurers should plan for dividend payments just as much as other cash payments.
5 Attention should be paid to dividend restrictions imposed by lenders.
6 Corporate managers should be aware of all sources of new funds, including bank borrowings, and not simply look to retained cash flows to finance new investment. Retained earnings are not 'free'. Shareholders expect a return on these funds and prefer that they should not be employed in the erection of monuments to managerial status.
7 Taxation and transaction costs tend to favour retentions as a source of new capital.
8 Corporate managers stress stability as an important determinant of dividends. Dividends are the active decision variable and retentions the residual.

Table 6.1 Considerations influencing the dividend decision

1 Information content
2 Target payout
3 Stability
4 Clientele effect
5 Market expectations
6 Financial institutions
7 New investment opportunities
8 Ability to make annual payments
9 Equity/Debt considerations
10 Restrictive covenants
11 Taxation
12 Legality
13 Cash flow versus profit flow
14 Control
15 Special circumstances

9 Individual investors may find cash dividends attractive for reasons such as lack of self-control and regret aversion.

10 There is some evidence of a *clientele effect* (see Elton and Gruber, 1970). Low and zero rate taxpayers appear to prefer high payout ratios, while high taxation groups prefer low dividends and hopefully subsequent realized capital gains.

11 Companies must continue to pay dividends, probably because they have always paid dividends. Such payments are an expensive way of communicating information to the stock market relating to the company's future cash flows. Corporate treasurers tend to pursue a target payout ratio over the long-term and changes in dividends convey new information to the market.

Questions to be Considered in Reviewing Dividend Payments

We recommend that boards of directors reviewing dividend policy and dividend changes should consider the following questions carefully. The headings under which the questions fall are listed in table 6.1.

1 Information content
   (a) What has been our historic dividend policy?
   (b) What information about our expectations of future net cash flows do we wish to communicate to the market?
   (c) What effect will a given increase or decrease in the dividend have on our share price?

(d) What dividend payment will have the optimal effect on share price, if any?

(e) Can we sustain any proposed increase?

(f) How can we best convey our intentions to shareholders?

2 Target Payout

(a) What is our target payout ratio over all time periods?

(b) Have we communicated our target to the market?

(c) Will the market believe it?

3 Stability

(a) By how much should our dividend increases lag behind our earnings/net cash flow increases?

(b) For how many periods should we pay the same dividend?

(c) By how much should earnings/net cash flows fall before we cut the dividend?

4 Clientele Effect

(a) Are our shareholders high, low or zero rate taxpayers?

(b) Do they prefer dividends or capital gains?

(c) What are the costs involved if shareholders choose to devise their own dividend policy?

5 Market Expectations

(a) What does the financial press predict?

(b) What is our dividend yield?

(c) How many times are dividends covered by earnings?

6 Financial Institutions

(a) Do we wish to encourage share ownership by financial institutions?

(b) Will they support us in merger battles?

(c) Can we use financial institutions as a source of loan capital?

(d) Should we ever consider paying no dividend at all given that this may bar certain financial institutions from holding our shares?

7 New Investment Opportunities

(a) What is our proposed investment schedule?

(b) How should we announce it?

(c) Can we really isolate the dividend decision from investment and other financing decisions?

8 Ability to make Annual Payments

(a) Do we need to convince shareholders of our ability to make annual dividend payments?

(b) Do we need to convince lenders of our ability to make annual payments?

(c) If we increase or decrease the dividend what effect will it have on our credit ratings?

9 Equity/Debt considerations

(a) To what extent have we replaced equity with debt?

(b) What is our target debt–equity ratio?

(c) How will the proposed dividend payout affect our debt–equity ratio?

(d) Do we need to increase our equity base to justify the issuing of more debt?

(e) At what price could we raise additional equity?

(f) Why should we pay dividends and consider issuing equity?

10 Restrictive Covenants

(a) Are there any restrictions on the amount of dividends we are allowed to pay?

(b) Should we negotiate any change?

11 Taxation

(a) What is the company's tax bill?

(b) Can we reduce it by the amount of tax deducted from dividends?

(c) What is the tax position of our shareholders?

(d) Can we reduce the shareholders' tax bill by justifying to the Inland Revenue a repayment of capital, rather than the payment of dividends?

12 Legality

(a) Is our proposed dividend payout legal?

(b) How will a change in dividend affect the risk to our creditors?

13 Cash Flow versus Profit Flow

(a) Are we making a clear distinction between the effect of dividend on cash balance and retained earnings?

(b) How many times will the dividend be covered by earnings?

(c) How many times will the dividend be covered by net cash flow?

(d) What will be the effect of the dividend payment on our cash balance?

14 Control

(a) If we need to issue more shares, what will be the effect on our controlling shareholders?

15 Special Circumstances

(a) Is the government asking companies to restrict dividend increases?

(b) Are employees or trade unions critical of our dividend policy?

(c) Will the proposed change in dividend affect our applications for special government grants?

(d) Will our dividend to overseas shareholders cause friction with the Treasury or Inland Revenue?

(e) Is our dividend policy out of step with policies pursued by other firms in the same industry?

(f) Do we wish to encourage or discourage the conversion into equity of outstanding convertible debt?

Summary

When the mathematical and graphical worlds of proofs under restrictive assumptions are deserted for reality, we are unable to resolve the most important issue in the dividend controversy: *what is the policy which maximizes shareholder wealth*? As Black (1976) points out, the role of cash payments to shareholders in pursuit of the objective of market value maximization remains something of a 'dividend puzzle'. However, it appears that three important ingredients in the dividend decision are information content, target payout and stability. *Our conclusion is that companies should probably pay low cash dividends, making such changes as are necessary to indicate directors' anticipations of future net operational cash flows.* Payment of a small dividend minimizes the need for additional external financing, whilst at the same time allowing ownership of the company's shares by institutional investors.

Appendix 1:   The Mathematical Proof of Dividend Irrelevance

The one-period returns of securities of all firms in a given risk class must be the same in any given period, otherwise investors would hold only the securities with the highest return, and this would be inconsistent with equilibrium in the sense of market clearing. So for any period t, and for all firms in a given risk class, we have

$$r_{t+1} = \frac{d_{t+1} + v_{t+1} - v_t}{v_t} \tag{6.4}$$

where r is the rate of return appropriate to the risk class, d is the dividend per share, and v is the price per share.

Rewriting equation (6.4) gives

$$v_t r_{t+1} + v_t = d_{t+1} + v_{t+1}$$

Therefore

$$v_t = \frac{1}{1 + r_{t+1}} (d_{t+1} + v_{t+1}) \tag{6.5}$$

Equation (6.5) shows the present value of a share. In order to obtain the total value of all the firm's shares, that is, current value of the firm, we simply multiply by n, the number of shares, giving

$$n_t v_t = \frac{1}{1 + r_{t+1}} (n_t d_{t+1} + n_t v_{t+1})$$

Therefore

$$V_t = \frac{1}{1 + r_{t+1}} (D_{t+1} + n_t v_{t+1}) \tag{6.6}$$

where $V_t = n_t v_t$ is the value of the firm, and $D_{t+1} = n_t d_{t+1}$ is the total dividend paid by the firm.

If m new shares are issued at time $t+1$ at the then ruling price v_{t+1} then

$$V_{t+1} = n_{t+1} v_{t+1}$$

$$= n_t v_{t+1} + m_{t+1} v_{t+1}$$

Hence

$$n_t v_{t+1} = V_{t+1} - m_{t+1} v_{t+1} \tag{6.7}$$

Substituting equation (6.7) into equation (6.6) gives

$$V_t = \frac{1}{1 + r_{t+1}} (D_{t+1} + V_{t+1} - m_{t+1} v_{t+1}) \tag{6.8}$$

that is, the value of shares existing at time t is equal to the present value of the dividend payable at time $t+1$, plus the present value of all shares existing at time $t+1$, minus the present value of new shares issued at time $t+1$.

Now sources of funds always equal applications of funds, so

$$R_{t+1} + m_{t+1} v_{t+1} = D_{t+1} + W_{t+1} + I_{t+1} \tag{6.9}$$

where R is operating receipts, W is wages and other operating expenses and I is capital investment.

Rearranging equation (6.9) gives

$$-m_{t+1} v_{t+1} = R_{t+1} - D_{t+1} - W_{t+1} - I_{t+1} \tag{6.10}$$

Substituting equation (6.10) into equation (6.8) yields

$$V_t = \frac{1}{1 + r_{t+1}} (R_{t+1} - W_{t+1} - I_{t+1} + V_{t+1}) \tag{6.11}$$

As D_{t+1} does not appear in equation (6.11), the value of the firm is completely independent of its dividend policy. The present valuation depends on the required rate of return appropriate to the risk class of the firm over the next time-period, the firm's operating income and investment outlays over the next time-period, and the market value of the company's shares at the end of the next time-period. However, this latter factor, V_{t+1}, simply depends upon future required rates of return, operating incomes and investment outlays. From equation (6.11) we get

$$V_{t+1} = \frac{1}{1 + r_{t+2}} (R_{t+2} - W_{t+2} - I_{t+2} + V_{t+2})$$

Given a firm's operating policies, the particular dividend policy adopted has no effect on the current market value of the firm. The value of the firm depends on its investment schedule. Given efficient capital markets and ignoring transaction costs and taxation, an increase in the dividend reduces the investment schedule, and, therefore, reduces the ex-dividend price of the equity by the same amount. It is the investment policy, not the financing arrangements, which determines the value of the enterprise. A change in dividend policy implies a change in the distribution of total returns between dividends and capital gains.

Appendix 2: The Graphical Proof of Dividend Irrelevance

Figure 6.3 depicts the dividend irrelevance argument. The curve X_1Z represents investment opportunities. More and more funds are invested as we move from right to left. Projects are ranked in accordance with their internal rates of return, with the most profitable projects being undertaken in the earlier stages. The firm will continue to invest up to the point X where the internal rate of return offered at that level of investment is equal to the required rate of return by shareholders. Reading from right to left, projects up to point X have positive net present values, whereas projects to the left of X have negative net present values and will therefore not be

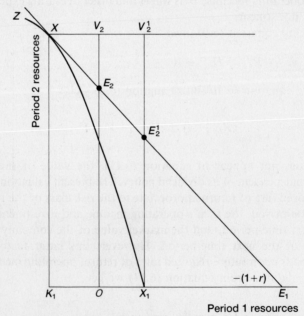

Figure 6.3 Graphical proof of dividend irrelevance

undertaken. The horizontal axis represents period 1 resources which must be invested to claim period 2 resources. To claim period 2 resources K_1X it is necessary to invest K_1X_1 in period 1. The present value of period 2 resources K_1X must be greater than the present value of period 1 resources K_1X_1. In fact, the present value of period 2 resources K_1X is K_1E_1. This present value is given by the present value line XE_1. The present value line XE_1 transforms K_1X (period 2 resources) to K_1E_1 (period 1 resources) by discounting at the required rate of return r. The required rate of return determines the angle marked $-(1+r)$, the greater the angle the less period 2 resources are worth in period 1. Management invests to the point X where the internal rate of return is equal to r.

Available resources in period 1 are OX_1, the required level of additional financing being K_1O. Let us assume in the first instance that management pays no dividend. All available cash OX_1 is retained in the business and new shares are issued amounting to K_1O. This entitles the new shareholders to V_2E_2 of the OV_2 period 2 resources, i.e. $K_1O(1+r)$, leaving OE_2 to the original shareholders. As $K_1O = XV_2$, and the angle V_2XE_2 is equal to the angle XE_1K_1, then the providers of K_1O must be entitled to V_2E_2. The point to note is that the present value of the firm to the original shareholders is OE_1 which is the present value of period 2 resources OE_2.

An alternative assumption is that the firm pays out all available resources in dividends. If available resources OX_1 are paid in dividends, then the firm must raise K_1X_1. The claim by new shareholders on period 2 resources becomes $K_1X_1(1+r)$ which is equal to V_2E_2, leaving period 2 resources X_1E_2 for existing shareholders. The present value of these resources to existing shareholders is X_1E_1. As they have already received a dividend of OX_1, then the present value of the firm to the original shareholders is $OX_1 + X_1E_1$ which is equal to OE_1. As this is also the present value of the firm to existing shareholders with no dividend, then changing the dividend has not changed the wealth of the original shareholders. For these two extremes of dividend policy, and all other intermediate policies, the change in dividend policy has not changed shareholder wealth. Hence dividend policy is irrelevant to the wealth of shareholders.

Study Questions

6.1 Present the mathematical proof of dividend irrelevance. Present the graphical proof of dividend irrelevance. Can incremental wealth be created by an effective dividend policy?

6.2 Discuss the important determinants of a company's payout policy.

6.3 As Financial Director of a public limited company, draft a report to your co-directors on the establishment of an effective dividend policy. Your report should include the implications of modern portfolio theory for dividend policy.

6.4 The New York Electric Utility Company is short of cash. It has a major programme for future capital expenditure. For many years, its capital expenditure has exceeded annual net income, which has not resulted in more users or greatly increased output. The State of New York is opposing the utility company's attempts to increase prices. The company would like the State to make a major contribution to its capital expenditure programme. Working capital has increased dramatically, and fuel costs are rising.

The company has paid dividends for many years. Many small shareholders rely on the dividend income. For the past few years, a quarterly dividend of 45¢ has been paid, and the share price is now $18. However, the directors are considering changing the dividend for the current quarter.

As Financial Director, draft a report to your co-directors outlining the factors to be considered in establishing an effective dividend policy, and make a firm recommendation for the current quarter.

Further Reading

Brigham, Eugene F. *Financial Management: Theory and Practice.* New York: Dryden Press, 1985, chapter 13.
Jensen, Michael C. and Smith, Jr, Clifford W. (eds) *The Modern Theory of Corporate Finance.* New York: McGraw-Hill, 1986, chapter 7.

7

Leasing Decisions

The Theory of Leasing Decisions

Firms achieve their objective of maximizing shareholder wealth by making successful investment decisions which generate positive net cash flows. The *leasing decision* concerns whether the firm should lease equipment or borrow money and buy the equipment, and is a *financing decision*. Now, as already noted, considerably greater importance generally attaches to investment decisions than financing decisions, but it is still advantageous to make good financing decisions. Thus, once a firm has decided to invest, corporate managers should then attempt to maximize the market value of the firm by examining the costs of both leasing and borrowing the money to buy, and selecting the cheaper method of financing.

In order to identify the cheaper source of financing – the lease or the loan – the financial manager should discount the after-tax cash flows for both the lease and the loan at the after-tax cost of borrowing, apart from the residual value which should be discounted at a higher rate. Lease payments, interest payments and capital repayments are all contractual obligations fixed in advance. By contrast the residual value of the purchased equipment at the end of the time period being considered is very uncertain, and thus should not be discounted at the risk-free rate of interest, but rather at, say, the same rate of return as was required on the investment decision, or alternatively at simply double the after-tax borrowing rate as an approximation. If the present value of the lease is cheaper than the present value of the loan, then the firm should lease the equipment, but if leasing is more expensive, then the firm should borrow the funds and buy the equipment.

In this chapter we restrict our attention to *finance leases* rather than operating leases. Finance leases are a source of long-term finance whereby the economic benefit of ownership over the life of the asset generally passes to the lessee, usually a commercial company or local authority, from the lessor, usually a bank subsidiary or large leasing company such as IBM or Rank Xerox, in return for the payment of specified sums over an obligatory period. Finance leases are regarded as an alternative to borrowing money and buying, and are generally non-cancellable. Operating leases, on the other hand, are short-term leases equivalent to renting for only a few weeks or months, and may relate to, for example, an exhibition hall or decorating equipment. Operating leases are regarded as expenses to be set against cash inflows, and are cancellable.

Practical Leasing Decisions

Major Influences on Leasing Decisions

The leasing industry has grown rapidly over the last twenty years, and this may be attributed to several factors. First, leasing may make economic sense when the lessee is not paying tax, or is paying tax at a lower rate than the lessor. Secondly, it is generally easier and quicker to lease an asset than to arrange a loan to finance its purchase. Thirdly, during periods of rising interest rates, if lease agreements have been made previously at interest rates which neither reflect these increases nor allow for changes in lease payments to compensate for increases in interest rates, then leases may turn out to be very cheap sources of finance. Fourthly, for many years all leases, including finance leases, were treated as expenses in the profit and loss account rather than as sources of financing in the balance sheet, and some financial managers felt that this was a valuable source of 'off the balance sheet' financing. These influences on the lease or buy decision are now discussed in more detail.

The tax factor has been extremely important in the UK because until recently a 100 per cent first year allowance (FYA) was available on plant and equipment. This has now been phased out, so only the usual 25 per cent writing-down allowance applies. When a company does not expect to pay corporation tax for the foreseeable future, the tax deduction is lost. It should be possible to negotiate a deal with a bank's leasing subsidiary whereby the bank buys the equipment, claims the tax allowance, and then passes on some of the benefits to the lessee in the form of a cheap lease, that is a lease which to the user is cheaper than borrowing the money and buying the equipment. When the user expects to pay corporation tax, then it can claim the tax allowance, and the leasing deal becomes much less attractive; in such cases it is usually advantageous to take the benefit of the available tax allowances and borrow to buy rather than lease. On the other hand, should the user not expect to get the benefit of the tax allowances, the financial manager should explore the leasing alternative.

The second factor affecting leasing decisions relates to the ability of firms to acquire funds for new investment. Finance is not always readily available for the acquisition of plant and machinery, and motor vehicles, particularly for the smaller company which lacks a track record and does not have a balance sheet asset base to offer as security for loans. Anticipated cash flows are not always enough to satisfy bank managers. A lease often proves easier to arrange than a bank loan to finance purchases by commercial enterprises. For example, expensive cars for company directors are often acquired through leasing rather than bank loans for purchase. This also makes good economic sense, since, generally, all the lease payments are allowed as a tax deduction, whereas the 25 per cent writing-down allowance available on cars is subject to a maximum of £2,000 per annum.

The third influence on the lease or buy decision is that fixed lease payments can turn out to be very cheap if interest rates rise. Clearly, however, the same benefit is attached to a loan arranged at a fixed rate of interest throughout the loan period. Bank lending has for many years been based on points above base rate and interest rates on loans have therefore changed during the life of the loan. By contrast, many early lease agreements involved lease payments which were fixed for the period of the lease. As interest rates rose many leases turned out to be very inexpensive. As a result, many lessors now adjust lease payments during the life of the lease to reflect changes in interest rates. Even if lease payments are fixed and interest rates variable, financial managers should not enter into leasing deals in the expectation that rising interest rates will result in the lease being inexpensive – interest rates move downwards as well as upwards.

The fourth reason offered for the growth in leasing over the last twenty years is that leasing has been 'off the balance sheet' financing. We recommend that financial managers should not be fooled by this aspect of leasing, as leasing involves making contractual payments in the same way as does borrowing. For most practical purposes the finance lease is a method of purchase because the lessee has the full economic use of the asset. Lease payments reduce net cash flows in a similar manner to payments of interest and repayments of capital. Lease payments are contractual, risk-free payments which the lessee fully intends to honour, and the lessor fully expects to receive. For practical purposes both leasing and borrowing increase the amount of leverage on a £1 for £1 basis and hence both add financial risk to business risk. We should not expect investors and bank managers to be fooled by balance sheet numbers. Accounting bodies in general have now recognized the problem, and have recently introduced standards which require accountants to include the capitalized amount of outstanding leases in their balance sheets.

An Example of the Lease or Buy Decision

A company wishes to invest in a new piece of equipment. It may either purchase the equipment for £40,000 using a bank loan to finance the purchase, or lease the equipment making four annual lease prepayments of £12,000. The rate of interest charged on the bank loan is 21 per cent. The equipment has a life of four years. Should the company lease or borrow and buy? Assume:

Case 1: the company does not expect to pay corporation tax for the foreseeable future and the equipment has no residual value.
Case 2: the company expects to pay corporation tax at 52 per cent approximately one year after earning its cash flows and a first year allowance of 100 per cent is available; the equipment has no residual value.
Case 3: the company expects to pay corporation tax at 52 per cent approximately one year after earning its cash flows and a writing-down allowance of 25 per cent is available; the equipment has a residual value.

Case 1 is illustrated in table 7.1. Here the net present value (NPV) of the lease over the loan is calculated. Column 2 shows the lease payments as negative numbers because they represent cash outflows. If these cash payments are made £40,000 is saved immediately, which is the present value of the loan if the equipment were purchased; £40,000 is the present value

Table 7.1 Lease or borrow and buy: (1) no corporation tax payable and no residual value

1	2	3	4	5	6	7	8
Period	Lease payments	Tax savings	Cost of loan	Tax allowance	Cash flow	Discount factor (21% interest)	Present value
0	(12,000)		40,000		28,000	1.000	28,000
1	(12,000)				(12,000)	0.826	(9,912)
2	(12,000)				(12,000)	0.683	(8,196)
3	(12,000)				(12,000)	0.564	(6,768)
					NPV of lease over loan		3,124

of a loan repayment schedule of £40,000 discounted at the cost of borrowing. This saving is shown in column 4. The after-tax cost of borrowing in column 7 is 21 per cent because in a world without taxation the tax shield on interest is lost. Discounting the annual cash flows by the after-tax cost of borrowing gives the present value of each year's cash flow in column 8. The sum of the cash flows is positive at £3,124 which means that the lease is cheaper than the loan, and therefore the user should lease rather than borrow and buy. An alternative approach is to examine each source of finance separately. The present value of the loan repayments is £40,000, whereas the present value of the lease payments is £12,000 immediately plus £12,000 × 2.073 giving a total of £36,876. Since the present value of the lease payments is £3,124 less than the present value of the loan repayments, the lease should be accepted because it is the cheaper source of financing.

Case 2 is illustrated in table 7.2, where again the NPV of the lease over the loan is calculated, but now the company expects to pay corporation tax. Columns 2 and 4 are the same as in table 7.1: again £40,000 is the present value of a loan repayment schedule of £40,000, this time with tax relief on interest but discounting at the after-tax rate of interest. Column 3 shows that the lease payments save tax at 52 per cent approximately one year later, and column 5 that the first year allowance (FYA) of 100 per cent is lost approximately one year later if the company leases; the FYA is claimed by the lessor, usually a bank subsidiary. The net cash flows in column 6 are discounted at the after-tax cost of borrowing, which in a world with taxes is 10.08 per cent (calculated as $(1 - 0.52) \times 21$ per cent), to give the present value of the cash flows in column 8. The sum of the cash flows

Table 7.2 Lease or borrow and buy: (2) corporation tax payable, 100 per cent FYA available and no residual value

1	2	3	4	5	6	7	8
Period	Lease payments	Tax savings	Cost of loan	Tax allowance	Cash flow	Discount factor (10.08% interest)	Present value
0	(12,000)		40,000		28,000	1.000	28,000
1	(12,000)	6,240		(20,800)	(26,560)	0.908	(24,116)
2	(12,000)	6,240			(5,760)	0.825	(4,752)
3	(12,000)	6,240			(5,760)	0.750	(4,320)
4		6,240			6,240	0.681	4,249
					NPV of lease over loan		(939)

Table 7.3 Lease or borrow and buy: (3) Corporation tax payable, 25 per cent writing-down allowance available and positive residual value

1	2	3	4	5	6	7	8	9	10	11
Period	Lease payments	Tax savings	Cost of loan	Tax allowance	Residual value	BC	Cash flow	Discount factor (10.08% interest)	Discount factor (20.16% interest)	Present value
0	(12,000)		40,000				28,000	1.000		28,000
1	(12,000)	6,240		(5,200)			(10,960)	0.908		(9,952)
2	(12,000)	6,240		(3,900)			(9,660)	0.825		(7,970)
3	(12,000)	6,240		(2,925)			(8,685)	0.750		(6,514)
4		6,240		(8,775)			(2,535)	0.681		(1,726)
4					(1,600)				0.480	(768)
5						832			0.399	332
								NPV of lease over loan		1,402

Note: For the purposes of this example all residual capital allowances are shown at £8,775 at the end of period 4. The tax allowance column totals £20,800, being 52 per cent of the £40,000 cost. In fact, if the equipment is purchased the tax benefit at 25 per cent would amount to £2,194 at the end of year 4 with a balancing allowance of £2,421 at the end of year 5, the total tax benefit amounting to £16,640, that is 52 per cent of £32,000 – the difference between the cost of £40,000 and the residual value of £8,000. Under the lease, a tax charge will arise at the end of year 5 amounting to £3,328, being 52 per cent of the lease refund of £6,400.

is negative at £939, which indicates that the lease is more expensive than the loan, and therefore the user should borrow and buy rather than lease. As discussed earlier, we should expect the company to buy rather than lease when the company can get the benefit of the 100 per cent first year allowance. Again, the present value of the lease opportunity and the present value of the loan alternative may be calculated separately. The present value of the lease payments is $(12,000 \times 1.000) + (5,760 \times 0.908) + (5,760 \times 0.825) + (5,760 \times 0.750) - (6,240 \times 0.681) = £22,053$. The present value of the loan repayments after subtracting the FYA is $40,000 - (20,800 \times 0.908) = £21,114$. Since the present value of the loan repayments is £939 less than the present value of the lease payments, the user should borrow the money and buy the equipment since it is the cheaper source of financing.

Case 3 is depicted in table 7.3. In the previous examples it is assumed that the equipment in which the company wished to invest had no residual value at the end of the time period considered. We now wish to examine the impact of introducing residual values on the lease or borrow and buy decision. As discussed at the beginning of this chapter, the residual value of the equipment at the end of the time period is very uncertain, and thus should be discounted at a rate appropriate to the residual value's quality, say the same rate of return as was required on the investment decision, or alternatively at simply double the after-tax borrowing rate as an approximation. Suppose that the estimated residual value of our £40,000 machine is £8,000 at the end of its four year life. If we own the machine we expect to obtain the full £8,000, which is taxed approximately one year later. If we lease the machine, let us assume that the lessors will refund the user 80 per cent of the residual value. Table 7.3 also shows the new situation with a 25 per cent writing-down allowance replacing the 100 per cent FYA.

The NPV of the lease is now £1,402. The introduction of a residual value increases the attractiveness of purchasing. This must be the case because the company receives 100 per cent of the residual value if it purchases rather than only 80 per cent. The after-tax borrowing rate is 10.08 per cent, so the residual value of the machine should be discounted at 20.16 per cent. There is a loss of $£8,000 \times 20$ per cent $= £1,600$ on the residual value if the company leases, but this is partially offset by a balancing charge (BC) for tax purposes of £832 less than would have been the case if the company had purchased. As the existence of a residual value increases the attractiveness of buying rather than leasing, but, overall, leasing has become preferable to the borrow and buy alternative (compared with Case 2 – 100 per cent FYA and no residual value – where borrowing and buying was preferable to leasing), the elimination of the 100 per cent FYA and its replacement by a 25 per cent writing-down allowance has increased the attractiveness of leasing. However, in practice there will be an offsetting increase in lease payments as the lessor loses the benefit of the 100 per cent first year allowance, thus reducing the attractiveness of leasing. We should expect that the net effect would be that borrowing and buying would be preferable to leasing when the company can obtain the benefit of the available tax allowance.

When the user does not expect to pay corporation tax, the replacement of the 100 per cent FYA by a 25 per cent writing-down allowance makes leasing less attractive than previously; as the lessor obtains a reduced tax benefit the lease payments will rise. However, as before, some of the tax benefit should be passed on so that leasing is still likely to be preferable to borrowing and buying.

It should be stressed that the leasing decision is a financing decision, not an investment decision. The acquisition of the equipment has been incorporated into a net present value calculation whereby the anticipated cash flows are discounted at some rate reflecting their economic risk. This investment has been made on the basis of net present value which has been found to be positive, or internal rate of return which has been found to be greater than the required rate of return. The current decision relates to the financing of the project – a lease or a loan to finance acquisition.

For and Against Leasing an Asset

1   *Obsolescence*   A firm which is concerned about the possible obsolescence of high technology equipment may not want to own the equipment. It may be possible to arrange a cancellable lease whereby the lessee has the option to terminate the lease during the lease period. The lessor may not be quite as concerned about obsolescence as the lessee because the lessor is familiar with the leasing industry and is likely to be aware of the existence of alternative lessees.

2   *Restrictive covenants*   Restrictions on managerial behaviour are often attached to loans but are less common and usually less rigorous under leases. Loan creditors may impose restrictions on dividend payments, additional loans, and the acquisition and disposal of assets. Therefore financial managers who are concerned about restrictive covenants on additional loans may be encouraged to lease.

3   *Reported earnings/balance sheet numbers*   Accounting profit has tended to be higher under lease financing rather than loan financing. Only the lease payments were charged in the profit and loss account, whereas when a company borrows and buys both the interest payments and depreciation charges on the asset acquired are charged as an expense. Hence, particularly in the early years of a loan, accounting profit tended to be higher under a lease arrangement. Similarly, the level of total assets appearing in the balance sheet has generally been lower under a lease

arrangement than a loan arrangement. All loans appear in the balance sheet as sources of finance and all purchased assets appear as part of total assets employed. However, with leased assets no lease obligation usually appeared in the balance sheet. Given that, in general, under such circumstances accounting profit was higher and total assets lower for a lease arrangement compared with a loan, reported return on capital employed was usually higher under a lease, and could be considerably higher. It should be noted, however, that wealth is not created by amending balance sheets and profit and loss accounts. This has now been recognized by the accounting bodies, and accounting standards have recently been modified so that lessees are required to include leased assets in their financial statements. A finance lease should be recorded in the balance sheet of a lessee as an asset and as an obligation to pay future rentals.

4 *Maintenance and insurance* Both leasing an asset and ownership of the asset usually impose upon the lessee the costs of maintenance and insurance so that the lease or borrow and buy decision can ignore such costs. If, however, the leasing arrangement imposes costs upon the lessor rather than the lessee, then the savings to the lessee should appear in the cash flows when evaluating the lease opportunity. Furthermore, the lessor may be able to offer the user more streamlined maintenance facilities than the manufacturer.

5 *The capital-revenue myth* Many local authorities and companies are fooled by the capital-revenue myth. Both leasing an asset and borrowing to buy the asset involve making contractual payments. Such payments are cash outflows regardless of whether they are charged against the revenue budget or the capital budget. Leasing has been encouraged in some areas because leasing is generally regarded as a revenue item rather than a capital item. In periods of financial distress organizations often impose restrictions on capital expenditure. Managers may be able to avoid restrictions on the acquisition of capital items by acquiring the same assets under a finance lease. We exhort people not to be fooled by the nonsense of capital-revenue budgeting systems.

6 *Secondary leases* The period of a lease is often referred to as the primary period. It may well be the case that the asset is not exhausted at the end of the primary period, and leasing agreements sometimes offer the lessee the right to continue using the asset for a secondary period for a purely nominal lease rental. Financial managers should try to secure such an arrangement when negotiating a lease; this would increase the attractiveness of leasing compared with purchasing. Lessors may well, however, charge an offsetting higher lease rental for the primary period.

7 *Flexibility of lease payments* Many leases now allow for changes in interest rates and taxation. Where this is not the case, financial managers should not enter into leases in the expectation that interest rates will rise and make the fixed lease payments a cheap source of finance; interest

rates can also move downwards. Similarly, forecasting taxation changes is difficult.

8   *Cash flow advantage*   There is no cash flow advantage to leasing if leasing simply replaces loan financing on a £1 for £1 basis. However, it is often the case that companies lease because they cannot borrow. This cash flow advantage should not be overstated, however, by assuming that leasing does not increase the extent to which the company is financed by borrowing. Lease payments are contractual payments which increase the financial risk to shareholders who demand a higher rate of return to reflect this additional risk. The hidden cost of additional lease or interest payments is the increasing required rate of return by shareholders.

9   *The lessor's year end*   A potential lessee should ideally seek a lessor just before the lessor's year-end. If the lessor buys an asset just before a year-end, then the benefit of the tax allowance is received at the earliest possible opportunity, which is an inducement to the lessor to arrange the deal.

10   *Lessor and lessee borrowing rates*   One of the advantages of bank leasing is that banks can generally borrow at lower rates than companies. However, this only accounts for a small portion of the leasing benefit. Of far greater importance is the tax allowance which the bank subsidiary can claim when the lessee cannot because insufficient taxable profits are being earned. Both the user and the bank can benefit at the expense of the Inland Revenue.

11   *Temporary non-taxpaying lessee*   A company may expect to pay no tax for the immediate future but to resume paying corporation tax in two or three years. When this is the case the financial manager must forecast the periods when taxation is expected to be paid and introduce the anticipated tax savings which would be lost into the lease evaluation.

12   *Loss of tax allowances*   One of the biggest incentives to leasing appears to be the loss of tax allowances when a company is not paying corporation tax. The 100 per cent first-year allowance was reduced in the 1984 budget to 75 per cent for expenditure incurred during the period March 1984 to March 1985, 50 per cent for expenditure incurred during the period April 1985 to March 1986, and eliminated thereafter (when only the usual 25 per cent writing-down allowance applied). This elimination of first-year allowance is likely to lessen the attractiveness of leasing, and it will be interesting to see whether, as a result, the growth in lease financing declines.

For further discussion of factors to be taken into consideration when evaluating leasing decisions see, for example, Johnson and Lewellen (1972), Schall (1974), Myers et al. (1976) and Franks and Hodges (1978).

Summary

The opportunity cost of leasing an asset is to borrow the money and buy the asset. In general, *a lease should be accepted when it is cheaper than borrowing and buying, although all additional factors should be taken into account.* In order to identify the cheaper financing method, the after-tax cash flows should be discounted at the after-tax cost of borrowing, apart from the residual value which should be discounted at a higher rate. *We should normally expect companies to borrow and buy rather than lease when it is expected that corporation tax will be paid*, although many financial managers emphasize the value of leasing as a source of immediate financing.

Study Questions

7.1 1 Explain the growth of leasing.
2 When does leasing make economic sense?
3 List all the known factors involved in considering a finance lease.

7.2 Your Board of Directors has decided to expand output by acquiring additional plant and equipment which will cost £400,000 and yield a cash flow return of approximately 30 per cent. The plant can be financed by a bank loan at 18 per cent interest, or your company can lease the equipment for four years by making four annual pre-payments of £125,000. At the end of the four year period the plant is expected to have a market value of £40,000. The leasing company proposes to refund your company 75 per cent of the market value. Your company pays tax at 30 per cent in those years when corporation tax is actually payable. (Assume a first year allowance of 100 per cent.)

As Financial Director draft a report to your board outlining all the factors to be considered in the lease versus buy decision, and comment on the implications of the 1984 tax changes (when the 100 per cent first year allowance was gradually changed to a 25 per cent annual allowance).

7.3 As Financial Director of West Morton Engineering Ltd, you are asked in February 1988 to draft a report to your board on the most appropriate method of financing plant for a new division. The purchase price of the plant is £800,000. The required rate of return on the total investment in the new division is 30 per cent, and the decision has been made to finance the new plant from an external source. The bank has offered to lend the company £800,000 at 3 per cent above base rate (base rate is 11 per cent). The bank loan can either be repaid over 3–5 years or a loan can be so structured as to have the same characteristics as a lease. Alternatively, Steeton Leasing Ltd, a subsidiary of the company offering to sell the plant, has offered a finance lease whereby West Morton Engineering Ltd can make four annual prepayments of £240,000. At the end of the lease period 90 per cent of the residual value (estimated at £150,000) would be refunded to WME Ltd by SL Ltd. You are not sure whether or not your company will be paying tax in the foreseeable future. If corporation tax is paid, it will be at the rate of 30 per cent. Plant acquisitions qualify for a 25 per cent annual allowance.

Draft your report to the board making a firm recommendation and outline all the factors involved.

7.4 As Financial Director of Ince Bootle plc you are asked to draft a report to your board on the most appropriate method of financing plant for an expansion of the company's operation. The plant will cost £500,000 and the required rate of return on the investment is 16 per cent. The decision has been made to finance the new plant either by a bank loan or a finance lease. Your bank has offered to lend the company £500,000 at 4 per cent over the base rate, base rate being 10 per cent at the present time. Your bank manager has offered a four year loan. You have also approached the bank's leasing subsidiary, which suggests that Ince Bootle can make three annual lease prepayments of £200,000. At the end of the lease period, 90 per cent of the residual value, such residual value being estimated at £100,000, would be refunded to Ince Bootle by the bank's leasing subsidiary. You cannot tell at the present time whether your company will be paying corporation tax over the next three or four years, but any tax payable will be at the rate of 30 per cent. A 25 per cent annual allowance is available on plant purchases.

As Financial Director, draft a report to your board making a recommendation, discussing any additional factors to be considered in making such a decision.

Further Reading

Franks, Julian R., Broyles, John E. and Carleton, Willard T. *Corporate Finance: Concepts and Applications.* Boston, Mass.: Kent Publishing, 1985, chapter 23.
Jensen, Michael C. and Smith, Jr, Clifford W. (eds) *The Modern Theory of Corporate Finance.* New York: McGraw-Hill, 1986, chapter 7.

8

Combining Investment and Financing Decisions

The Theory of Combining Investment and Financing Decisions

In Part I of this book we considered *investment* decisions and so far in Part II we have considered *financing* decisions. In practice, however, investment and financing decisions *interact* and need to be taken simultaneously. A straightforward approach to combining investment and financing decisions is the *adjusted present value* technique. (For further discussion see Myers (1974, 1977) and Bar-Yosef (1977).)

As noted earlier, the objective of the firm is to maximize its current market value, that is to maximize shareholder wealth. Firms create wealth by making successful investment decisions which generate positive net cash flows. Investment decisions are, in general, far more important than financing decisions because it is the investment decisions which decide the level of future cash flows generated from successful trading. However, it is still necessary to make good financing decisions, and in certain situations these *can* be of *prime* importance. Financial management is concerned with the making of wealth-creating investment decisions and devising a sensible financing strategy; investment and financing decisions need to be taken at the same time. A financial management programme is outlined in figure 8.1.

Investment decisions can be made within the framework of the net present value (NPV) formula which attempts to measure the present value of wealth created by taking on an investment opportunity. This NPV formula can then be modified to take into account the impact of financing decisions, which gives the adjusted present value (APV) of the investment opportunity. Once the effects of financing the investment opportunity have been identified and valued, the calculation of APV merely involves addition to or subtraction from the NPV. APV is simply NPV adjusted for anything special about the financing decision, such as government grants, tax allowances, cheap loans, issuing costs, and the ability to sustain additional debt. The

145

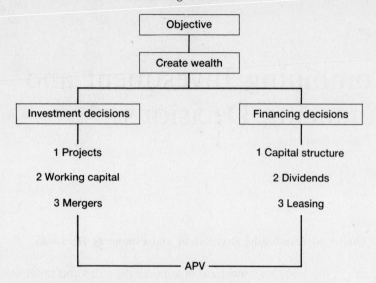

Simultaneous solution of investment and financing problems

Figure 8.1   Financial management programme

NPV of a project is calculated on the assumption that the project is financed entirely with *equity*, and when modified to take into account the present value of financing decisions yields APV.

$$\text{APV} = \text{NPV} + \text{present value of (benefits – costs) of financing decisions caused by project acceptance} \qquad (8.1)$$

Combining Investment and Financing Decisions in Practice

The application of the adjusted present value technique is best illustrated by practical examples.

Example 1

A project has a net present value of £50m. However, as the project is considered socially desirable, it qualifies for a *tax-free government grant* of £10m. This is a special financing arrangement and hence needs to be taken into account.

$$\text{APV} = \text{NPV} + \text{£10m} = \text{£60m}$$

Example 2

A project has a net present value of £100m. With a view to raising capital to finance the project it is necessary to incur *issuing costs* amounting to £5m (assume not tax-deductible). The issuing costs relate entirely to the financing decision, but they are an incremental cost of accepting the project.

$$APV = NPV - £5m = £95m$$

At the margin such financing costs can be important. If our project has a positive NPV of £3m but it is necessary to incur financing costs of £5m, then the adjusted present value is negative, and the project should not be undertaken.

Example 3

A project has a net present value of £100m. The project will sustain *perpetual debt* of £4m per annum at 10 per cent interest. The tax rate is 50 per cent. From chapter 5 (Capital Structure Decisions), we know that the value of the firm with debt is equal to the value of the firm without debt plus the present value of the tax savings (if any anticipated incremental costs of financial distress are ignored). Now the present value of the tax savings is equal to the market value of debt multiplied by the tax rate for a company with tax savings on interest in perpetuity. The concept of debt increasing the value of the *firm* applies to *individual projects* within the firm also. Thus a project which will sustain debt has a higher present value than a similar project which will not sustain debt, because the tax shield on debt has a positive present value. In our example, the project has a net present value of £100m ignoring the present value of the tax shield. The anticipated perpetual interest payments amount to £400,000 per annum, and so the resulting tax shield is £200,000 per annum. The present value of that tax shield discounted at 10 per cent is £2m. Hence

$$APV = NPV + £2m = £102m$$

The benefit of using debt finance has probably been overstated because the present value of the anticipated incremental costs of financial distress has been ignored; this needs to be subtracted from the APV. Furthermore, the tax shield would be lost if the company were not in a tax-paying position.

For simplicity, perpetual debt has been assumed, but for debt which is not perpetual it is necessary to work out the interest repayment schedule and calculate the annual tax savings. These are discounted at the going rate of interest to give the present value of the tax shield, which is then added to the net present value of the project to give the adjusted present value.

Example 4

A project has a net present value of £200m. A specialist financial institution offers a cheap loan of £24m at 6 per cent interest rather than the market rate of 10 per cent. There is clearly an *element of gift* in the financing arrangements. A perpetual loan of £24m offered at three-fifths the going rate of interest includes a gift element of £9.6m. Savings in annual interest payments of £0.96m discounted at 10 per cent have a present value of £9.6m. Thus, so far,

$$APV = NPV + £9.6m = £209.6m$$

If the project can sustain this amount of debt without any increase in the anticipated costs of financial distress, then the adjusted present value should also be increased by the present value of the tax shield. Assuming a 50 per cent tax rate, annual interest payments of £1.44m give a tax shield of £0.72m per annum, which discounted at 10 per cent have a present value of £7.2m. The final adjusted present value is therefore

$$APV = £209.6m + £7.2m = £216.8m$$

As in example 3, the loan is assumed to be perpetual for simplicity of illustration, and the benefit of using debt finance has probably been overstated.

Summary

Adjusted present value is a useful technique for combining investment and financing decisions. The approach involves making a *series of present value calculations*. First, the net present value of the project is obtained. Secondly, the effects of financing the project are identified and the present value of the cost or benefit of each effect to the firm is calculated. Finally, all the present values are combined to give APV. *The firm should only accept projects with positive APVs*.

The *APV rule* explicitly takes into account the interaction between a firm's investment and financing decisions and gives the *correct decision rule concerning the firm's investment strategy*.

Study Questions

8.1 Distinguish between investment and financing decisions.

8.2 List the factors which could change NPV to APV.

8.3 A company has decided to increase output by acquiring a plant costing £10 million immediately. After-tax incremental cash inflows are expected to amount to £4 million per annum for five years, and the required rate of return on scale expansion programmes is 20 per cent. The project will be financed partly by an issue of equity amounting to £6 million, plus £400,000 issuing costs. A government grant of £1 million is available, and the remaining £3 million will be made available by Barclays Bank at 6 per cent, rather than the market rate of 12 per cent, repayable in five instalments at the end of each of the five years. The company pays tax at 30 per cent. Calculate the NPV and APV.

Further Reading

Brealey, Richard and Myers, Stewart. *Principles of Corporate Finance*. New York: McGraw-Hill, 1984, chapter 19.
Franks, Julian R., Broyles, John E. and Carleton, Willard T. *Corporate Finance: Concepts and Applications*. Boston, Mass.: Kent Publishing, 1985, chapter 22.

9

International Financial Management

Introduction

International financial management is essentially the same as any other kind of financial management. The objective is to make money satisfying consumer wants in competitive markets by matching the resources of the organization to the needs of the market-place. In international financial management we consider those aspects of wealth creation which are not present in purely domestic financial management. These additional factors include:

1 dealing in different currencies with countries with different interest rates;
2 dealing with greater problems of debt collection;
3 dealing with different legal systems, tax rules, and different degrees of economic stability.

Exchange Rates

Exchange rates express the relationships between different currencies. For example, the exchange rate between US dollars and pounds sterling can be stated as 1.600 dollars per pound sterling, or £0.625 per dollar. Exchange rates appear daily in the financial press including the *Financial Times*.

Spot Rates

The spot rate is today's rate of exchange for 'immediate' delivery, usually within two working days.

Forward Rates

These are rates agreed today for delivery of currency at some time in the future, usually 30, 90, and 180 days. The forward rate may be at a premium or a discount on the spot rate, depending upon the market's expected future currency movements. If the 180 day forward rate for the dollar against the pound is £0.641 as against the spot rate of £0.617 then the forward rate premium expressed as an annual rate is:

$$P = \frac{F-S}{S} \times \frac{12}{n(\text{months})} \times 100$$

$$P = \frac{0.641 - 0.617}{0.617} \times \frac{12}{6} \times 100$$

$$P = 7.8 \text{ per cent}$$

A forward discount would show as a negative premium when the forward pound equivalent rate is less than the spot rate.

Cross Rates

If the British pound equals 1.5 US dollars and 8 French francs are equivalent to one dollar, then the cross rate which relates pounds to francs is $1.5 \times 8 = 12$ French francs per British pound.

Fixed and Floating Exchange Rates

Under the Bretton Woods system of exchange rates established in 1949, the major trading nations were required to maintain fixed exchange rates against the US dollar, only small fluctuations being allowed. The fixed exchange rate system was administered by the International Monetary Fund (IMF). The US dollar was tied to the price of gold at 35 dollars per ounce, the dollar linked to gold therefore being the foundation of the system. Through the US dollar all currency values were linked with gold. Occasionally governments found it necessary to devalue (or even revalue) their currencies owing to the pressure of inflation and permanent deficits in their trading with the rest of the world. In 1967 the continuing balance of trade deficits led the British government to devalue the pound sterling from $2.8 to $2.5 per pound. This made exported goods cheaper and imports into the United Kingdom more expensive. Also in the 1960s, West Germany twice revalued its currency after continued export surpluses.

In 1971 the Nixon administration devalued the US dollar against gold, and in 1973 the major trading nations adopted a system of floating exchange rates. Exchange rates are now allowed to fluctuate according to market forces. Exchange rates are occasionally subject to government interference, hence the name 'dirty float'. For managers, the comparative certainty of fixed exchange rates has been removed, and exchange rates are now far more volatile. An overseas contract or transaction which promises to generate a cash flow of $10,000 from the USA in six months is subject to the additional risk that the dollar will change in value *vis-à-vis* the pound.

Factors which Influence Exchange Rates

Exchange rates are determined in the foreign exchange markets by supply and demand for different currencies. Supply and demand are influenced by the currency needs of individuals making payments or travelling overseas, speculators dealing in currency, and government intervention. Some of the factors which are believed to influence exchange rates are listed below.

1 *Inflation (Purchasing power parity theorem)* In a perfectly free and competitive world £100 should buy the same quantity of goods in any country, since the pound can be exchanged for its equivalent foreign currency. We all know that such a world does not exist, but if the rate of inflation in the UK is expected to be higher than the rate of inflation in the USA, then we should expect the pound to decline relative to the dollar. Relative inflation rates therefore affect exchange rates.

2 *Interest rates (Interest rate parity theorem)* Relative interest rates and expected changes in interest rates also influence exchange rates. We must expect exchange rates to move so as to reduce the interest rate differential between different countries. For example, if interest rates are higher in the UK than in the USA, investors will prefer to switch funds from the USA to the UK. Dollars will be used to buy pounds, and the buying pressure should strengthen the pound against the dollar.

3 *Government intervention* Governments exert tremendous pressure on exchange rates, not only by direct buying and selling, but also by their restrictions on currency dealings, restrictions on currency movements, and by their taxation and monetary policies. These in turn affect interest rates and the level of inflation.

4 *Balance of trade* Currency depreciation is expected when a country's imports are regularly greater than its exports. During the period of fixed exchange rates, pressure on the British pound followed balance of trade deficits which led to the devaluation of the pound against other major currencies.

5   *Overseas investment*   Overseas investment by British companies and individuals, when financed with the domestic currency, increases the supply of pounds for foreigners, putting downward pressure on the pound. Investment in the UK by foreigners will tend to strengthen the pound. Currency flows between different countries chasing high yields on government securities, bonds and equities are referred to as 'hot' money.

6   *Speculation*   Speculators, including the Treasury managers of international banks, influence movements in exchange rates by buying and selling in the expectation of making positive returns by correctly forecasting movements in exchange rates, and by exploiting any market inefficiencies.

Covered Interest Arbitrage

A US investor has $1,000 to invest at the risk-free rate for six months. Interest rates are 10 per cent in the UK and 5 per cent in the USA. The US investor can buy pounds at the spot rate of $2 to one pound. The £500 investment earns approximately £25 interest in 180 days, and the investor has £525 to convert back into dollars. If the spot rate is still $2, then the investor has earned 10 per cent which is better than the 5 per cent available in the USA. However, the investor is exposed to exchange rate risk. His or her position is 'uncovered'. If the spot rate is $1.8 after six months, then the £525 will be converted into $945. This compares badly with the investment which could have been made in the USA. If the investor had invested the $1,000 in the USA at 5 per cent, he or she would have $1,025 at the end of the 180 day period. If the spot rate is $2.2, the £525 will be converted into $1,155 which fortunately is much better than the $1,025 available in the USA.

An investor can avoid exchange rate risk by a forward contract to convert £525 into $US in 180 days. If the forward rate is $1.970, the £525 will be exchanged for $1,034.25 in 180 days, a gain of $9.25 over the domestic investment. Transactions of this kind are referred to as covered interest arbitrage. Such activity by arbitrageurs helps to maintain equilibrium in international exchange markets. Arbitrage is the buying and selling of the same commodity in different markets. From this example, we can imagine how the international Treasury manager can use foreign exchange markets to hedge against currency risk. Future markets can be used to buy and sell at the forward rate to avoid exposure to exchange rate fluctuations.

Avoidance of Exchange Rate Risk

Practical financial management involves hedging against exchange rate risk. The simplest way to avoid exchange rate risk is to insist on cash with order which can be exchanged at the spot rate. Alternatively, the price can be agreed in one's own domestic currency, thereby placing the exchange rate risk on the customer. Some companies selling in many parts of the world can adopt a 'swings and roundabouts' approach to foreign exchange management, i.e. gains are expected approximately to cancel out losses.

It is not usually possible to arrange for cash with order or to agree for payment in the exporter's domestic currency. Most international transactions involve delayed payment and exchange rate risk to the exporter. There is no exchange rate risk to the importer when the amount payable is fixed in the importer's own currency. The exporter may well wish to avoid exchange rate risk, i.e. the risk that his or her domestic currency will strengthen against the importer's currency resulting in a smaller amount eventually receivable when the importer pays. The exporter can avoid exchange rate risk by today selling a forward contract to supply the importer's currency in the future. For the vast majority of individuals and firms, foreign exchange transactions are arranged by commercial banks. Financial managers wishing to engage in foreign exchange dealings will do so through their bank's foreign exchange departments.

An Example of Hedging

A British company expects to receive $10,000 from the USA in six months. The following rates of exchange are quoted:

	$ per pound	£ per dollar
Spot	1.620	0.617
30 days	1.600	0.625
90 days	1.580	0.633
180 days	1.560	0.641

The financial manager can wait to receive the $10,000 in 180 days and therefore risk loss or gain at the spot rate in six month's time. The company would bear the foreign exchange risk. Alternatively the manager can now sell the $10,000 receivable in 180 days at the future rate of 1.560, i.e. £6,410. This amount would be receivable regardless of the spot rate existing in 180 days. By hedging in the forward currency market, the financial manager knows exactly how much will be received or paid in 180 days. The paperwork will be managed by the foreign exchange department of the company's commercial bank.

Alternatively the company may expect to pay $10,000 in 180 days. If the financial manager buys the $10,000 at the 180 day rate, he or she will eventually pay £6,410. Again, the contract is made now and the funds will be converted at the agreed rate in 180 days, regardless of the spot rate existing on that day.

A different approach is for the exporter exposed to exchange rate risk to borrow in the customer's currency an amount which with principal and interest will equal the amount receivable in the future. The immediate proceeds of the loan can be converted into the amount receivable in the domestic currency, thereby avoiding exchange rate risk. The overseas currency receivable on the due date can be used to repay the loan.

Currency Options

Another course of action has become available in recent years. When a firm bids for an overseas contract the financial manager may wish to purchase a currency option. This gives the holder the right, but not the obligation, to sell the foreign exchange which it will receive if it wins the overseas contract. If the firm is successful in its bid for the contract, the option may be exercised. If the bid fails, the option may be allowed to lapse. Currency options are available in some major currencies. They can be used when the forward currency market does not provide an appropriate hedge.

Overseas Investment by Multinational Companies (MNCs)

Recent years have witnessed considerable growth in international investment by multinational companies, particularly by companies based in the USA, the UK, Japan, West Germany, and Switzerland. Foreign investment is associated with the following additional risks:

1 expropriation of assets;
2 loss or diminution of control;
3 destruction by war or revolution;
4 loss of currency convertibility;
5 inability to transfer funds out of the overseas country;
6 exchange rate risk affecting domestic valuation of overseas assets and liabilities;
7 exchange rate risk associated with transactions;
8 tax discrimination and import controls.

Domestic Valuation of Overseas Assets and Liabilities

With reference to (6), a USA company might acquire assets in the UK costing £1,000m and take on liabilities amounting to £500m, when the exchange rate stands at $2 per pound. The net dollar investment is therefore $2,000m less $1,000m equals $1,000m. If the pound weakens to $1, then the £1,000m assets are converted into a domestic $1,000m and the liabilities to $500m, a decrease in the net domestic translation amounting to $500m. Alternatively, if the pound strengthens to $3 then the £1,000m assets are translated into $3,000 and the £500m liabilities into $1,500, a net overseas investment of $1,500m, resulting in a translation gain of $500m over the original net overseas investment of $1,000m.

If the US company expects the value of the pound to rise in terms of US dollars, then it should increase its assets in the UK and reduce its liabilities. If the pound is expected to fall *vis-à-vis* the US dollar, then the company should reduce its assets in the UK and increase its liabilities. The US company, and other multinational companies, can avoid this exchange risk by financing assets in the UK with UK liabilities, i.e. reducing the net equity position to zero.

Exchange Rate Risk Affecting Transactions

If a firm does not invest overseas, but only has overseas transactions, then there are still greater risks than those associated with the domestic situation. These include:

1 exchange rate risk;
2 less reliable information relating to the credit worthiness of customers;
3 greater difficulty in enforcing cash collections;
4 longer delivery times where goods are in transit.

Protection against foreign exchange business risk can be achieved by international diversification across a wide range of currencies, so that gains and losses on exchange, to some extent, are offset. Furthermore, a company can avoid exchange rate risk by dealings in the forward rate markets.

(Irrevocable) Letter of Credit

The problem of cash collection is usually solved by the use of the letter of credit. An exporter may demand cash with order or, at the other extreme, deliver goods to an overseas customer on open account for payment in the usual way, giving perhaps one to three months' credit. Between these two extremes, a variety of methods has been devised to assist in the financing of international transactions, the most popular being the letter of credit. This is a document prepared by a bank for an importer promising to pay a specified amount to an exporter once certain stated conditions have been met. An exporting firm presents the letter of credit to its own bank which arranges payment from the importer's bank once the conditions of the transaction are met by the exporter. The letter of credit can be irrevocable once the conditions have been met.

International Cash Management

Multinational companies manage their cash balances in the same way as domestic companies. Additional complications include:

1 cash balances exist in several countries;
2 multinational banks help companies to manage and transfer funds;
3 deposits may be channelled to areas of high interest yield, safety, and strong currency;
4 cash flows generated from successful trading may be channelled to areas of low tax rates, perhaps by transfer pricing;
5 loans can be raised in areas of low interest rates.

Eurocurrency Markets

Eurodollars are US dollar denominated deposits with banks outside the United States. The Eurodollar market is not regulated by any government and is therefore an international currency. A British firm with a subsidiary in the US could raise funds in the UK and then transfer the funds to the United States for use in that country. The company could also raise funds in the United States, denominated in dollars. Alternatively, the firm could raise funds in the Eurodollar market. The Eurodollar market therefore enables companies to borrow dollars outside the United States. Other Eurocurrencies are available in addition to the Eurodollar.

The Overseas Investment Decision

Just as in the case of domestic investment, the objective is to generate cash flows which compensate for the risk of the investment. Apart from the normal business risk, additional risks are inherent in foreign investments including the political risk of expropriation, and the volatility of foreign exchange. The foreign investment decision can be viewed from the points of view of the multinational company making the investment, the overseas company evaluating its domestic investment, and the government of the overseas country evaluating the effect on its economy. In evaluating capital projects overseas, attention should be directed towards:

1 additional complexity of cash flows from overseas operations;
2 exchange rate volatility;
3 possibility of restrictions on repatriation of funds and probability of effect on abandonment value.

Repatriation of Funds

The objective of overseas investment is usually to generate cash flows from successful trading for domestic shareholders. Problems can arise when a multinational company attempts to repatriate funds since overseas countries have a wide range of rules to prevent or slow down repatriation. Multinationals repatriate funds by:

1 management fees;
2 payment of goods and services by transfer pricing between companies in different countries;
3 royalties for the use of patents, names, and copyrights;
4 loan repayments with interest;
5 payment of dividends.

Conclusion

Just as in the case of domestic financial management, international financial management involves making sensible investment and financing decisions with a view to making money satisfying consumer wants in competitive markets by matching the resources of the organization to the needs of the market-place. Practical financial managers should be aware of opportunities for hedging against exchange rate risk, additional financing opportunities in Eurocurrencies, exchange rate risk relating to overseas assets and liabilities, and additional factors involved in making foreign investment decisions.

Study Questions

9.1   Interest rates in Zedland are 24 per cent per annum. However, in the UK interest rates stand at only 8 per cent. You have £100,000 to invest for 180 days in Zedland securities, but you are naturally worried about exchange rate movements. In the *Financial Times* you note the following:

Zedland (dollar)	0.2000
30 days	0.1980
90 days	0.1970
180 days	0.1900

1   What is your net gain in UK pounds from investing in the Zedland securities assuming that after 180 days the exchange rate is the same as the spot rate?

2 If the Zedland dollar depreciates by 10 per cent against the British pound, what is your net gain or loss relative to an investment in British securities?

3 What is the net gain or loss from a covered position?

9.2 Bradley Manufacturing, a British company, has a subsidiary in the USA, Bradley (USA) Inc. The subsidiary has assets of 500,000 dollars, and liabilities of 300,000 dollars. The exchange rate is 1.5 US dollars to the British pound.

1 What is the Bradley (USA) net equity position (assets less liabilities) in dollars and pounds?

2 What is the Bradley (USA) position in dollars and pounds if the exchange rate moves to 1.25 US dollars to the British pound? What is the gain or loss to the British company?

3 What is the gain or loss if the dollar moves from 1.5 to the British pound, to 1.75 US dollars to the British pound?

4 Make the same calculations for a second subsidiary of Bradley Manufacturing in the USA which has assets of 300,000 dollars and liabilities of 200,000 dollars.

Further Reading

Brealey, Richard and Myers, Stewart. *Principles of Corporate Finance*. New York: McGraw-Hill, 1984, chapter 32.

Eiteman, David K. and Stonehill, Arthur I. *Multinational Business Finance*. Reading, Mass.: Addison-Wesley, 1986.

Part III

Financial Planning and Control

10

Profit Planning and Control

The Theory of Profit Planning

As managers we are aware that sales minus total costs equals profit.

$S - TC = P$, where

S = sales,

TC = total costs, and

P = profit.

The theory of profit planning suggests that total costs can be split between those costs which vary with the level of output and those costs which tend not to vary with the level of output. Those costs which do vary with the level of output or sales are called *variable* costs and include the cost of materials, piece-work labour and factory power. Those costs which do not tend to vary with the level of output are called *fixed* costs, and would normally include managerial and office salaries, rent and rates, and straight-line depreciation. The theory of profit planning suggests that we should first deduct the variable costs from sales to identify the *contribution* towards fixed costs and profit.

$S - VC = C$, where

S = sales,

VC = variable costs, and

C = contribution towards fixed costs and profit.

Having identified the contribution we can deduct the fixed costs to give the profit.

$C - FC = P$, where

$C =$ contribution,

$FC =$ fixed costs, and

$P =$ profit.

Profit Planning Equations

$S - TC = P$

$VC + FC = TC$

$S - VC = C$

$C - FC = P$

For breakeven:

$S - TC = 0$

$C - FC = 0$

Once we have identified the fixed and variable costs, it is possible to plan for profit. For example, on the launch of a new product or opening of a new division, a manager will usually want to know the level of sales required for break-even, where the venture makes no profit, but at least does not result in a loss. From the above, we can identify two definitions of break-even. Firstly, when sales and total costs are equal, the profit is zero. Secondly, when the contribution (sales less variable costs) is just enough to cover the fixed costs ($C - FC = 0$), the venture shows neither profit nor loss.

Example 1

Consider the case of Miss MP Nosbor who buys 20 snibbods at £20 each, and sells them at £25 each. She incurs fixed office expenses of £40, £40 straight-line depreciation, and a fixed annual interest charge of £15.

MP Nosbor

Sales: 20 snibbods at	£25
Cost of sales: 20 snibbods at	£20
Fixed office expenses	£40
Fixed annual depreciation	£40
Fixed interest charge	£15

1 How much profit does Miss Nosbor earn by selling 20 snibbods?
2 What will be the profit if sales volume is doubled?
3 What is the required sales volume for break-even?
4 How many snibbods must be sold to earn a profit of £200?

1   *20 snibbods sold*

Units	20	% Sales
Sales (20 × £25)	500	100
Variable costs (20 × £20)	400	80
Contribution (20 × £5)	100	20
Fixed costs	95	
Profit	5	

The contribution is £100 and the profit is £5. There is a number used by accountants called the profit/volume ratio. In fact, the profit-volume ratio should be called the contribution-sales percentage. In our example, the contribution is £100, and the level of sales is £500. The contribution-sales percentage is therefore 20 per cent. This means that each £1 of sales yields a 20p contribution towards fixed costs and profit. Each £100 in sales results in a £20 contribution towards fixed costs and profit.

2   *40 snibbods sold*

Units	40	% sales
Sales (40 × £25)	1,000	100
Variable costs (40 × £20)	800	80
Contribution (40 × £5)	200	20
Fixed costs	95	
Profit	105	

If the level of sales is doubled, then the profit does not simply double (unless all our costs are variable). In our example, if we double the level of sales, the profit increases 21 times to £105. At 40 units sold, sales income doubles to £1,000, variable costs double to £800, and the contribution doubles to £200. However, the fixed costs remain at £95. The contribution is still 20 per cent, the contribution-sales percentage is still 20 per cent.

3   *Break-even sales*   To estimate the break-even level of sales, we can use the contribution-sales percentage (profit–volume ratio). The fixed costs are £95 and the contribution-sales percentage is 20 per cent, i.e. 0.2. If we divide £95 by 0.2, this gives us the break-even level of sales at £475. Alternatively, since the contribution per unit is £5, then we will need to sell 19 units to achieve a contribution of £95, which is just enough to cover the fixed costs.

Units	19	
Sales (19 × £25)	475	$\frac{95}{0.2}$ = £475
Variable costs (19 × £20)	380	
Contribution (19 × £5)	95	
Fixed costs	95	
Profit	—	

4   *Target profit = £200*   To achieve a profit of £200, we must earn a contribution of £295. At £5 per unit we must therefore sell 59 units to achieve our profit target. Alternatively, if we divide our target contribution of £295 by 0.2, this reveals a level of required sales at £1475.

Units	59	
Sales (59 × £25)	1,475	$\frac{295}{0.2}$ = £1,475
Variable costs (59 × £20)	1,180	
Contribution (59 × £5)	295	
Fixed costs	95	
Profit	200	

Once we have some reasonable estimates of our variable and fixed costs, it is possible to plan for profit. For any target level of sales we can estimate the resulting profit, and for any profit target we can estimate the required level of sales or units sold. When a firm has not analysed its fixed and variable costs in detail, it is possible to estimate the periodic fixed and variable costs using a profit chart as illustrated in figure 10.1.

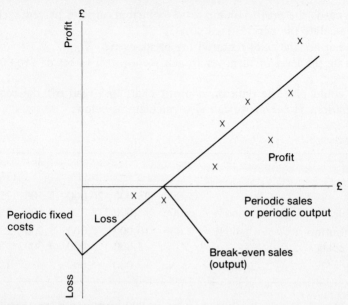

Figure 10.1 The profit chart

Periodic sales, or periodic units sold, are measured along the horizontal axis and periodic profits and losses on the vertical axis. Higher periodic sales are associated with higher periodic profit. We should expect a reasonably clear association between sales and profit, and in figure 10.1 a line of best fit through the coordinates illustrates the trade-off as expected. Our best estimate of periodic sales for break-even is that level of sales which is associated with a zero profit. Theoretically, the fixed costs are those which the firm incurs when sales are zero. The vast majority of firms would cease trading long before periodic sales fall to zero, but figure 10.1 does show our best estimate of accounting loss when no sales are effected. The level of loss is equal to the fixed costs since no variable costs are charged against sales when invoiced sales are zero.

Example 2

The following sales and profit figures relate to Horton Engineering for the months of November and December.

Period	1	2
Sales (£)	25,000	20,000
Net profit (£)	7,000	5,000

1 What is the profit-volume ratio (contribution-sales percentage)?
2 Calculate the period fixed costs.
3 What are the sales required for break-even?
4 State the level of turnover to achieve a profit target of £10,000.

We could plot the data on a profit chart and read off the required information. However we can also calculate as below.

Summary

		1	2	3	4
Sales		5,000	25,000	20,000	7,500	32,500
Variable costs	60%	3,000	15,000	12,000	4,500	19,500
Contribution	40%	2,000	10,000	8,000	3,000	13,000
Fixed costs			3,000	3,000	3,000	3,000
Profit			7,000	5,000	—	10,000

1 A reduction in the level of sales of £5,000 results in a lower profit of £2,000. Since the fixed costs remain constant, then the contribution has also fallen by £2,000. The contribution-sales percentage is therefore 40 per cent, £10,000 in Period 1 and £8,000 in Period 2. Alternatively the total costs change by £3,000 and the variable costs as a percentage of sales are 60 per cent.
2 Since the contribution is 40 per cent, and we are given the profit figures, then the fixed costs must be £10,000 − £7,000 in Period 1, and £8,000 − £5,000 in Period 2, i.e. £3,000.
3 For break-even we require a contribution of £3,000, just enough to cover the fixed costs. Since the contribution–sales percentage is 40 per cent, then we can divide £7,000 by 0.4 to give the estimated break-even sales at £7,500.
4 For a profit target of £10,000 we require a contribution of £13,000. Dividing by 0.4 gives a sales target of £32,500.

Example 3

Dick Robbins carries on business as a snibbo vendor. He has £1,000 invested in the business tied up in stock, debtors and equipment. Before selling anything he has to meet annual running costs such as rent, rates and office expenditures, amounting in total to £500.

The selling price of a snibbo is £35.

The cost to Dick of a snibbo is £30.

1 How many snibbos must Dick Robbins sell each year to break-even on trading?
2 How many snibbos must Dick Robbins sell each year to make the business viable, assuming he expects a return on capital employed of 20 per cent?
3 Suppose he expects a return on capital employed of 40 per cent. What is the new required volume for viability?
4 In an effort to increase volume to 300/400 units, Dick reckons he will either:
    (a)   Take on a salesman at £1,000 per annum, or
    (b)   Reduce his selling price by £3.
Which course of action would you recommend?

Summary

	1	2	3	4 (a)	(b)	4 (a)	(b)
Units	100	140	180	300		400	
Sales	3,500	4,900	6,300				
Variable cost	3,000	4,200	5,400				
Contribution	500	700	900	1,500	600	2,000	800
Fixed costs	500	500	500	1,500	500	1,500	500
Profit	–	200	400	–	100	500	300

1 For break-even we require a contribution of £500 to cover the fixed costs. With a contribution of £5, we must sell 100 units for break-even.
2 A 20 per cent return on capital employed suggests a profit of £200. For a required contribution of £700 we must sell 140 units.
3 If the profit target is increased to 40 per cent, then we need to sell 180 units.
4 At 300 units, a reduction in selling price gives the greater profit. At 400 units, we achieve a greater profit by taking on the salesman. At some level of unit sales we would achieve the same profit as follows:

Let x be the number of units. If we take on the salesman then we achieve a contribution of £5 for each unit sold ($5x$). After deducting the fixed costs of £1,500 we achieve a profit. With the price reduction we achieve a contribution per unit of £2 ($2x$). After deducting the fixed costs of £500 we achieve the same profit. The number of unit sales for the same profit is therefore 333 units.

Salesman: $\qquad 5x - 1,500 = P$

Price reduction: $\quad 2x - 500 = P$

$$5x - 1,500 = 2x - 500$$

$$3x = 1,000$$

$$x = 333 \text{ units.}$$

Example 4

You are a self-employed financial consultant. Brenda Trader asks you to help her plan for profit in her new venture. She plans to open a private nursing home in Harrogate. With your assistance, Brenda estimates annual costs as follows:

Variable costs per resident year		Fixed costs	
	£		£
Food	1,000	Nursing staff	24,000
Medical expenses	200	Fixed heating	11,000
Heating (additional)	300	Telephone	2,000
Cleaning and repairs	400	Office staff	4,000
Incidentals	100	Maintenance	13,000
	2,000	Loan interest	5,000
		Depreciation	4,000
		Rates	1,000
			64,000

Brenda estimates the full setting-up costs as follows:

	£
Property at cost (including alterations)	50,000
Furniture and equipment	20,000
Working capital	20,000
	90,000

She plans to write off the furniture and equipment over five years (see fixed costs).

Brenda hopes to finance the setting-up as follows:

	£
Permanent loan (interest at 10% in fixed costs)	50,000
Own capital introduced	40,000
	90,000

Apparently, the going rate in Harrogate for similar accommodation and service is about £6,000 per resident year.

1　How many residents does Brenda need to break-even in terms of accounting profit?

2　A closer examination of the premises suggests that the maximum number of residents maintainable during the full year is 24. What will the accounting profit be if Brenda attracts (a) 10, (b) 14, (c) 24 patients?

3　If she expects a 40 per cent return on her capital introduced in year one, how many full-time residents will be required for break-even?

1　The fixed costs are £64,000 and the contribution per resident year is £4,000 (£6,000 − £2,000). Therefore 16 residents are required for break-even.

Residents	16
Income	96,000
Variable costs	32,000
Contribution	64,000
Fixed costs	64,000
Profit	—

2 Residents	10	14	24
Income	60,000	84,000	144,000
Variable costs	20,000	28,000	48,000
Contribution	40,000	56,000	96,000
Fixed costs	64,000	64,000	64,000
Profit (loss)	(24,000)	(8,000)	32,000

3   Capital introduced into the business is £40,000 and the profit target therefore £16,000. To achieve this profit target she must attract the equivalent of 20 residents.

Residents	20
Income	120,000
Variable costs	40,000
Contribution	80,000
Fixed costs	64,000
Profit	16,000

Absorption (Total) Costing versus Marginal Costing

Total Costing

		Products		
	Total	A	B	C
Sales £000	500	200	200	100
Material cost	250	100	75	75
Other variables	100	35	50	15
Overheads (fixed) (100%) of wages)	100	35	50	15
Total costs	450	170	175	105
Profit (loss)	50	30	25	(5)

1   What course of action does the above analysis suggest?
2   State the alternative bases on which overheads may be absorbed.

Profit planning, as discussed earlier, is often called marginal costing. We use marginal costing for profit planning. Many companies use total or absorption costing for reporting periodic profit and loss. Under this system, the fixed costs are allocated on some rational basis between different products and divisions. Consider the three products to which the above data apply. Products A and B are profitable, but after absorbing the fixed costs as a percentage of wages, product C shows an accounting loss. However, the fixed costs can be allocated on several different bases, e.g. percentage of materials, percentage of sales, number of employees, floor space. Different bases of allocation will lead to different profit figures. It is generally agreed that marginal costing, rather than absorption costing, should be used for profit planning and for considering the success of products and divisions in terms of their contribution rather than their reported profit after the discretionary allocation of fixed costs. Product C does in fact make a contribution of 10 towards fixed costs and profit. If product C is discontinued, and if we simply lose sales of 100 and save variable costs of 90, then the profit of the firm falls from 50 to 40.

Marginal Costing

	Total	Products A	B	C
Sales £000	500	200	200	100
Material cost	250	100	75	75
Other variables	100	35	50	15
Variable costs	350	135	125	90
Contribution	150	65	75	10
Fixed costs (overheads)	100			
Profit	50			
Profit: Volume ratio (Contribution: sales %)	30	32½	37½	10
Contribution per £ Other variables	1.5	1.9	1.5	0.7
Contribution per £ Material	0.6	0.7	1.0	0.1
Contribution per machine hour	0.7	0.7	0.7	1.0
Machine hours ('000)	200	90	100	10

The marginal costing approach to profit planning does not include the discretionary allocation of fixed costs between individual products and divisions. Product A makes a contribution of 65 towards fixed costs and profit, product B makes a contribution of 75, and product C a contribution of 10. Product B has the best contribution–sales percentage at 37½ per cent. Product A achieves the greatest contribution per £1 of labour input. Product B achieves the greatest contribution per £1 of material input. Product C, in fact, achieves the greatest contribution per machine hour. These statistics can be useful in profit planning. Where materials, labour and machine hours are in short supply (limiting factors), managers are anxious to get the maximum contribution from available resources.

The Break-Even Chart

It is common practice for financial management texts to demonstrate the theory of profit planning by use of a break-even chart. The profit planning equations introduced earlier in this chapter were:

$S - VC = C$, and

$C - FC = P.$

We know that the fixed costs tend not to change within small changes in volume or sales. These are demonstrated as the horizontal curve in figure 10.2. The variable costs do increase with sales, and we also expect the sales curve to be upwards sloping (hopefully at a steeper slope than the variable costs). Section A of figure 10.2 includes the curves for fixed costs, sales and total costs (fixed costs plus variable costs). The break-even level of sales arises where sales are equal to total costs ($S = TC$). If we have statistics on volume, then the break-even volume can also be estimated from the break-even chart.

A slightly different presentation of figure 10.2 section A, appears in section B. The fixed costs are added to the variable costs to give the total costs curve. The sales curve is exactly as in section A. We can identify exactly the same level of sales and output for break-even, but we also have a little bit extra. We also see that the contribution ($S - VC$) equals the fixed costs at the break-even volume. This is our second definition of break-even, i.e. $C - FC = 0$.

Accounting Policies

The theory of financial management suggests that financial decisions should be based on the assessment of cash flow and risk. On the other hand, financial accounting is concerned with the measurement of accounting profit in the profit and loss account and with a list of a company's assets and sources of finance in the balance sheet. Practical financial management often involves the making of decisions based on accounting profit and balance sheet effect. Since a good deal of importance has traditionally been attached to a company's published financial statements, several principles, postulates, conventions, or concepts have been developed over the centuries to provide a framework for financial reporting.

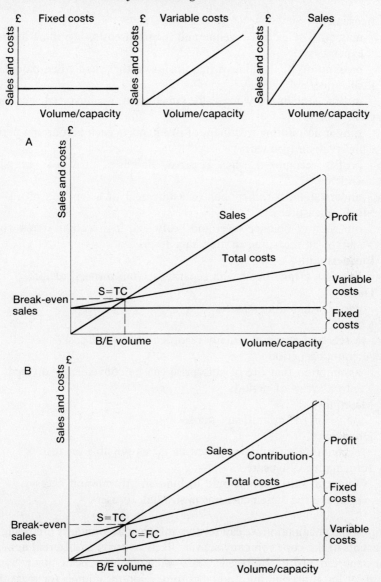

Figure 10.2 The break-even chart

The Principles, Postulates, Conventions and Concepts of Financial Accounting

1 Going concern
   expected continuance of operations
   distinction between capital and revenue

2 Accruals
matching of earned revenue and incurred costs, including accrued expenses
recognition of liabilities when arising, rather than when paid

3 Realization
income recognized when value transferred, i.e. invoiced, not paid

4 Consistency
similar accounting treatment of like items in each accounting period

5 Conservatism (prudence)
profits recognized when realized, liabilities provided for when anticipated
understatement rather than overstatement of assets and profit

6 Money measurement
omission of balance sheet and profit and loss account items which cannot be measured in monetary terms

7 Business entity
business affairs dealt with separately from owners' affairs

8 Duality
capital + liabilities = assets

9 Cost
assets and expenses usually recorded at historic cost

10 Accounting period
assumption that life of enterprise can be conveniently divided into a series of periods

11 Materiality
omission of insignificant items

12 Objectivity
accounting information based as far as possible on fact

13 Informative disclosure
financial statements should include all information necessary to make the statements not misleading to users

With some imagination we can see that different accountants preparing the accounts of the same company are very likely to arrive at different numbers for reported profit. In recent years attempts have been made by the publication of accounting standards to develop techniques for measuring profit across different companies on a consistent basis. Reported profits are still to some extent a function of accounting policies. Nevertheless, in the real world firms often judge their performance in terms of accounting profit, set targets in terms of accounting profit, and spend a good deal of time analysing and making decisions on the basis of accounting profit. Measures of performance and targets are often expressed in terms of return on capital employed and earnings per share. Neither cash flow nor risk are ingredients in return on capital employed and earnings per share calculations. One of the major problems with the use of accounting profit is that it is subject to some extent to the methods chosen for measuring profit. The major headaches in measuring accounting profit include stock valuation, the measurement of depreciation, and the effect of inflation. There are also many other problems.

Some Problems in Profit Measurement

1 *Stock valuation* We may assume that the last goods to enter the warehouse are the first ones to leave (LIFO), that the highest cost items are the first ones to leave (HIFO), that the first goods to arrive are the first to go out (FIFO), or that we should use the cost of our next purchase to charge goods to production (NIFO). Alternatively, we could use average cost, we could develop a unit or standard cost, we could use adjusted selling price, or the net realizable value. In valuing stock we may choose to add on an amount to cover overhead expenses. The general rule in accounting is that we value stock at the lower of cost or net realizable value.

2 *Depreciation* Several methods have been devised for estimating depreciation including the straight line method, reducing balance method, machine hour rate, labour hour rate, the sum of the digits method, and numerous complicated annuity systems.

3 *Inflation* A great deal of time and effort has been spent in trying to determine a reasonable method for adjusting accounting numbers for inflation. No universally accepted method has been developed, and we emphasize that the method adopted will affect the level of reported profit, but it will not affect cash flow.

4 *Research and development* This may be written off in one period, or spread over a number of years.

5 *Long-term contracts* The profit on a long-term contract may be apportioned over the life of the contract, or perhaps only recognized on completion of the contract.

6 *Expenditure provisions* Accounting profit is invoiced sales less invoiced cost of sales and depreciation. We can take an optimistic or pessimistic view of after-sales service, liabilities likely to arise under guarantees or warranties, and other expenditures likely to arise in the future.

7 *Deferred taxation* We may or may not include a charge in the accounts for the taxation which would be payable if we disposed of our fixed assets.

8 *Hire purchase charges* The profit and interest may be spread over the life of the agreement by different methods.

9   *Rental income*   Sometimes a substantial premium is received at the commencement of a rental agreement. The total amount of the premium may be included in this year's profit and loss account or perhaps spread over the life of the agreement.

10   *Reserve accounting*   We may choose to charge rationalization and other non-recurring costs not against this year's profit and loss account, but against balances on profit and loss account and general reserves brought forward from previous years. This will increase the amount of reported profit for the current period.

The following example of a problem in profit measurement has been used extensively to demonstrate the effect of different accounting policies on reported accounting profit.

Computer Services Co. Ltd: Example

As chief accountant of the Computer Services Co Ltd you are aware of conflicts of opinion between the Marketing and Financial Directors as to the accounting policies to be adopted in preparation of the firm's accounts for its first trading year. The Marketing Director is anxious that the first year of operations should appear to be as successful as possible whereas the Financial Director expresses his belief that both profit and financial position should be presented conservatively.

Marketing Director

Depreciation of programs purchased:
Write off over useful life, i.e. five years

Depreciation of premises:
None. Add annual increase in value to profit and loss account

Depreciation of equipment:
20% of valuation. Add valuation increase to profit and loss account

Pure research costs:
Write off over five years

Long-term contract profit allocation:
Credit estimated profit to profit and loss account. Treat contract valuation as debtor

Contingent liabilities:
Write off when actually paid

Rental income receivable:
Credit all to profit and loss account when received

Formation expenses:
Capitalize

Program development costs:
Capitalize

After sales costs:
Write off when paid

Financial Director

Depreciation of programs purchased:
Write off over useful life, i.e. four years

Depreciation of premises:
5% straight-line depreciation on valuation. Credit increases in value to capital reserve

Depreciation of equipment:
20% of replacement value. Credit valuation increases to capital reserve

Pure research costs:
Write off in expenditure period

Long-term contract profit allocation:
Take profit when contract completed. Treat accumulated expenditure as work-in-progress

Contingent liabilities:
Make reasonable provision

Rental income receivable:
Allocate to appropriate income period

Formation expenses:
Write off

Program development costs:
Write off

After sales costs:
Make reasonable provision, treating as distribution cost

Computer Services Co. Ltd

The firm's trial balance at 30 June 1988 is given below:

	Assets and expenses £000	Liabilities and income £000
Sales		600
First year's expenditure on 3 year contract	50	
Cost of programs purchased	200	
External services	70	
Salaries and wages	300	
Administrative expenses	70	
Selling and distribution	20	
Financial expenses	5	
Program development costs	80	
Premises (Cost 1.7.87)	150	
Equipment (Cost 1.7.87)	200	
Company formation	1	
Pure research costs	35	
Rental income		8
Trade debtors	177	
Trade creditors		85
Share capital		670
Cash at bank	5	
	1,363	1,363

1 Freehold premises were professionally valued on 30.6.88 at £160,000.
2 The replacement cost of equipment is estimated at £220,000.
3 The expenditure on the long-term contract is expected to contribute £65,000 to the final settlement.
4 Expenditure amounting to £8,000 is expected to arise in the correction of computing errors relating to computer services for which invoices have been dispatched.
5 The company guaranteed the bank overdraft for one of its suppliers to the extent of £10,000. A liquidator has been appointed and the Computer Services Co. Ltd will probably be called upon to honour the guarantee.
6 The rental income received relates to the 2 years to 30 June 1989.

Answer

Computer Services Co. Ltd

Balance Sheet as at 30 June 1988

		Marketing Director £000	Financial Director £000
Sources of Funds:			
Share capital		670	670
Capital reserve		—	30
Profit and loss account (loss)		97	(97)
		767	603
Employment of Funds:			
Fixed assets:			
Freehold property		160	152
Equipment		176	176
Pure research		28	—
		364	328
Current assets:			
Programs	240		150
Work-in-progress	—		50
Debtors	242		177
Cash at bank	5		5
	487		382
Less Current Liabilities:			
Trade creditors	85		97
Contingent liability	—		10
	85		i07
Net Current Assets		402	275
Formation Expenses		1	—
		767	603

Answer

Computer Services Co. Ltd

Profit and Loss Account for the year ended 30 June 1988

		Marketing Director £000		Financial Director £000
Sales			600		600
Less Cost of Sales:				
Salaries and wages	300		300	
External services	70		70	
Program development	—		80	
Pure research	7		35	
Depreciation – programs	40		50	
– premises	—		8	
– equipment	44		44	
Cost of sales		461		587
Gross profit		139		13
Add: Profit on long-term				
contract		15		—
Rental income		8		4
		162		17
Less:				
Administration	70		70	
Selling and distribution	20		28	
Finance	5		16	
		95		114
Net profit on trading (loss)		67		(97)
Add: Increase in value of				
fixed assets		30		—
Net profit for year (loss)		97		(97)

1 *Profit measurement* Clearly, different accounting policies have led to very different reported accounting profits. For the same company, the Marketing Director reports a profit of £97,000, whereas the Financial Director reports a loss of £97,000.

2 *Performance measurement* If we use a basic performance ratio such as net profit as a percentage of sales, then the Marketing Director reports a positive return on sales of $\frac{97}{600} \times 100 = 16.2$ per cent, whereas the Financial Director reports a negative return on sales of $\frac{(97)}{600} \times 100 = (16.2)$ per cent.

3 *The dividend decision* The Marketing Director, reporting a profit of £97,000, could recommend a dividend of perhaps £30,000 whereas the Financial Director would probably not recommend a dividend payment. Dividends, however, are not paid 'out of profits'. They are paid out of cash. Both Marketing and Finance Directors agree that the cash balance is £5,000. Cash dividends are often measured as a percentage of accounting profit, but we emphasize that dividends are paid out of the cash balance.

4 *Cash flow* Cash flow is not subject to the problems of profit measurement. If the company commenced trading by issuing shares for £670,000 in cash, then the annual cash flow is negative at £665,000, the difference between the opening and closing cash balances. In summary, profit is an opinion, but cash flow is a fact.

Standard Costing

At the end of each trading period, managers need to measure actual performance against the target performance. One widely-used approach for measuring performance is known as standard costing. It involves setting standard costs for labour, materials, variable and fixed overheads, as well as standard selling prices and target quantities to produce and sell. Once we have assembled statistics relating to actual achievement, the actual performance can be measured against the standards. The objective of the exercise is to reconcile the budget or target profit with the actual profit by measuring favourable and adverse variances between actuals and standards.

Sales Variances (in terms of profit)

Textbook Definitions of Variances

1 Sales price variance (SPV):
   Quantity sold × (actual selling price less standard selling price)

2 Sales quantity variance (SQV):
(Actual quantity less budget quantity) × standard profit per unit
3 Total sales (sales value) variance (TSV):

	Actual sales
Less	Standard cost of actual sales
=	Standard profit (given actual sales)
Less	Budget profit
=	Total sales variance

Sales quantity variance + sales price variance = Total sales variance

Asking the Right Question: Sales Variance (in terms of profit)

● Sales price variance:

What is the actual sales figure?
What is the budget selling price of the actual quantity sold?

● Sales quantity variance:

What is the actual sales quantity?
What is the budget sales quantity?
What is the standard profit per unit?

● Total sales (sales value) variance:

What is the actual sales figure?
What is the standard total cost per unit?
What is the standard total cost of the actual sales?
What is the budget profit?

Sales Variances: Examples

1	Budgeted sales	1,000 units
	Standard selling price	£2
	Actual sales	1,200 units
	Standard cost	£1.50 per unit
	Actual selling price	£1.75 per unit

Calculate sales price, quantity and total sales (sales value) variances.

2   A company budgets to produce 10,000 units per month at a standard cost of £12, and to sell all units produced at £18 per unit. In November actual production is 9,800 units all of which were sold at £19 per unit. Calculate sales price, quantity and total sales (sales value) variances for the

month and prepare a statement reconciling budgeted and actual profit assuming production was effected at standard cost.

Answers

1	SPV	1,200 (1.75 – 2.00)	300(A)
	SQV	1,200 – 1,000 (0.5)	100(F)
	TSV		200(A)

	Check:	Actual sales	2,100
		Standard cost of actual sales	1,800
		Standard profit (given actual sales)	300
		Less Budget profit	500
		TSV	200(A)

2	SPV	9,800 (19 – 18)	9,800(F)
	SQV	(9,800 – 10,000)6	1,200(A)
	TSV		8,600(F)

	Check:	Actual sales	186,200
		Standard cost of actual sales	117,600
		Standard profit (given actual sales)	68,600
		Less budget profit	60,000
		TWV	8,600(F)

(F) = Favourable variance
(A) = Adverse variance

Materials Variances

Textbook Definitions of Variances

1 Materials price variance (MPV):
 Standard cost of material used less actual cost of material used
2 Materials usage variance (MUV):
 Standard cost of standard material usage less standard cost of actual material used i.e. (Standard material for actual output less actual quantity of material used) × standard unit cost of the material
3 Materials cost variance (MCV):
 Standard cost of output less actual cost of output
 Material price variance + materials usage variance = materials cost variance

Asking the Right Question: Materials Variances

● Materials price variance:

What is the standard cost of the materials actually used?
What is the actual cost?

● Materials usage variance:

What quantity of materials should have been used for the actual production?
What quantity of materials has been used?
What is the standard cost per unit of input?

● Materials cost variance:

What is the standard material cost of the output?
How much did it cost?

Materials Variances: Examples

1	Actual production	2,000 units
	Standard material input for 2000 units	2,030 lbs @ 50p per lb
	Actual material input	2,050 lbs
	Actual cost of material input	52½ per pound

Calculate material price, usage, cost variances.

2   The standard material input in the manufacture of a product is 8 lb costing 30p per lb. In November 3,600 units were produced using 30,000 lb of material costing £9,150.
Calculate material price, usage and cost variances.

Answers

1	MPV 2,050 (0.525 − 0.500)	51.25(A)
	MUV (2,050 − 2,030) 0.5	10.00(A)
	MCV 2,030 (0.5) − 2,050 (0.525)	61.25(A)
2	MPV 30,000 (0.3) − 9,150	150(A)
	MUV [3,600(8) − 30,000] 0.3	360(A)
	MCV 3,600 (2.4) − 9,150	510(A)

Labour Variances

Textbook Definitions of Variances

1 Rate of pay variance (RPV):
Standard cost of hours worked less actual cost of hours worked i.e. actual hours worked × difference in rate of pay
2 Labour efficiency variance (LEV):
Standard cost of standard hours produced less standard cost of actual hours worked i.e. (standard hours produced less actual hours worked) × standard rate of pay
3 Labour cost variances (LCV):
Standard cost of output less actual cost of output
Labour rate of pay variance + labour efficiency variance = labour cost variance

Asking the Right Question: Labour Variances

● Rate of pay variance:

What is the standard cost of the hours actually worked?
What is the actual cost?

● Labour efficiency variance:

How many standard hours have been produced?
How many hours have been worked?
What is the standard labour hour rate?

● Labour cost variance:

What is the standard labour cost of the output?
What is the actual cost?

Labour Variances: Examples

1	Actual production	240 units
	Standard time per unit	4 hours
	Standard labour rate	60p per hour
	Hours actually worked	1,000
	Wages paid	£587

Calculate labour rate, efficiency, cost variances.

2 A product is budgeted to use 6 labour hours at 40p per hour. In November 4,200 units are produced using 25,470 labour hours at 35p per hour. Calculate labour rate, efficiency and cost variances.

Answers

1	LRV/RPV 1,000 (0.6) − 587	13(F)
	LEV [240(4) − 1,000]0.6	24(A)
	LCV 240(2.4) − 587	11(A)
2	LRV/RPV 25,470(0.40 − 0.35)	1,273.5(F)
	LEV [4,200(6) − 25,470]0.4	108.0(A)
	LCV 4,200 (2.4) − 25,470(0.35)	1,165.5(F)

LRV = Labour rate variance
RPV = Rate of pay variance

Variable Overhead Variances

Textbook Definitions of Variances

1 Variable overhead expenditure variance (VOEXV):
Standard cost of hours worked and output less actual cost
2 Variable overhead efficiency variance (VOEV):
Standard hours produced at standard less standard cost of actual hours worked i.e. (Standard hours produced less actual) × standard variable overhead *time* rate
3 Variable overhead cost variance (VOCV):
Standard cost of output less actual cost of output
Variable overhead expenditure variance + variable overhead efficiency variance = variable overhead cost variance

Asking the Right Question: Variable Overhead Variances

● Variable overhead expenditure variance:

What is the variable overhead hourly rate?
What is the allowed cost for the actual hours worked?
What is the actual cost?
What is the variable overhead rate per unit of output?
What is the allowed cost for the actual output?
What is the actual cost?

● Variable overhead efficiency variance:

How many standard hours have been produced?
How many hours have been worked?
What is the variable overhead hourly rate?

● Variable overhead cost variance:

What is the standard variable overhead cost of the output?
What is the actual cost?

Variable Overhead Variances: Examples

1	Variable overhead accruing with time	£6,000 (Budget)
	Variable overhead accruing with output	£4,000 (Budget)
	Budgeted output	10,000 standard hours
	Actual variable overhead – time	£5,240
	Actual variable overhead – output	£4,120
	Standard hours produced	10,400
	Actual hours worked	8,800

Calculate variable overhead expenditure, efficiency and cost variances.

2	Budget variable overhead accruing with time	£24,000
	Budget variable overhead accruing with output	£54,000
	Budget output	30,000 standard hours
	Actual variable overhead – time	£23,400
	Actual variable overhead – output	£55,600
	Standard hours produced	30,200
	Actual hours worked	29,500

Calculate variable overhead expenditure, efficiency and cost variances.

Answers

1	VOEXV – Time $8,800(0.6) - 5,240$	40(F)
	– Output $10,400(0.4) - 4,120$	40(F)
	VOEXV	80(F)
	VOEV $(10,400 - 8,800)0.6$	960(F)
	VOCV $10,400(1) - 9,360$	1,040(F)

1	VOEXV – Time 29,500(0.8) – 23,400	200(F)
	– Output 30,200(1.8) – 55,600	1,240(A)
	VOEXV	1,040(A)
	VOEV 30,200 – 29,500(0.8)	560(F)
	VOCV 30,200(2.6) – 79,000	480(A)

Fixed Overhead Variances

Textbook Definitions of Variances

1 Fixed overhead volume efficiency variance (VEV):
Standard hours produced at standard less actual hours worked at standard
i.e. (standard hours produced less actual hours) × standard fixed overhead
rate
2 Fixed overhead capacity usage variance (CUV):
Actual hours at standard less budgeted hours at standard i.e. (actual hours
less budget hours) × standard fixed overhead rate
3 Fixed overhead volume variance (VV):
Standard hours produced at standard less budgeted hours at standard
i.e. (standard hours produced less budgeted hours) × standard fixed
overhead rate
4 Fixed overhead expenditure variance (EXV):
Budgeted fixed overhead cost less actual cost
5 Fixed overhead cost variance (CV):
Standard cost of output less actual cost of output
6 Volume efficiency variance + capacity usage variance = volume variance
Volume variance + expenditure variance = cost variance

Asking the Right Question: *Fixed Overhead Variances*

● Fixed overhead volume efficiency variance:

How many standard hours have been produced?
How many hours have been worked?
What is the standard fixed overhead rate per hour?

● Fixed overhead capacity usage:

How many hours have been worked?
How many hours were budgeted to be worked?
What is the standard fixed overhead rate per hour?

- Fixed overhead expenditure variance:

What is the budget fixed overhead cost?
What is the actual cost?

- Fixed overhead cost variance:

What is the standard fixed overhead cost of the output?
What is the actual cost?

Fixed Overhead Variances: *Examples*

1   Budgeted fixed overhead   £10,000
    Budget hours   500
    Actual hours worked   520
    Standard hours produced   540
    Actual fixed overhead   £10,200

Calculate fixed overhead volume efficiency, capacity usage, volume expenditure and cost variances.

2   Budgeted fixed overheads   £16,000
    Budgeted output   12,000 standard
                                             hours
    Actual output   9,600 standard
                                             hours
    Hours worked   9,270
    Actual fixed overheads   £16,242

Calculate fixed overhead volume efficiency, capacity usage, volume, expenditure and cost variances.

Answers

1   VEV 540 – 520 (20)   400(F)
    CUV 520 – 500 (20)   400(F)
    VV 540 – 500 (20)   800(F)
    EXV 10,000 – 10,200   200(A)
    CV 540 (20) – 10,200   600(F)

2   VEV 9,600 – 9,270 (1.333)   440(F)
    CUV 9,270 – 12,000 (1.333)   3,640(A)
    VV 9,600 – 12,000 (1.333)   3,200(A)
    EXV 16,000 – 16,242   242(A)
    CV 9,600 (1.333) – 16,242   3,442(A)

The Shipley Manufacturers Case: Example

(A comprehensive example reconciling budget profit with actual profit) The following information relates to Shipley Manufacturers Ltd for December

	Budget	Actual
Production (units)	10,000	9,800
Production (standard hours)	20,000	19,600

	£	£
Labour	20,000(20,000 hours)	19,740(19,500 hours)
Material	12,000(60,000 lbs)	11,920(59,400 lbs)
Variable overhead –		
time	10,000	9,910
output	8,000	8,040
Total variable costs	50,000	49,610
Fixed costs	25,000	24,800
Total costs	75,000	74,410
Sales	100,000 (10,000 units)	97,020 (9,800 units)
Profit	25,000	22,610

Prepare a statement reconciling the budget and actual sales, costs and profit.

Shipley Manufacturers Ltd
Profit and Loss Statement for December

	£	£
Budget profit		25,000
Sales Variances:		
Price variance (SPV) 98,000 – 97,020		980(A)
Quantity variance (SQV) (10,000 – 9,800)2.5		500(A)

Shipley Manufacturers Ltd
Profit and Loss Statement for December *continued*

	£	£
Total variance (TSV) $97,020 - 9,800(7.5) - 25,000$		1,480(A)
Standard profit given actual sales		23,520

Production variances:	£ (i)	£ (ii)	£ (iii)
Materials variances:	(F)	(A)	(C)
Price variance (MPV) $11,880 - 11,920$		40	
Usage variance (MUV) $(58,800 - 59,400)20p$		120	
Cost variance (MCV) $(11,760 - 11,920)$			160(A)
Labour variances:			
Rates of pay variance (RPV) $19,500 - 19,740$		240	
Efficiency variance (LEV) $19,600 - 19,500$	100		
Cost variance (LCV) $19,600 - 19,740$			140(A)
Variable overhead variances:			
Expenditure variance-time $9,750 - 9,910$		160	
Expenditure variance – output $7,840 - 8,040$		200	
(EXV)		360	
Efficiency variance (EV) $(19,600 - 19,500)50p$	50		
Cost variance (CV) $17,640 - 17,950$			310(A)

continued

Shipley Manufacturers Ltd
Profit and Loss Statement for December *continued*

	£	£	£	£	£
Fixed overhead variances:					
Volume efficiency variance (VEV)					
(19,600 − 19,500)1.25	125				
Capacity usage variance (CUV)					
(20,000 − 19,500) 1.25		625			
Volume variance (VV)					
(20,000 − 19,600)1.25	500				
Expenditure variance(EV)					
25,000 − 24,800	200				
Cost variance			300(A)		
24,500 − 24,800					
Net production variance					
9,800(7.5) − 74,410				910(A)	
Actual profit				22,610	

1 (F) = Favourable, (A) = Adverse, (C) = Cost.
2 Net production variance = standard cost of output less actual cost of output

Standard costing is widely used throughout industry to monitor profit by companies, on a regular basis, by comparing actual performance with target performance. The fixed overhead variances are often criticized because they tend to assume that fixed costs are 'recovered' on an hourly basis or on a unit of production basis, whereas in fact we recover fixed costs by generating positive cash flows from successful trading satisfying consumer wants. The calculation of variances is sometimes restricted to operational revenues and costs, as in the following example.

Lancashire Metals: Example

As management accountant of Lancashire Metal Services, you are responsible for collecting the following data for June 1988.

	Target	Actual
Sales (units)	10,000	11,000
Sales	£120,000	£129,516
	£	£
Cost of Sales:		
Materials	30,000	34,118
(60,000 lbs)		(64,000 lbs)
Labour	50,000	57,560
(20,000 hrs)		(23,000 hrs)
Operating Costs	80,000	91,678
Operating Profit	£40,000	£37,838

Prepare a statement for your Board of Directors reconciling the budget (target) operating profit with the actual operating profit.

Answer

Budget profit				£	£
Sales variances					40,000
SPV 11,000(12) –				2,484(A)	
129,516					
SQV (11,000 – 10,000)4				4,000(F)	
TSV					1,516(F)
					41,516

	(F)	(A)	(C)		
Materials variances					
MPV 64,000(.5) – 34,118		2,118			
MUV [11,000(6) –	1,000				
64,000]15					
MCV 11,000(3) – 34,118			1,118(A)		
Labour variances					
RPV 23,000(2.5) –		60			
57,560					
LEV [11,000(2) –		2,500			
23,000]2.5					
LCV 11,000(5) – 57,560			2,560(A)		
Net production variance:					
11,000(8) –					3,678(A)
91,678					
Actual profit					37,838

Although standard costing and budgetary control are very widely used, they are often unpopular for the following reasons:

1 Creativity
Managers strive to meet budget requirements and tend to overlook opportunities to be innovative.

2 Waste
Surplus funds tend to be spent in a flurry of year-end activity so as not to jeopardize the budget requirement for the following period.

3 Emphasis on mistakes
It sometimes appears that the objective of budgetary control systems is to illustrate all our mistakes.

4 Standard setting
Should standards of performance be 'slack' or 'tight'?
The achievement of targets depends as much on the target set as the ability of management.

5 Consistent failure and apathy
Many budgetary control systems are discredited because the figures always appear to be 'doctored' to show unrepresentative performance, e.g. increased management fees from head office.

6 Can we alter the past?
Undue emphasis on the past is unproductive. We can only act to alter the future.

7 There is always a reason why
Investigations into adverse variances usually reveal quite reasonable explanations. Again, undue emphasis is not constructive.

8 Where do the numbers come from?
Who sets the standards? They tend to be last year's actuals.
Are they meaningful in a changing technology?

9 Cost
Standard costing and budgetary control systems are costly procedures.

Study Questions

10.1 After fourteen years' devoted service to the Wikeroyd Yorkshire (and International) Clog Company Limited, Ingleborough Thumpernought has finally persuaded the board to appoint him as chief executive of a new division in distant Keighbeckwhistle. Clogs will be invoiced from head office to the new division at £9 per pair, plus £1 transport. It will cost £200,000 to acquire premises in Keighbeckwhistle and install all necessary office and storage equipment. Salesmen will be paid commission on sales of 25 per cent of the selling price, and will stand all their own expenses. The recommended selling price is £20. Annual running costs at the new division are estimated at £25,000.

1 How many pairs of clogs must Ingleborough sell to earn the 30 per cent required rate of return on the head office initial outlay?
2 Calculate the break-even volume.
3 If head office decides it must claw back all expenses and the initial investment over two years, how many pairs of clogs must be sold over the two years?
4 Ingleborough estimates that he can achieve the maximum level of sales (15,000 pairs) by either reducing the selling price to £19, or spending £10,000 per annum on promotion. What would you recommend?
5 List six reasons why profit flow and cash flow are different.

10.2 Distinguish between marginal and total costing.
From the data below calculate:

1 the period fixed costs
2 The profit-volume ratio (C/S%)
3 The period unit sales for break-even.

Period	1	2
Unit sales	100	150
	£	£
Sales	5,000	7,500
Total costs	4,000	4,500
Profit	1,000	3,000

You are the sole director of a company producing and selling a high quality leather case. The following data are your 1987 estimates:

Productive capacity	300 units	Salesman's salary	£10,000 pa
Selling price	£40 per unit	Commission	£1 per unit sold
Material costs	£8 per unit	Director's salary	£15,000 pa
Other variables	£3 per unit	Other office expenditures	£1,500 pa
Rent and rates	£3,000 pa	Vehicle expenses	£4,000 pa
Straight-line depreciation	£2,000 pa	Director labour costs	£24,000 pa
		Promotion costs	£15,000 pa

Prepare a profit plan for 60 per cent, 80 per cent and 100 per cent output. How many cases must be sold for break-even?

10.3 You are a self-employed financial consultant. A friend, Marcia, asks you to help her plan for profit in her new venture. She plans to open (yet) another old people's home in Ilkley. Marcia, with your assistance, estimates annual costs as follows:

Variable costs per guest year	£	Fixed costs	£
Food	1,500	Nursing staff	21,000
Medical expenses	500	Fixed heating	6,000
Heating (additional)	200	Telephone	1,000
Cleaning and repairs	200	Office staff	6,000
Incidentals	100	Maintenance	13,000
	2,500	Loan interest	10,000
		Depreciation	4,000
		Rates	3,000
			64,000

Marcia estimates the full setting-up costs as follows:

	£
Property at cost (including alterations)	100,000
Furniture and equipment	20,000
Working capital	10,000
	130,000

She plans to write off the furniture and equipment over 5 years (see fixed costs).

Marcia hopes to finance the setting-up as follows:

	£
Permanent loan (interest at 10% in fixed costs)	100,000
Own capital introduced	30,000
	130,000

Apparently, the going rate in Ilkley for similar accommodation and service is about £6,500 per guest-year.

1 How many guests does Marcia need to break-even in terms of accounting profit?

2 A closer examination of the premises suggests that the maximum
number of guests maintainable during the full year is about 34.
What will the accounting profit be if Marcia achieves (a) 14, (b)
24, (c) 34?

3 If she expects a 40 per cent return on total capital employed in
year one, how many guests will be required for break-even?

4 After a great deal of wrangling you finally get her to estimate that
if she puts the price at £6,250 she will attract the equivalent of
30 full-time guests, at £6,500 26 guests, and at £6,750 20 guests.
What would you recommend?

5 List the reasons why the accounting profit break-even and the cash
flow break-even will be different.

10.4 From the following information relating to Gargrave Antique
Restorers Ltd, prepare a profit and loss account for the year ended
31 December 1987 and a balance sheet as at that date.

Trial Balance as at 31.12.87

Assets and Expenses	£	Sources of Funds and Income	£
Trade debtors	17,000	Invoiced sales	152,000
Purchases	65,000	Share capital	50,000
Opening stock, 1.1.87	21,000	Creditors for antiques	13,000
		Directors' loans	22,000
Property at cost	110,000	Bank overdraft	18,000
Equipment (cost)	26,000	Balance on profit and loss account 31.12.86	46,000
Motor vehicles (cost)	34,000	Accumulated depreciation to 31.12.86 on equipment	16,000
Directors' salaries	20,000		
Shop salaries	12,000		
Administration expenditures	3,000	Accumulated depreciation on motor vehicles to 31.12.86	14,000
Promotion expenses	21,000		
Finance charges	2,000		
	£331,000		£331,000

---

1 Stock on hand at 31.12.87 is valued at cost, £28,000.

2 Depreciation on fixtures and fittings for 1987 is calculated at 20
per cent of cost.

3 Accrued administration expenditures (heat and light, telephone) are estimated at £2,000.
4 Depreciation on motor vehicles is calculated at 25 per cent of book value (cost less depreciation).
5 'Administration expenditures' include £1,500 for insurance paid in advance for the year to 31.12.88.

The directors expect the first 6 months of 1988 to be very difficult (until the Americans arrive). What can the directors do to avoid a cash crisis?

10.5 As management accountant of the Bethlehem Nut and Screw Company, you are responsible for collecting the following data for December 1987.

	Target		Actual
Sales (units)	10,000		8,000
Sales	£120,000		£99,516
	£		£
Cost of Sales:			
Materials	30,000		24,118
(60,000 lbs)		(52,000 lbs)	
Labour	50,000		47,560
(20,000 hours)		(18,000 hours)	
Operating Costs	80,000		71,678
Operating Profit	£40,000		£27,838

Prepare a statement for your Board of Directors reconciling the budget (target) operating profit with the actual operating profit and prepare a brief report outlining the month's events.

10.6 As management accountant of Heaton Water Beds Ltd, you are responsible for collecting the following data for December 1987.

	Target		Actual
Sales (units)	200		220
Sales	£50,000		£53,750
	£		£
Cost of Sales:			
Materials	16,000		19,650
(4,000 lbs)		(4,950 lbs)	
Labour	12,000		14,900
(3,000 hours)		(3,600 hours)	
Operating Costs	28,000		34,550
Operating Profit	£22,000		£19,200

1 Prepare a brief report for your Board of Directors reconciling the budget (target) operating profit with the actual operating profit.
2 State the working capital problems often experienced by expanding businesses.

Further Reading

Brealey, Richard and Myers, Stewart. *Principles of Corporate Finance.* New York: McGraw-Hill, 1984, chapter 26.
Schall, Lawrence D. and Haley, Charles W. *Introduction to Financial Management.* New York: McGraw-Hill, 1986, chapter 13.

11

Cash Planning and Control

Introduction

Planning just has to be better than not planning if managers wish to succeed. The theory of finance teaches that the objective of the firm is to make money satisfying consumer wants in competitive markets. Managers, to a large extent, pursue objectives relating to growth in sales, growth in the quantity of the firm's assets, growth in the number of employees, and even growth in departmental expenditure. Furthermore, individuals pursue their own career development and job satisfaction within organizations. Over the past twenty years management development programmes have taught that companies should:

1 set objectives;
2 devise strategies to achieve objectives;
3 plan;
4 perform;
5 review performance with plan;
6 continuously review objectives, strategies, plan and performance.

In the early days we called it 'management by objectives (MBO)' which became 'corporate planning' and is now 'strategic management'. One of the important ingredients is planning, and one of the most difficult aspects is the setting of objectives. What is our business? What are our skills? What are our strengths and weaknesses? Is there a market for our skills? Do we sincerely want to be rich? Once we have set objectives, then we can devise strategies to achieve objectives, make plans, perform and review.

Even if the firm has only the modest objective of survival, cash flow must be carefully planned for and monitored. Profit and cash flow are different.

Many firms have survived for long periods without making much profit, but they have successfully managed cash. Firms which have run out of cash have not survived. The day you stop paying wages tends to coincide with the day employees stop working for your company. The day you stop paying bills tends to coincide with the day suppliers stop supplying or demand cash with order. The day your bank manager decides to call in the overdraft tends to be the start of liquidation proceedings for companies, bankruptcy for individuals. Firms can survive without making a profit by disposing of fixed assets, sale and lease-back of property, sale of the fleet of cars and then leasing, mortgaging property, cutting back on investment in stock and debtors, extending supplier credit, borrowing, issuing more shares, disposing of subsidiaries, and cutting back on plant replacement and research and development. We encourage firms to make profit, but for survival cash management is essential. Many authors emphasize that for the small and new business, cash flow is far more important than profit flow.

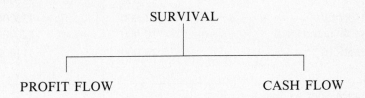

In this chapter we prepare cash flow plans and forecast financial statements including profit and loss account, balance sheet, and statement of sources and applications of funds. We are particularly concerned here with cash planning, and one of the easiest ways of forecasting the future cash balance is to forecast everything except cash, the cash balance being the final balancing figure or 'plug' which actually makes the balance sheet balance.

Financial Statement Planning

George Wynberg: Example

George Wynberg is managing director of the Stoke Electrical Company Limited. He asks you to prepare forecast financial statements for an urgent board meeting late this afternoon. The marketing director has just come up with a sales forecast of £300,000 for 1989.

Profit and loss accounts

	1987 £		1988 £
Turnover		190,000		240,000
Opening stock	24,000		28,000	
Add purchases	116,000		150,000	
	140,000		178,000	
Less closing stock	28,000		36,000	
Cost of sales		112,000		142,000
Gross profit		78,000		98,000
Less:				
Other variables	22,000		27,000	
Fixed costs (including depreciation)	23,000		28,000	
		45,000		55,000
Net profit		33,000		43,000
Less dividend paid		10,000		12,000
Retentions		23,000		31,000

Balance Sheets

	1987		1988
Sources of Capital				
Share capital		60,000		60,000
Retained earnings		104,000		135,000
Shareholders' funds		164,000		195,000
Long-term loans		100,000		100,000
		264,000		295,000
Employment of Capital				
Property (cost)		190,000		190,000
Plant and equipment (net of depreciation)		28,000		38,000
Motor vehicles (net)		24,000		34,000
		242,000		262,000
Current Assets:				
Stock	28,000		36,000	
Debtors	32,000		40,000	
Cash at bank	—		3,000	
	60,000		79,000	

Balance Sheets *continued*

	1987 £		1988 £
Current Liabilities:			
Creditors	36,000		46,000
Bank overdraft	2,000		—
	38,000		46,000
Net Current Assets		22,000	33,000
		264,000	295,000

Use ratio analysis to forecast the profit and loss account and closing balance sheet for 1989.
Note: Cash at bank (bank overdraft) is the balancing figure. Make reasonable assumptions such as available capacity, no issues of shares or more loans, dividend paid £15,000.

Answer

Profit and loss account

		1989 £
Turnover		300,000
Opening stock	36,000	
Add purchases	185,000	
	221,000	
Less closing stock	44,000	
Cost of sales		177,000
Gross profit		123,000
Less:		
Other variables	33,000	
Final costs	34,000	
(including depreciation)		
		67,000
Net profit		56,000
Less dividend paid		15,000
Retentions		41,000

Balance Sheet

	1989 £
Sources of Capital	
Share capital	60,000
Retained earnings	176,000
Shareholders' funds	236,000
Long-term loans	100,000
	336,000
Employment of Capital	
Property (cost)	190,000
Plant and equipment (net)	50,000
Motor vehicles (net)	46,000
	286,000

Current assets:		
Stock	44,000	
Debtors	50,000	
Cash at bank	14,000	
	108,000	
Current liabilities:		
Creditors	58,000	
Bank overdraft	—	
	58,000	
Net current assets		50,000
		336,000

Workings

		£
1	Turnover	300,000
2	Opening stock (1988 closing stock)	36,000
3	Gross profit = 41 per cent of sales	123,000
4	Cost of sales = sales − gross profit	177,000
5	Closing stock = cost of sales ÷ 4	44,000
6	Purchases = balancing figure	185,000
7	Other variables = 11% of sales	33,000
8	Fixed costs $28,000 + 5,000 \times \dfrac{60}{50}$ (See note)	34,000
9	Net profit = sales − total costs	56,000
10	Dividend paid	15,000

£

11 Retained earnings 135,000 + 41,000   176,000

12 Plant and equipment 38,000 + 10,000 $\left(\dfrac{60}{50}\right)$ 50,000

13 Motor vehicles 34,000 + 10,000 $\left(\dfrac{60}{50}\right)$ 46,000

14 Debtors 300,000 ÷ 6(sales/debtors)   50,000
15 Creditors 185,000 ÷ 3.2(purchases/creditors)   58,000
16 Cash at bank/overdraft = balancing figure   14,000

Note: Fixed assets increased by £5,000 when turnover increased by £50,000 from £190,000 to £240,000. The proposed increase for 1989 is £60,000.

In the George Wynberg example we use ratio analysis to forecast next year's financial statements. A most difficult item to forecast is the cash balance, which is therefore left as the balancing figure. Clearly, the sales forecast for 1989 is of critical importance. Most of the estimates are, as we should expect, directly related to the level of the firm's activity. In the Allerton Traders example which follows we are required to prepare a detailed cash flow forecast and a forecast statement of sources and applications of funds as well as the balance sheet and profit and loss account.

Allerton Traders Ltd: Example

The balance sheet of Allerton Traders Ltd at 30 June 1988 was as follows:

Employment of Funds		
Fixed Assets:		
Freehold premises (cost)		28,000
Plant and equipment (cost)	60,000	
Less depreciation	20,000	40,000
		68,000
Research and development		10,000
Trade investments (cost)		18,000
Current Assets:		
Stock on hand	44,000	
Debtors	63,000	
	107,000	
Less Current Liabilities:		
Creditors	22,000	
Bank overdraft	25,000	
	47,000	

continued

Employment of Funds *continued*

Net Current assets	60,000
	156,000
Sources of Funds	
Issued share capital	100,000
General reserve	35,000
Balance on profit and loss account	21,000
	156,000

From the following information prepare the cash budget, budgeted profit and loss account for the 6 months ended 31 December 1988, budgeted balance sheet as at that date, and statement of sources and applications of funds.

1 Research and development is written off at the rate of £100 per month.
2 Depreciation of plant and machinery calculated at 1% per month on cost.
3 The capital expenditure budget provides for payments for plant costing £4,000 in July and £8,000 in November.
4 Advertising budget – £120 per month.
5 Creditors at 30.6.88 are for purchases.
6 Debtors at 30.6.88. May sales £27,500. June sales £35,500.
7 Credit periods are expected to be the same in the second half of 1988, i.e. one month for suppliers, two months for customers.
8 Sales are anticipated at £180,000 for the 6 months. August and September sales will be twice those in other months.
9 Fixed costs – £900 per month.
10 Variable costs – 10% of monthly turnover.
11 Gross profit on turnover is budgeted at 20%.
12 Closing stocks of purchases at cost are budgeted to be:

Jul 31	£50,000	Aug 31	£30,000	Sep 30	£15,000
Oct 31	£25,000	Nov 30	£35,000	Dec 31	£40,000

13 The annual dividend of 10% on paid up share capital is payable on 31.12.88.
14 Income from trade investments is expected to amount to £1,500 receivable on 31 December.
15 At 31.12.88 General Reserve to be increased from £35,000 to £40,000.
16 No expenditure on research and development is anticipated.

Answer

Allerton Traders Ltd 1988 (Summary)

Monthly Trading Accounts	July	Aug	Sept	Oct	Nov	Dec	Total
Sales	22,500	45,000	45,000	22,500	22,500	22,500	180,000
Cost of Sales:							
Opening stock	44,000	50,000	30,000	15,000	25,000	35,000	44,000
Add purchases (balance)	24,000	16,000	21,000	28,000	28,000	23,000	140,000
	68,000	66,000	51,000	43,000	53,000	58,000	184,000
Less closing stock	50,000	30,000	15,000	25,000	35,000	40,000	40,000
Cost of sales	18,000	36,000	36,000	18,000	18,000	18,000	144,000
Gross profit (20%)	4,500	9,000	9,000	4,500	4,500	4,500	36,000
Note: Depreciation	600	640	640	640	640	720	3,880

Allerton Traders Ltd

Cash Flow for the six months ended 31 December 1988

(Summary)

	July	Aug	Sept	Oct	Nov	Dec	Total
Opening Overdraft	(25,000)	(26,770)	(20,790)	(19,810)	920	6,650	(25,000)
Cash Inflow:							
Sales (debtors)	27,500	35,500	22,500	45,000	45,000	22,500	198,000
Investment income	—	—	—	—	—	1,500	1,500
Total Inflow	27,500	35,500	22,500	45,000	45,000	24,000	199,500
Cash Outflow:							
Purchases (creditors)	22,000	24,000	16,000	21,000	28,000	28,000	139,000
Fixed costs	900	900	900	900	900	900	5,400
Variable costs	2,250	4,500	4,500	2,250	2,250	2,250	18,000
Advertising	120	120	120	120	120	120	720
Capital expenditure	4,000	—	—	—	8,000	—	12,000
Dividends	—	—	—	—	—	10,000	10,000
Total Outflow	29,270	29,520	21,520	24,270	39,270	41,270	185,120
Change $\begin{array}{c}+\\-\end{array}$	1,770	5,980	980	20,730	5,730	17,270	14,380
Closing Overdraft	(26,770)	(20,790)	(19,810)	920	6,650	(10,620)	(10,620)

Note: No depreciation or research and development write-off as no cash flow is involved.

Allerton Traders Ltd

Budgeted profit and loss account for the six months ended 31.12.88

			£
(1)	R	Sales	180,000
		Less cost of sales:	
(2)	L	Opening stock 1.7.88	44,000
(3)	L	Purchases	140,000
(4)	L		184,000
(5)	L	Less closing stock 31.12.88	40,000
(6)	R	cost of sales	144,000
(7)	R	gross profit on trading	36,000
		Less:	
(8)	L	Variable costs	18,000
(9)	L	Fixed costs	5,400
(10)	L	Research and development	600
(11)	L	Advertising	720
(12)	L	Depreciation	3,880
(13)	R		28,600
(14)	R	Net profit on trading	7,400
(15)	R	Add income from trade investments	1,500
(16)	R	Net profit available for shareholders	8,900
(17)	L	Less dividend (paid 31.12.88)	10,000
(18)	L	Transfer to general reserve	5,000
(19)	R		15,000
(20)	R	Increase in balance on profit and loss account (reduction)	(6,100)
(21)	R	Profit and loss account balance brought forward	21,000
(22)	R		14,900

R = right hand column
L = left hand column

Allerton Traders Ltd

Budgeted balance sheet as at 31 December 1988

		£ 31.12.88		£ 30.6.88
Sources of Funds				
Issued share capital		100,000		100,000
General reserve		40,000		35,000
Balance on profit		14,900		21,000
and loss account				
		154,900		156,000
Employment of Funds				
Fixed assets:				
Freehold premises		28,000		28,000
(Cost)				
Plant and equipment	72,000		60,000	
(Cost)				
Less depreciation	23,880	48,120	20,000	40,000
		76,120		68,000
Research and		9,400		10,000
development				
Trade investments		18,000		18,000
Current Assets:				
Stock on hand	40,000		44,000	
Debtors	45,000		63,000	
	85,000		107,000	
Less current liabilities:				
Creditors	23,000		22,000	
Bank overdraft	10,620		25,000	
	33,620		47,000	
Net current assets		51,380		60,000
		154,900		156,000

Sources and Applications of Funds for the six months to 31.12.88

Sources of Funds

Funds from operations:

Profit and loss account (self-generated)	(6,100)
General reserve (self-generated)	5,000
Dividend (self-generated)	10,000
Depreciation (non-cash)	3,880
R&D (non-cash)	600
Funds from operations	13,380
Stock reduction	4,000
Reduction in debtors	18,000
Increase in creditors	1,000
	36,380

Applications of Funds

Reduction in overdraft	14,380
Purchase of plant and equipment	12,000
Dividend	10,000
	36,380

Notes

1 The monthly trading accounts are based entirely on invoices, not cash.
2 August and September sales are twice as high as in other months: Therefore, a 'normal' month's sales figure is £180,000 divided by 8 = £22,500.
3 The purchases figure is the balancing amount in the monthly trading accounts.
4 Depreciation at 1 per cent per month is increased one month after new plant is acquired.
5 The summary is for 6 months. The opening stock is the opening stock on 1 July. Managers often simply cast all the figures to the right as a check on the arithmetic.
6 In the cash flow statement, cash is collected two months after invoicing.
7 Creditors for purchases (from the monthly trading account) are paid one month after invoicing.
8 A positive or negative cash flow for each month is calculated, and the opening balance adjusted to give the closing balance which is then carried forward to the start of the following months.

9 The profit and loss account is based on invoices. Invoiced sales less invoiced cost of sales and depreciation gives the profit which is then allocated to either general reserve or balance on profit and loss account and against which dividends (paid in cash) are charged.

10 Lines 1–7 are reproduced from the monthly trading accounts summary.

11 Variable costs, fixed costs, and advertising are taken direct from the cash summary since there are no outstanding invoices.

12 Research and development and depreciation are non-cash items but they are part of the cost of producing and selling goods to consumers.

13 The net profit for shareholders is £8,900 against which a £10,000 dividend paid in cash is charged. Dividends paid in cash must not exceed the level of reported profit but we can pay the £10,000 dividend because we have £21,000 of retained earnings from previous years against which no dividend has been charged in previous years.

14 The transfer to general reserve is inconsequential. Every £1 transferred to general reserve is £1 less balance on profit and loss account. No cash is involved. There is no money in a financial reserve. Such amounts represent accounting profits against which no dividend has been charged. These amounts show the extent to which the firm's fixed and current assets have been financed from retained earnings.

15 The balance sheet is a snapshot of the company's assets and sources of finance at one particular moment. The balance sheet does not show the value of the business, this being based on the company's ability to generate cash. A successful hairdressing business may have a high market value because it generates excellent cash flows, although there may be very little in the way of balance sheet assets. An engineering company which makes trading losses can have a very low market value, but vast quantities of assets in the balance sheet.

16 Plant and equipment are shown at accumulated historic cost less accumulated depreciation.

17 Research and development represents the amount of capitalized (put in the balance sheet) expenditure not yet written off to profit and loss account.

18 Debtors are the November and December sales.

19 Creditors are the December purchases.

20 The bank overdraft is extracted from the cash flow forecast.

21 'Funds' is a much misunderstood word in finance. It means cash or cash equivalent. An increase in trade credit is a source of funds, although it is not a source of actual cash.

22 The statement of sources and applications of funds is based on balance sheet changes. Since the balance sheet balances at the beginning of the period and at the end of a period, then the differences from one period to another should cancel out to give the sources of funds during the period and the destinations or applications of those funds.

23 To the closing figure at the bottom of this year's profit and loss account we add back non-cash items such as depreciation and the research and development charge. We also add back appropriations of profit such as the dividend and transfer to general reserve to give the funds generated from successful trading. The amount of £13,380 represents funds generated from operations.

24 Additional sources of funds include reduction in stock and debtors, and an increase in trade credit.

25 Applications of funds include the payment of dividends, purchase of plant and equipment, and a reduction in the overdraft. The overdraft reduction is an increase in the stock of cash from negative £25,000 to negative £10,620.

Now that we can forecast financial statements, we must not assume that we can run the business. Figure 11.1 shows that preparation of the forecast financial statements takes place after all the important decisions have been made. Corporate objectives must be set and the strategies devised to achieve objectives. We need long-range sales forecasts as well as short-term forecasts.

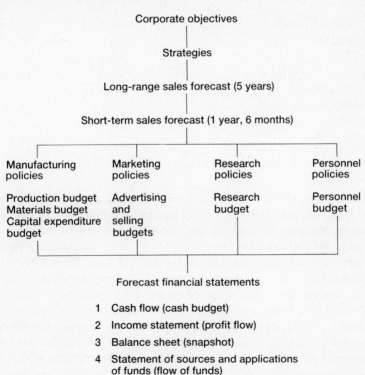

Figure 11.1 The planning process

Policies must be established for manufacturing, marketing, research and personnel. Budgets must be prepared for each division and each activity. In the Allerton Traders example we have brought together all the budgets for each activity and prepared forecast financial statements for the following six months. If the forecasts are unacceptable to management, then many changes can be made before a final plan is agreed.

Strategy for Financial Emergencies

Balance Sheet					
Sources of Funds		£000	Assets		£000
Shareholder's Funds:			Fixed Assets		
Share capital		50	Property		100
Retained earnings		75	Plant & equipment		60
		125	Motor vehicles		20
					180
Lease finance	20				
Loans	50				
		70	Current Assets		
Current Liabilities			Stock	40	
Creditors	80		Debtors	70	
Instalment credit	10		Cash	5	
Bank overdraft	10	100			115
		295			295

All firms should have a strategy for financial emergencies. All firms are in the risk business. They have good periods and bad periods. As far as we know, no firm has exponential growth, although we have all met managers who assume that the great growth years will continue forever. We constantly remind managers that if Rolls Royce, Penn Central and British Leyland can go bust, then anybody can go bust. A glance at the prosperous growth years of these companies might suggest that they would survive into the twenty-first century. Any company can experience financial problems, and managers should therefore have a strategy for financial emergencies, even if it is simply an awareness of the balance sheet adjustments that can be made to generate cash. When faced with a cash crisis, many of us think only of cost reduction or price increase. A glance at the balance sheet should suggest additional opportunities.

1 *Property*
   Sell surplus property, raise a mortgage, sale to a pension fund and leaseback, move out of the city into a low-cost area where grants may be available.
2 *Plant and equipment*
   Sell and lease or hire, sell and re-purchase on instalment credit, dispose of unused plant and equipment.
3 *Motor vehicles*
   Sell existing vehicles and arrange lease or hire.
4 *Stock*
   Reduce the number of lines, reduce the level of stock held.
5 *Debtors*
   Reduce the credit period, offer higher discounts for quick payment.
6 *Share capital*
   New issue, if possible.
7 *Lease finance*
   Lease rather than purchase.
8 *Loans*
   Arrange bank debenture.
9 *Creditors*
   Extend the credit period taken from creditors.
10 *Instalment credit*
   Buy on instalment credit rather than purchase.
11 *Bank loan/overdraft*
   Negotiate additional loans and overdrafts.

In a financial emergency we should explore the sale of patents, sale of research and development knowledge, sale of trade marks, issuing of licenses to produce our products, disposal of the 'crown jewels', disposal of subsidiaries, expansion of sub-contract work, and application for government grants. One final point we must mention again is that the firm must never run out of cash.

Study Questions

11.1 Arthur McGinty is disturbed that his shirt manufacturing company has made excellent accounting profit but is experiencing cash problems. From the following Balance Sheets, prepare a Statement of Sources and Applications of Funds for the year ended 31 December 1987.

McGinty Shirts Ltd

		1987 £000		1986 £000
Sources of Capital				
Share of capital		80		60
Profit and loss account		105		40
Shareholders' funds		185		100
Long-term loans		20		60
		205		160
Employment of Capital				
Fixed Assets:				
Freehold property at cost		120		90
Plant and equipment – cost	84		60	
– Depreciation	40	44	32	28
Motor vehicles – cost	42		24	
– Depreciation	22	20	12	12
		184		130
Current Assets:				
Stock	42		22	
Debtors	24		18	
Cash at bank	—		30	
	66		70	
Less Current Liabilities:				
Creditors	42		40	
Bank overdraft	3		—	
	45		40	
Net Current Assets		21		30
		205		160

As management accountant explain to Arthur why the cash problem has arisen.

11.2 Colin Wallsgrove is managing director of Crosshills Towel Services Limited. He asks you to prepare forecast financial statements for an urgent board meeting. The sales director has won new contracts which will add about £60,000 to existing turnover in 1987.

Profit and Loss Accounts

	1985 £		1986 £	
Turnover		242,000		250,000
Opening stock	30,000		40,000	
Add purchases	152,000		147,000	
	182,000		187,000	
Less closing stock	40,000		42,000	
Cost of sales		142,000		145,000
Gross profit		100,000		105,000
Less:				
Other variables	30,000		31,000	
Fixed costs	28,000		30,000	
		58,000		61,000
Net profit		42,000		44,000
Less dividend paid		15,000		18,000
Retentions		27,000		26,000

Balance Sheets

	1985 £	1986 £
Sources of Capital		
Share capital	100,000	100,000
Retained earnings	94,000	120,000
Shareholders' funds	194,000	220,000
Long-term loans	90,000	70,000
	284,000	290,000
Employment of Capital		
Property (cost)	180,000	183,000
Plant and equipment (net)	40,000	42,000
Motor vehicles (net)	32,000	30,000
	252,000	255,000

continued

11.2   *Balance Sheets* continued

	1985 £		1986 £	
Current Assets:				
Stock	40,000		42,000	
Debtors	42,000		43,000	
Cash at bank	—		—	
	82,000		85,000	
Current Liabilities:				
Creditors	48,000		46,000	
Bank overdraft	2,000		4,000	
	50,000		50,000	
Net Current Assets		32,000		35,000
		284,000		290,000

1 The data relate to 1985 and 1986. Use ratio analysis to forecast the profit and loss account and closing balance sheet for 1987.
2 Present calculations for six of your 1987 estimates.
3 List the key financial ratios which can help you run your business.

Note: Cash at bank (bank overdraft) is the balancing figure. Make reasonable assumptions such as available capacity, no issues of shares or more loans, dividend proposed £20,000.

11.3   Twyford Eradicator is managing director of Toilette Masonry Ltd. She asks you to prepare forecast financial statements for a board meeting late this afternoon. The marketing director has just come up with a sales forecast of $200,000 for 1988.

Profit and Loss Accounts

	1986 $		1987 $	
Turnover		170,000		190,000
Opening stock	23,000		24,000	
Add purchases	101,000		116,000	
	124,000		140,000	
Less closing stock	24,000		28,000	
Cost of sales		100,000		112,000
Gross profit		70,000		78,000

11.3 *Profit and Loss Accounts* continued

	1986 $		1987 $
Less:			
Other variables	19,000		22,000
Fixed costs	21,000		23,000
		40,000	45,000
Net profit		30,000	33,000
Less dividend paid		10,000	10,000
Retentions		20,000	23,000

Balance Sheets

	1986 $		1987 $
Sources of Capital			
Share capital		60,000	60,000
Retained earnings		81,000	104,000
Shareholders' fund		141,000	164,000
Long-term loans		100,000	100,000
		241,000	264,000
Employment of Capital			
Property (cost)		190,000	190,000
Plant and equipment (net)		24,000	28,000
Motor vehicles (net)		20,000	24,000
		234,000	242,000
Current Assets:			
Stock	24,000		28,000
Debtors	28,000		32,000
	52,000		60,000
Current Liabilities:			
Creditors	31,000		36,000
Bank overdraft	14,000		2,000
	45,000		38,000
Net Current Assets		7,000	22,000
		241,000	264,000

1 The data relate to 1986 and 1987. Use ratio analysis to forecast the profit and loss account and closing balance sheet for 1988.
2 Present calculations for six of your 1988 estimates.

   Note: Cash at bank (bank overdraft) is the balancing figure. Make reasonable assumptions such as available capacity, no issues of shares or more loans, dividend paid $12,000.

   Distinguish between trading as sole proprietor and as a director/major shareholder of a private company.

11.4   Budgeting at Gargrave Furniture Retailers Ltd. The balance sheet of Gargrave Furniture Retailers Ltd at 30 June 1987 was as follows:

Employment of Funds		
Fixed Assets:		
Freehold premises (cost)		48,000
Plant and equipment (cost)	120,000	
Less depreciation	60,000	60,000
		108,000
Research and development		40,000
Trade investments (cost)		20,000
Current Assets:		
Stock on hand	80,000	
Debtors	120,000	
	200,000	
Less Current Liabilities:		
Creditors	40,000	
Bank overdraft	55,000	
	95,000	
Net current assets		105,000
		273,000
Sources of Funds		
Issued share capital		170,000
General reserve		55,000
Balance on profit and loss a/c		48,000
		273,000

From the following information prepare the cash budget and budgeted profit and loss account ended 30 June 1988 and budgeted balance sheet as at that date, together with a statement of sources and applications of funds.

1 Research and development is written off at the rate of £1,000 per month.
2 Depreciation of plant and machinery is calculated at 2% per month on cost.
3 The capital expenditure budget provides for purchases of plant costing £8,000 in July and £20,000 in December (purchased at month end).
4 Advertising budget – £300 per month.
5 Creditors at 30.6.87 are for purchases.
6 Debtors at 30.6.87. May sales £40,000. June sales £80,000.
7 Credit periods are expected to be the same, i.e. one month for suppliers, two months for customers.
8 Sales are anticipated at £400,000 for 1987/88. November and December sales will be twice those in other months.
9 Fixed costs – £2,000 per month.
10 Variable costs – 15% of monthly turnover.
11 Gross profit on turnover is budgeted at 25%.
12 Closing stock of purchases at cost are budgeted to be:

July 31	£100,000	Aug 31	£70,000	Sept 30	£40,000
Oct 31	£150,000	Nov 30	£120,000	Dec 31	£40,000
Jan 31	£60,000	Feb 28	£70,000	Mar 31	£80,000
Apr 30	£100,000	May 31	£100,000	June 30	£90,000

13 The annual dividend of 10% on paid up share capital is payable on 30.6.88.
14 Income from trade investments is expected to amount to £2,500 receivable on 31 December.
15 At 30.6.88 General Reserve to be increased from £55,000 to £75,000.
16 No expenditure on research and development is anticipated.

Further Reading

Brealey, Richard and Myers, Stewart. *Principles of Corporate Finance.* New York: McGraw-Hill, 1984, chapter 27.
Franks, Julian R., Broyles, John E. and Carleton, Willard T. *Corporate Finance: Concepts and Applications.* Boston, Mass.: Kent Publishing, 1985, chapter 26.

12

Ratio Analysis in Financial Management

The Theory of Ratio Analysis

One measure of corporate success or failure used by just about all companies
is return on capital employed. Accounting profit is traditionally used as
the measure of return, and capital employed is often defined as total capital
used in the business. However, there are several definitions of profit
including gross profit, profit before interest and tax, profit after interest
and tax, and there are several definitions of capital employed including total
capital, long-term capital (i.e. ignore current liabilities) and shareholders'
funds. Nevertheless, return on capital employed (ROCE) is widely used as
one important performance indicator. This measure compares accounting
profit measured against total capital with interest earned on a bank deposit.
If a bank deposit of £100 earns £10 in interest, then the return on invested
capital is 10 per cent. Similarly, if a company earns £10m on a total
capital investment of £100m, then the return on capital employed is
10 per cent.

The theory of ratio analysis suggests that return on capital employed
is determined by two other ingredients. Firstly, one important measure
of operational success or failure is the accounting profit as a percentage
of sales. This is one important measure of the firm's ability to buy
and sell or produce and sell goods and services at a profit. The sales
figure in the accountant's profit and loss account is the quantity of
invoiced sales. Accounting profit is invoiced sales less the cost of
sales including depreciation. The second determinant of return on capital
employed is the number of times the capital employed in the business
(total capital) is turned over in terms of invoiced sales. This statistic
is calculated by dividing invoiced sales for the period by the total
capital employed. Ratio analysis is therefore based on the following
equation:

$$\frac{P}{S} \times \frac{S}{CE} = \frac{P}{CE}$$

where

P = accounting profit,

S = invoiced sales, and

CE = capital employed.

A very crude summary would be that $\frac{P}{S}$ is a measure of operational success, and $\frac{S}{CE}$ is a measure of the firm's ability to manage its total assets or total capital employed. The ROCE is determined by multiplying the return on sales by the sales/capital employed statistic. Once we have calculated these business ratios we have the basis of all ratio analysis. We can develop many more ratios as we shall see later.

The reader may well have already concluded that the theory of ratio analysis is not much of a theory, when we consider earlier chapters. No mention has been made of either cash flow or risk, the two key variables in the modern theory of financial management. We may not think a great deal of the theory of ratio analysis, but business ratios are widely used in practical financial management, and for good reason. Many excellent teachers of finance suggest that the objective of the firm is to maximize net operational cash flows – subject to risk. Operations managers, therefore, should maximize cash flows or accounting profit. Operations managers need not concern themselves with taxation, sources of finance, interest payments, dividend payments, or leasing decisions. These can be left to finance specialists under the supervision of the Board of Directors. The primary allegiance of the Board is to shareholders. Directors will try to minimize tax payments, pay lower rather than higher interest charges, and therefore, try to maximize net cash flows available for shareholders. Operations managers use ratios to analyse and control costs and revenues. Financial managers, working alongside production and marketing managers, use ratios to analyse and control the rates at which fixed and current assets are 'turned over' in terms of invoiced sales. This traditional approach to financial management should lead to decisions similar to those advocated by the modern approach which focuses on cash flow and risk. Traditionalists suggest that sales (cash flows) should be maximized for any level of investment (initial outlay), and that that investment should be minimized for any level of sales (cash flows).

Practical Ratio Analysis

Introducing Some Popular Ratios: Example

From the following information prepare the trading and profit and loss account for Thornton Manufacturing Ltd for the year ended 31 December and a balance sheet at that date:

Turnover	£24m
Current assets: total assets	1:5
Stock at 1 January	£1m
Gross profit on turnover	25%
Fixed assets: turnover	1:1
Ordinary share capital (25p each) as % of total assets	50%
Loan stock as percentage of total assets	10%
Credit from suppliers	3.6 months
Debt collection period	1 month
Closing stock: turnover	1:8
Net profit on turnover	10%

From your completed balance sheet and profit and loss account calculate the following:

1 Current ratio i.e. $\dfrac{\text{current assets}}{\text{current liabilities}}$

2 Liquidity ratio i.e. $\dfrac{\text{cash} + \text{debtors}}{\text{current liabilities}}$

3 Debt as % of long-term funds

4 Return on total assets i.e. $\dfrac{\text{net profit} \times 100}{\text{total assets}}$

5 Earnings per share i.e. $\dfrac{\text{net profit available for shareholders}}{\text{number of shares}}$

Assuming the market value of the shares to be 20p and the annual dividend to be 2p per share, calculate the following:

1 Earnings yield i.e. $\dfrac{\text{earnings per share} \times 100}{\text{price per share}}$

2 Price-earnings ratio i.e. $\dfrac{\text{price per share}}{\text{earnings per share}}$

3 Dividend yield i.e. $\dfrac{\text{dividend per share} \times 100}{\text{price per share}}$

4 Dividend cover i.e. $\dfrac{\text{earnings per share}}{\text{dividend per share}}$

Thornton Manufacturing Ltd
Balance Sheet as at 31 December

	£m
Sources of Capital:	
(1) R Share capital	×
(2) R Retained earnings	X
(3) R Shareholders' funds	×
(4) R Loan stock	X
(5) R	X
Employment of Capital:	
(6) R Fixed assets	×

		£m
Current Assets:		
(7) L Stocks	×	
(8) L Debtors	×	
(9) L Cash	X	
(10) L	X	
Current Liabilities:		
(11) L Creditors	X	
(12) R Net current assets		X
(13) R		X

Thornton Manufacturing Ltd
Trading, Profit and Loss Account for the year ended 31 December.

		£m
(1) R Sales		×
(2) L Stock at 1 January	×	
(3) L Add purchases	X	
(4) L	×	
(5) L Less closing stock	X	
(6) R Cost of sales		X
(7) R Gross profit		×
(8) R Expenses		X
(9) R Net profit for year		×
(10) R Retained earnings from previous years		X
(11) R		X

L = Left
R = Right

Answer

Thornton Manufacturing Ltd
Balance Sheet as at 31 December

		£m
Sources of Capital:		
(1) R Share capital		15.0
(2) R Retained earnings		6.0
(3) R Shareholders' funds		21.0
(4) R Loan stock		3.0
(5) R		24.0
Employment of Capital:		
(6) R Fixed assets		24.0
Current Assets:		
(7) L Stock	3.0	
(8) L Debtors	2.0	
(9) L Cash	1.0	
(10) L	6.0	
Current Liabilities:		
(11) L Creditors	6.0	
(12) R Net current assets		—
(13) R		24.0

Thornton Manufacturing Ltd
Trading, Profit and Loss Account for the year ended 31 December

		£m
(1) R Sales		24.0
(2) L Stock at 1 January	1.0	
(3) L Add purchases	20.0	
(4) L	21.0	
(5) L Less closing stock	3.0	
(6) R Cost of sales		18.0
(7) R Gross profit		6.0
(8) R Expenses		3.6
(9) R Net profit for year		2.4
(10) R Retained earnings from previous years		3.6
(11) R		6.0

1 In the profit and loss account the sales figure of £24.0m is given.
2 The opening stock at 1 January is given at £1.0m.
3 The gross profit is 25 per cent of sales, i.e. £6.0m.
4 Given sales of £24.0m and gross profit of £6.0m, the cost of sales is £18.0m.
5 As the closing stock is 'turned over' 8 times in terms of sales, then the closing stock is £3.0m.
6 Purchases for the year are £20.0m, the balancing figure.
7 Net profit is 10 per cent of sales, i.e. £2.4m.
8 Expenses or overheads are the difference between gross profit and net profit, i.e. £3.6m.
9 In the balance sheet we have already calculated the closing stock at £3.0m. This figure appears in both the profit and loss account and the balance sheet.
10 The debt collection period is one month, and given sales of £24.0m for the year, debtors amount to £2.0m, i.e. one month's sales.
11 Credit taken from suppliers is 3.6 months. Given purchases of £20.0m, the trade creditors are:

$$\frac{20}{12} \times 3.6 = £6.0m$$

12 Fixed assets are the same as sales, i.e. £24.0m.
13 We know that the fixed assets are £24.0m, and that the ratio of current assets to total assets is 1:5. Since the figure for total assets is current assets plus fixed assets, the fixed assets to total assets must be 4:5. The fixed assets are £24.0m, and the total assets must be £30.0m. Current assets are £6.0m.
14 The balancing figure under current assets for cash is £1.0m.
15 Both sides of the balance sheet total £24.0m.
16 Share capital is 50 per cent of total assets, i.e. £15.0m.
17 Loan stock is 10 per cent of total assets, i.e. £3.0m.
18 Shareholders' funds are therefore £21.0m, and retained earnings £6.0m.
19 Returning to the profit and loss account, the bottom line figure for retained earnings is £6.0m, and the retained earnings from previous years are therefore £3.6m.

$$\text{Current ratio i.e.} \quad \frac{\text{current assets}}{\text{current liabilities}} = \frac{6}{6} = 1$$

This statistic gives an indication as to whether the company can pay its creditors in the short-term. Cash is extremely useful for paying bills. Usually, the nearest item to cash found in the balance sheet is the amount of debtors who are expected to pay in the near future. The balance sheet item preceding cash in the working capital cycle is stock which we hope to sell to debtors who will eventually pay us in cash. Current liabilities are trade creditors for goods and services supplied plus other amounts payable in the near future including taxation, dividends, and accrued expenses such as telephone and heating bills. In our example the current assets are just enough to cover the current liabilities. The traditional rule of thumb is that current assets are expected to cover current liabilities about twice. It is important that we do not jump to hasty conclusions when interpreting financial ratios. There are often perfectly reasonable explanations for 'good' and 'bad' current ratios. We must always look beyond the figures for interpretation. In our example the current ratio is 1.0. This is not a ratio, and in fact we should say that the current ratio is 1:1. However, many ratios are often expressed as whole numbers, percentages, decimals and fractions.

$$\text{Liquidity ratio i.e. } \frac{\text{cash} + \text{debtors}}{\text{current liabilities}} = \frac{3}{6} = 0.5$$

This ratio is sometimes referred to as the acid test, quick ratio, or solvency ratio. As with the current ratio it is an attempt to answer the question: can the company pay its way in the short–term? The liquidity ratio calculation ignores the stock figure. Stock valuation is a major problem in profit measurement and it may take several months to turn the stock into cash. The acid test is therefore a more harsh assessment of the company's ability to meet its current obligations. In our example, the current liabilities are twice the amount of the figure for cash plus debtors. Traditionally, we would expect the liquidity ratio to be approximately 1.0. Again, the ratio is expressed as a number rather than as a ratio of 1:2. Again, we must not jump to hasty conclusions on first examination of the liquidity ratio.

$$\text{Debt as percentage of long-term funds } = \frac{3}{24} = 12\tfrac{1}{2}\,\%$$

The debt–equity 'ratio' measures the amount of long-term debt as a percentage of the equity plus the long-term debt. It measures the extent to which long-term finance is represented by long-term borrowings, and is therefore a measure of gearing. The traditional approach uses balance sheet numbers because they are readily available. The theory of finance suggests that we should use the market values of debt finance and equity as the correct measure of gearing. Market values are often not available, particularly for unquoted companies. Another important measure of gearing is the amount of fixed financial charges as a percentage of operational cash flow. This can also be measured as the number of times operational cash flows cover fixed financial charges. In our example, the long-term debt is £3m and the balance sheet debt plus equity amounts to £24m. The gearing is therefore 12½ per cent. The 'correct' debt–equity ratio for a company depends on the level and volatility of the firm's operational cash flows. In the broadest terms we suggest that the volatile engineering jobbing shop should finance with 30 per cent borrowings, whereas the property company which has more stable cash flows and a substantial asset base for security, can finance with 70 per cent borrowings.

Earnings per share i.e.:

$$\frac{\text{net profit available for shareholders}}{\text{number of shares}} = \frac{£2.4m}{60} = 4p$$

A widely-used measure of corporate performance is earnings per share (EPS). All other things being equal we prefer EPS to rise rather than fall. As we saw in the merger chapter, all other things are not always equal, and the objective of increasing earnings per share can lead to decisions which are not necessarily wealth-creating. As with many other ratios, EPS can be plotted over time (trend analysis) and compared with corporate forecasts. For Thornton Manufacturing the net profit for shareholders is £2.4m. The share capital is £15m made up of 25p shares. There are 60 million shares. Earnings amount to 4p per share.

Earnings yield i.e.:

$$\frac{\text{earnings per share}}{\text{price per share}} \times 100 = \frac{4}{20} = 20 \text{ per cent}$$

If the shares of Thornton are purchased at 20p and the company earns 4p per share, then the earnings yield is 20 per cent. Clearly, the share price is usually a volatile number, as is earnings per share. We must not assume that actual yield is the expected yield. Earnings per share is a historic number whereas the market price of the share is based on expectations. We cannot simply accept the earnings yield as the required rate of return on the company's investments. As we saw in earlier chapters, capital expenditure analysis is based on cash flow, risk, and the level of investment required.

$$\text{Price–earnings ratio i.e. } \frac{\text{price per share}}{\text{earnings per share}} = \frac{20}{4} = 5(\text{years})$$

The price–earnings ratio is a much used and much misunderstood statistic. If we take today's market price of 20p and divide it by the historic number for earnings per share we arrive at the number 5. If the company always earns 4p per share then it will take 5 years to earn today's market price. The P–E ratio of 5 is a sort of payback indicator, giving the number of years it would take for the company to earn the current share price if earnings remain at 5p per share. This is a very strange number. Earnings per share is a historic number, whereas the market price per share depends on expectations. If the company achieves break-even, achieving neither profit nor loss, then the price–earnings ratio is infinite. If the company makes a loss then the price–earnings ratio is a negative number. Sometimes the price–earnings ratio, which is the reciprocal of the earnings yield, is used to estimate the average required rate of return on the firm's investments. This is clearly dangerous. In our example the earnings yield is 20 per cent, but this cannot be used as the discount rate in the capital budgeting decision. In the most general terms we can suggest that a long or high price–earnings ratio suggests that the firm's future is judged by the market to be brighter than its past, i.e. a growth company. A short price–earnings ratio suggests that recent profits are not expected to be maintained.

$$\text{Dividend yield i.e. } \frac{\text{dividend per share}}{\text{price per share}} \times 100 = \frac{2p}{20p} = 10 \text{ per cent}$$

If the company always pays a dividend of 2p per share on a market share price of 20p, then the equivalent interest rate is 10 per cent. Of course, the share price is volatile and the dividend will change. Nevertheless, the dividend yield is a widely used financial ratio.

$$\text{Dividend cover i.e. } \frac{\text{earnings per share}}{\text{dividend per share}} = \frac{4p}{2p} = 2$$

The dividend cover is a financial indicator of the safety of the dividend. The more times the dividend is covered by earnings (cash flow would be preferable), the safer appears to be the dividend. Dividend cover could also be the total earnings of £2.4m divided by the total dividend of £1.2m or the earnings yield of 20 per cent divided by the dividend yield of 10 per cent.

Using Ratio Analysis to Relate Variables

Practical financial managers use ratio analysis to relate one variable to another. For example, in table 12.1 we identify two companies A and B. A makes a profit of £200, while B makes a profit of £100. Which is better? A has created more wealth, but if we wish to discuss the profitability of

Table 12.1   Profit v Profitability

Company		A	B
Profit	(£)	200	100
Which is better?			
Turnover	(£)	2,000	1,000
Which is better?			
Profit/Sales	(%)	10	10
Capital employed	(£)	2,000	500
Which is better?			
Profit/capital employed	(%)	10	20
Why is profit/capital employed better for B than A?			
Sales capital employed	(Times)	1	2
B operates on lower capital employed for its level of sales			

$$\frac{\text{Profit}}{\text{Sales}} \times \frac{\text{Sales}}{\text{Capital employed}} = \frac{\text{Profit}}{\text{Capital employed}}$$

$$A\ \frac{P}{S} \times \frac{S}{CE} = \frac{P}{CE} \qquad\qquad B\ \frac{P}{S} \times \frac{S}{CE} = \frac{P}{CE}$$

$$10\% \times 1 = 10\% \qquad\qquad\qquad 10\% \times 2 = 20\%$$

B uses its assets more effectively.

each company, then we must relate the profit to some variable or variables. The turnover (invoiced sales) for company A is £2,000, and for company B £1,000. Which is better? Both companies earn 10 per cent on sales or turnover, and therefore appear to be equally profitable. Once we introduce the capital employed of £2,000 for company A and £500 for company B, then company B appears to be more profitable. Company A earns 10 per cent on its capital employed, whereas company B earns 20 per cent on capital employed. Both profit as a percentage of sales and return on capital employed are widely-used measures of corporate performance. There is a link between the two variables, and the link is sales divided by the level of capital employed. This is sometimes called the capital–turnover ratio. It is the number of times we have turned over the capital employed in terms of sales. Company A with turnover of £2,000 and capital employed of £2,000 has turned over its capital employed only once, whereas company B has turned over its capital employed twice. If we accept return on capital employed as *the* measure of corporate performance, then B is the more efficient or profitable company. Both companies have the same return on sales, but B has operated on a lower level of capital employed for its level of sales. It has turned over its capital employed twice.

We have immediately identified the three key ratios used by financial managers. These are the profit as a percentage of sales, the number of times we have turned over our capital employed, and the return on capital employed. Having identified these three key statistics, we can proceed to develop many more financial ratios. For example, we can measure the gross profit, net profit, and cash flow as a percentage of sales. We can take the turnover for the period and divide it by the fixed assets, the current assets, the average stock level, the average debtors, and the number of employees. We can measure the gross profit, net profit, and cash flow as a percentage of capital employed. We can calculate material costs, labour costs, other variable costs, and fixed costs as a percentage of sales. We can divide the fixed assets, current assets, and total assets by the number of employees. Managers show a great deal of imagination in generating business statistics.

The three business ratios we have identified can give us greater understanding of different businesses. For example, a supermarket operating in a competitive environment may earn only 2 per cent on its sales but may turn over its capital employed (mainly invested in stock) 20 times each year. This will give a 40 per cent return on capital employed. On the other hand, if a builder wants to earn 40 per cent on capital employed, then the building firm must earn more than 2 per cent on sales. The builder may turn over capital employed only twice each year, and must therefore earn 20 per cent on sales to achieve a 40 per cent return on capital employed.

We can see from the above ratios why managers use ratio analysis to try and improve profitability. Some of the more obvious applications of ratio analysis in improving profitability appear in table 12.2. Return on capital employed can be improved by either increasing the profit as a percentage of sales or by increasing the number of times we turn over our capital employed in terms of sales. Profitability can be improved by either increasing selling prices or reducing costs. This is fairly obvious. However, selling prices are largely market determined, and we may have exhausted the possibilities for cost reduction. We can still achieve an improvement in return on capital employed by using our assets more efficiently. For a given level of turnover and profit, we need the minimum investment in fixed assets. We require careful control of raw materials, work-in-progress, and finished goods. We also need to control the level of debtors, and negotiate the best possible credit terms from our suppliers. We can often improve the return on capital employed by concentrating on the reduction in capital employed, rather than attempting to reduce costs and increase selling prices.

Most practising managers understand sales and costs, but are not as familiar with the ingredients of capital employed. Figure 12.1 identifies total assets and total capital. Under the heading 'employment of capital' are listed all the things a company owns. These things are called assets by accountants. Some assets are for permanent use in the business. Permanent assets include

Table 12.2   How to improve profitability

$$\frac{\text{Profit}}{\text{Sales}} \quad \times \quad \frac{\text{Sales}}{\text{Capital employed}} \quad = \quad \frac{\text{Profit}}{\text{Capital employed}}$$

When seeking improved profitability we tend to think of the following action:

1 Increase selling prices
2 Reduce costs

As we can see from the above equation, increased turnover and reduced costs will improve profit and therefore increase the profit/capital employed percentage.

However, in an effort to improve the return on capital employed it is important that the level of assets (capital employed) is not overlooked. Reduction of the level of assets for a given turnover may be the most effective way of improving the return on capital employed.

Capital Employed = Fixed capital + Working capital

To improve the return on capital employed:

1 Fixed assets - minimum level required for a given turnover.
2 Stock - minimum level required for a given turnover.
3 Work-in-progress - minimum level required for a given turnover.
4 Finished goods - minimum level required for a given turnover.
5 Debtors - minimum level required for a given turnover.

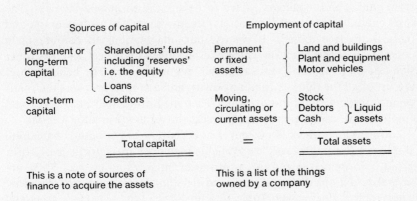

Figure 12.1   Balance sheet

land and buildings, plant and machinery and motor vehicles. Accountants call these permanent assets the fixed assets. These assets are not for sale, and tend to be used by the business over several accounting periods. Other assets are not for permanent use in the business. These include stock, work in progress, finished goods, debtors and cash. These are the moving or circulating assets. Cash is used to acquire raw materials which are converted into finished goods, which are sold to our customers, who eventually pay us in cash. Accountants refer to these assets as the current assets. If we add the fixed assets to the current assets, then this gives us total assets.

In economics, nothing is free. All the assets owned by a business must be financed using somebody's money. These funds come from various sources. One important source of finance is the equity, which is the shareholders' funds. The equity is made up of share capital plus reserves. The share capital is the cash paid into the company by the shareholders when the company was first formed, plus any additional cash paid for additional shares after formation. 'Reserves' is a much misunderstood word. Reserves are often described as ploughed back profits, retained earnings, general reserve, and balance on profit and loss account. Since formation, we hope the company has traded successfully and made profits. Dividends paid in cash by the company are deducted from the level of corporate profit. Any undistributed amounts increase the level of shareholders' funds, and the amount is referred to as ploughed back profit, balance on profit and loss account, reserves etc. There is no money in a financial reserve. There may be petrol in a reserve petrol tank, but we repeat that there is no money in a financial reserve. This is simply a note where the money came from to acquire assets in the business. If we wish to know the amount of cash owned by a business, then we must look at the current assets under the item 'cash'. Under the heading 'sources of capital' are listed the sources of funds to acquire assets. Other sources of funds include long-term loans usually from banks, and 'creditors' which is the amount of unpaid invoices. The total capital must equal total assets because there are no free assets and there is no free money. If we use our imaginations to conjure up a description of this sheet on which one side always balances with the other side, then we might as well call it the 'balance sheet'. The balance sheet is a list of all the things a company owns, and a note as to where the funds came from to acquire those assets. When measuring the return on capital employed we can use either total assets (investment) or total capital.

Unfortunately there is no universal definition of the return on capital employed. Several returns are available including gross profit, net profit, profit before interest and tax, profit after interest and tax etc. There are several definitions of capital employed including total capital, shareholders' funds, and the net assets. Table 12.3 includes a typical balance sheet and a summary profit and loss account. The balance sheet includes fixed and

Table 12.3 Which return on which capital employed?

	Balance Sheet			Profit and Loss Account	
Capital		Assets		Trading profit	500
Shareholders	1,000	Fixed	1,000	Less interest	75
Borrowings					
(15%)	500			'Available' for	
Creditors	500	Current	1,000	shareholders	425
	2,000		2,000		

Return on shareholders' funds:
$$\frac{425}{1,000} \times 100 = 42.5\%$$

Return on long-term funds:
(Net assets)
$$\frac{500}{1,500} \times 100 = 33.3\%$$

Return on total capital employed:
$$\frac{500}{2,000} \times 100 = 25\%$$

Return to borrowers:
$$\frac{75}{500} \times 100 = 15\%$$

1 Creditors receive no reward specifically for providing the firm with funds. Their reward is the profit they make by charging for goods and services.
2 When we find references to return on capital employed it is important to determine which return and which capital employed.

current assets. The firm is financed by shareholders' funds, borrowings at a 15 per cent rate of interest, and creditors. In the profit and loss account, the trading profit is £500 against which interest is charged at 15 per cent on £500, to give the net profit 'available' for shareholders. This is an unfortunate description because profit available for shareholders implies to many managers that £425 is available in cash. In fact, the profit available for shareholders means the profit legally available for share-holders against which dividends can be charged. Profit and cash are different. The firm has a profit of £425, but included in the current assets is the cash balance which can be large, small, positive or even negative. At this stage our objective is to calculate the return on capital employed.

The return on shareholders' funds is 42.5 per cent. Profit available for shareholders is £425, and the shareholders' funds amount to £1,000. The long-term finance in the company is the total of shareholders' funds and long-term loans. This total is £1,500. The interest on the loan is £75, and net profit available for shareholders is £425. The return is £500, and the long-term finance £1,500, the return on the long-term funds being 33.3 per cent. The total profit is £500 and the total capital employed £2,000. This measure of return on capital employed yields 25 per cent. It is clear that when managers discuss return on capital employed it is essential that they define return and also define the capital employed. Three managers working for the same company could be under the impression that the return on capital employed is 25 per cent, 33.3 per cent, or 42.5 per cent!

This example shows how gearing or leverage can gear up or lever up the return to shareholders. Gearing is the use of low-cost debt. We usually associate a lower required rate of return on borrowed funds than on equity. Equity is the risk capital. However, there is a hidden cost of debt finance, i.e. the increasing probability of financial distress. It is important that we understand that wealth is created by satisfying consumer wants, and not

Gearing (or leverage) refers to the extent to which the firm is financed by borrowings as opposed to financing by shareholders. The illustration below presents graphically the calculations in table 12.3

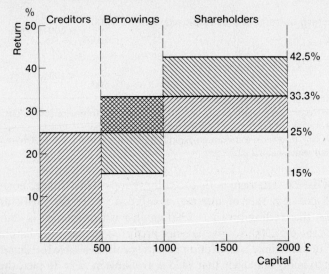

Notes:

1 The return on total capital employed is 25%.

2 Creditors receive no financial reward. The use of their funds levers up the return on long-term funds to 33.3%.

3 Borrowers receive only 15% on their investment, not 33.3%. The use of their funds levers up the return on shareholders' funds to 42.5%.

4 By the use of borrowings and creditors' funds the return to shareholders is levered up to 42.5% although the return on total capital employed is only 25%.

Figure 12.2   How borrowings can gear up (or lever up) the return to shareholders

by juggling with the numbers on the left-hand side of the balance sheet. The mix of debt and equity is usually referred to as the capital structure. Figure 12.2 illustrates how, in our example, the return to shareholders is increased by the judicious use of debt finance, although the profit created by marketing and production effort is £500 regardless of the method of finance. In figure 12.2 return is measured along the vertical axis and capital along the horizontal axis. Our creditors provide £500, loan creditors £500, and shareholders £1,000. The return on total capital employed is 25 per cent, the profit cake being £500 in total. We pay neither dividends nor interest to our creditors, and the use of their funds gears up or levers up the return on the long-term finance to 33.3 per cent. The profit cake is still £500. We only pay 15 per cent on our borrowings, and this therefore levers up the return to shareholders to 42.5 per cent. Again, the profit cake is £500, £75 for loan creditors and £425 'available' for shareholders. The capital structure does not decide the size of the profit cake, but it does decide the distribution between the various providers of capital. Since interest is allowed as a tax deduction, then there is a real benefit to borrowing which is the tax savings on interest payments. Readers are reminded that in chapter 5 we discussed the capital structure decision, concluding that there is a trade-off between the current value of the tax savings and the increasing probability of financial distress.

We remind readers that the theory of finance suggests that there is a trade-off between risk and return. When a company introduces debt into its capital structure, it increases the volatility of returns to shareholders. In financial jargon, the company adds financial risk to operational or business risk. All companies have business risk even if they are financed entirely with equity. In fact, we refer to business or operational risk as the risk associated with the all-equity financed company. Borrowing money increases the volatility of return to shareholders and this is illustrated in table 12.4. Company A is highly geared, company B has some gearing, company C has no borrowings. If all companies earn £60, then the earnings for shareholders are £15, £55, and £60 respectively. The return on shareholders' funds is 15 per cent for company A, 6.1 per cent for company B, and 6 per cent for C. Assuming a 10 per cent fall in return on net assets from 6 per cent to 5.4 per cent, then there is a significant swing in the earnings per share statistic for company A. In fact, earnings per share fall by 40 per cent. The fall is 11 per cent for company B and 10 per cent for company C. Company C is the all-equity financed company. In summary, an increase in borrowings increases the volatility of returns to shareholders. It adds financial risk to business risk. Shareholders do not like risk, and will therefore expect a higher rate of return on their invested funds where gearing is higher.

One of the underlying ideas in the modern theory of finance is that there is a trade-off between risk and return. The relationship between risk and

Table 12.4   The leverage effect (an extreme case)

Company	A	B	C
Shareholders' funds	100	900	1,000
Borrowings (5%)	900	100	—
	1,000	1,000	1,000
Profit on trading	60	60	60
Less interest	45	5	—
Earnings for shareholders	15	55	60
Return on shareholders' funds	15%	6.1%	6%
Earnings per share	£0.15	£0.061	£0.06
Return on net assets	6%	6%	6%
Assume a 10% fall in return on net assets from 6% to 5.4%			
Profit on trading	54	54	54
Less interest	45	5	—
Earnings for shareholders	9	49	54
Return of shareholders' funds	9%	5.44%	5.40%
Earnings per share	£0.09	£0.0544	£0.054
Return on net assets	5.4%	5.4%	5.4%
Fall in return on net assets	10%	10%	10%
Fall in earnings per share	40%	11.0%	10%

In the case of the more highly levered company A, a 10% fall in return on net assets yields a 40% fall in earnings per share.

Note: Leverage can lever downwards as well as upwards.

Summary: Leverage increases the variability of returns, i.e. the financial risk. Investors are averse to risk.

The ability of management to increase the stock market value of the firm by the use of low-cost borrowings is a controversial area of financial management reviewed in chapter 5.

expected return is illustrated in figure 12.3. The manager's objective is to find projects above the line. Such wealth-creating projects are represented by B and 1. Investments R_F, 4, 2, and C, earn returns which just compensate the investor for risk. The investment R_F could be a bank deposit, 4 could be a mix of bank deposits and a unit trust, 2 could be a unit trust investment, and C could be a widely diversified portfolio financed partly by borrowings. We would really like to find Project B but such investment opportunities are rare. Many of the modern ideas in finance including the assessment of risk are ignored in ratio analysis, to which we now return.

The following investment opportunities are available to a manager.

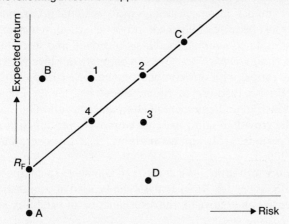

1 Consider A, B, C and D.

Which opportunity is the most risky?
C. High risk and high return.
Which investment do we wish to avoid?
D. High risk and low return.
For which investment are we searching?
B. High return and low risk.
Which is the investment in a bank or building society account under inflationary conditions?
A. Negative return and no risk.

2 Consider 1, 2, 3 and 4.

Why would we always choose 4 before 3, and 1 before 2?
Same return for lower risk.
Why would we always choose 1 before 4, and 2 before 3?
Higher return for same risk.
Why would we always choose 1 before 3?
Higher return and lower risk.
How can we decide between 4 and 2?
It depends on the decision-maker's attitude towards risk and return. The choice is for the investor.

3 Which investment do normal, healthy, risk-averse people choose?
R_F, Three-month Treasury bills, building society and bank deposits.

Figure 12.3 Risk v return

Uses of Ratio Analysis

Ratios can be extremely useful in four areas of management.

1 *Trend analysis* The historic ratios of a company can be plotted on a graph, thereby revealing historic variability and trends. Familiar examples would include sales, sales per employee, changes in sales, market share,

output per man, capital invested per employee, earnings per share, share price, debt collection period, price-earnings ratio, material prices, number of employees, days lost because of illness or industrial action, return on capital employed, gross and net margins, total asset turnover, and stock turnover.

2   *Inter-firm comparison (IFC)*   We can compare our own performance as illustrated by ratios, with our competitors and other firms in the same industry. The British Institute of Management has many IFC schemes available for industrial and commercial companies to join. Our particular interest would be growth in sales, sales per employee, various costs per unit of sales, credit periods, gross and net margins, asset turnover, and return on capital employed.

3   *Performance appraisal*   We encourage managers to compare actual performance with targets set. Ratio analysis can be used in conjunction with, or as a less expensive alternative to, the determination of variances generated by a standard costing system.

4   *Forecasting*   Ratios can be used as an aid to forecasting, particularly financial statement forecasting. We can use historic and projected ratios to forecast future cash flows, profit and loss accounts, balance sheets, and statements of sources and applications of funds.

Trend Analysis

Many people find historic financial trends intrinsically interesting. Others find signals which stimulate thought for greater efficiency in making money satisfying consumer wants in competitive markets. Some popular ratios are listed below. We suggest that managers should generate the statistics from historic sources and study the trends. Are there any messages there? Please do not extrapolate the trends into the future in a simplistic attempt at predicting the future. If trends could predict the future, then companies would not need managers!

1   *Profit/Profitability*   1985   1986   1987   1988   1989

$$\frac{\text{Profit} \times 100}{\text{Sales}}$$ $$\frac{\text{Gross profit}}{\text{Sales}}$$

$$\frac{\text{Net profit before interest and tax}}{\text{Sales}}$$

$$\frac{\text{Net profit after interest}}{\text{Sales}}$$

$$\frac{\text{Net profit after interest and tax}}{\text{Sales}}$$

Profit/Profitability (continued) 1985 1986 1987 1988 1989

$$\frac{\text{Profit}}{\text{Capital employed}} \times 100 \qquad \frac{\text{Various profit figures as above}}{\text{Total capital employed at year-end}}$$

$$\frac{\text{Various profit figures}}{\text{Opening total capital employed}}$$

$$\frac{\text{Various profit figures}}{\substack{\text{Average total capital employed} \\ \text{i.e. (opening} + \text{closing)} \div 2}}$$

$$\frac{\text{Various profit figures}}{\substack{\text{Long-term finance/net assets} \\ \text{(Opening, closing or average)}}}$$

$$\frac{\text{Net profit after interest and tax}}{\substack{\text{Shareholders' funds} \\ \text{(Opening, closing or average)}}}$$

Earnings per share $\dfrac{\text{Net profit after interest and tax}}{\text{Number of shares}}$

Earnings per employee $\dfrac{\text{Various profit figures}}{\substack{\text{Number of employees} \\ \text{(Opening, closing or average)}}}$

$\dfrac{\text{Value added}}{\text{Sales}}$ $\dfrac{\text{Sales} - \text{external costs}}{\text{Sales}}$

Value added = Sales − external costs (bought-in materials and services)
 = retained earnings + dividends + tax + interest + lease
   payments + hire charges + depreciation + wages + salaries.

Change in $\dfrac{\text{profit}}{\text{Sales}}$ $\dfrac{\text{This year's profit/sales} - \text{last year's profit/sales}}{\text{Last year's profit/sales}}$

Change in $\dfrac{\text{Profit}}{\text{Capital employed}}$ $\dfrac{\text{This year's P/CE} - \text{last year's P/CE}}{\text{Last year's P/CE}}$

1 *Profit/Profitability*   1985 1986 1987 1988 1989
(continued)

Change in earnings per share $$\frac{\text{This year's EPS} - \text{last year's EPS}}{\text{Last year's EPS}}$$

Change in earnings
per employee $$\frac{\text{This year's statistic} - \text{last year's statistic}}{\text{Last year's statistic}}$$

Change in $\dfrac{\text{Value added}}{\text{Sales}}$ $$\frac{\text{This year's VA/S} - \text{last year's VA/S}}{\text{Last year's VA/S}}$$

Overview:

$$\frac{\text{Profit}}{\text{Sales}} \times \frac{\text{Sales}}{\text{Capital employed}} = \frac{\text{Profit}}{\text{Capital employed}}$$

$$\frac{\text{Value added}}{\text{Sales}} \times \frac{\text{Sales}}{\text{Capital employed}} = \frac{\text{Value added}}{\text{Capital employed}}$$

2 *Cash Flow*   1985 1986 1987 1988 1989

$\dfrac{\text{Cash flow} \times 100}{\text{Sales}}$ $\dfrac{\text{Operational cash flow}}{\text{Sales}}$

$\dfrac{\text{Cash flow}}{\text{Capital employed}}$ $\dfrac{\text{Operational cash flow}}{\text{Various capital employed figures}}$

Cash flow per share $\dfrac{\text{Operational cash flow}}{\text{Number of shares}}$

Cash flow per employee $\dfrac{\text{Operational cash flow}}{\text{Various numbers of employees}}$

Overview: $$\frac{\text{Cash flow}}{\text{Sales}} \times \frac{\text{Sales}}{\text{Capital employed}} = \frac{\text{Cash flow}}{\text{Capital employed}}$$

3 *Sales*   1985   1986   1987   1988   1989

Increase in sales   This year's sales – last year's sales
                                                   Last year's sales

Market share   Corporate sales as percentage of total market sales

Commission/sales   Commission as percentage of sales

Bad debts   Bad debts as percentage of sales
                            Bad debts as percentage of debtors

4 *Costs*

Wages/sales   Payroll costs as percentage of sales
Materials/sales   Material costs as percentage of sales
Gross profit/sales   Gross profit as percentage of sales
Distribution costs/sales   Distribution costs as percentage of sales
Advertising/sales   Advertising costs as percentage of sales
Marketing costs/sales   Marketing costs as percentage of sales
Commissions/sales   Salesmen's commissions as percentage of sales
Fixed costs/sales   Fixed costs as percentage of sales
Finance charges/sales   Finance charges as percentage of sales
Variable costs/sales   Variable costs as percentage of sales
Contribution/sales   Contribution as percentage of sales
Net profit/sales   Net profit as percentage of sales
Dividends/sales   Dividends as percentage of sales
Tax/sales   Taxation as percentage of sales

Changes in wages, materials,
gross profit, distribution
costs, advertising, marketing,   This year's – last year's
commissions, fixed costs,   Last year's
finance charges, variable
cost, contribution, net profit,
dividends, taxation.

Analysis of variable   Materials etc. as percentage of variable costs
   costs
Analysis of fixed costs   Accounts Dept. costs etc. as percentage of
                                    fixed costs

4 *Costs* (continued)	1985	1986	1987	1988	1989

Wages/value added — Wages as percentage of value added

Dividends/value added — Dividends as percentage of value added

Tax/value added — Tax as percentage of value added

Finance charges/value added — Finance charges as percentage of value added

Depreciation/value added — Depreciation as percentage of value added

Retentions/value added — Retentions as percentage of value added

5 *Growth*

Increase in sales, market share, output, number of employees, quantity of assets, number of customers, number of transactions, profit, cash flow, value added.

$$\frac{\text{This year's statistic} - \text{last year's statistic}}{\text{Last year's statistic}}$$

New investment

New investment as percentage of existing investment

New investment per employee

New investment as percentage of operational cash flow

6 *Asset Utilization/Efficiency*

$$\frac{\text{Sales}}{\text{Capital employed}} \qquad \frac{\text{Sales}}{\text{Various capital employed figures}}$$

Fixed asset turnover

$$\frac{\text{Sales}}{\text{Various fixed asset figures}}$$

Current asset turnover

$$\frac{\text{Sales}}{\text{Various current asset figures}}$$

Stock turnover

$$\frac{\text{Sales}}{\text{Various stock figures}}$$

Stock turnover

$$\frac{\text{Cost of sales}}{\text{Various stock figures}}$$

6 *Asset Utilization/Efficiency*   1985   1986   1987   1988   1989
   (continued)

Debtors' turnover

$$\frac{\text{Sales}}{\text{Various debtors' figures}}$$

Debt collection period

$$\frac{\text{Debtors} \times 365}{\text{Sales}} = \text{days}$$

Creditors' turnover

$$\frac{\text{Credit purchases}}{\text{Creditors}}$$

Creditors' payment period

$$\frac{\text{Creditors}}{\text{Credit purchases}} \times 365 = \text{days}$$

Employee efficiency   Per employee – sales, output, remuneration, gross and net profit, value added, operational cash flow, fixed assets, total assets (capital employed).

Increase in fixed assets, stock, debtors, and cash balances.

$$\frac{\text{This year's statistic} - \text{last year's statistic}}{\text{Last year's statistic}}$$

7 *Capital Structure* (Balance sheet)

Shareholders' funds	Equity as percentage of total capital employed
Loan capital	Long-term loans as percentage of capital employed
Short-term loans (overdraft)	Short-term loans as percentage of capital employed
Creditors	Creditors as percentage of total capital employed
Other	Other as percentage of total capital employed

Total capital employed   <u>100</u>   <u>100</u>   <u>100</u>   <u>100</u>   <u>100</u>

8 *Capital Structure*
   (Market values)

Equity	Market value of equity
Debt	Market value of debt

Market value of securities   <u>100</u>   <u>100</u>   <u>100</u>   <u>100</u>   <u>100</u>

9　*Gearing*　　　　　　　　　　1985　1986　1987　1988　1989

Gearing (1)　　　　　　　　$$\frac{\text{Long-term loans}}{\text{Total capital employed}}$$

　　　(2)　　　　　　　　　$$\frac{\text{Long-term loans}}{\text{Long-term loans} + \text{equity}}$$

　　　(3)　　　　$$\frac{\text{Long-term} + \text{short-term loans} + \text{overdraft}}{\text{Total capital employed}}$$

　　　(4)　　　　　　　　　$$\frac{\text{Fixed finance charges}}{\text{Operational cash flow}}$$

　　　(5)　　　　　　　　$$\frac{\text{Fixed finance charges}}{\text{Net profit before interest and tax}}$$

10　*Asset Structure*　　　　　1985　1986　1987　1988　1989

Land and property　　　　Land and property as percentage
　　　　　　　　　　　　　of total assets

Plant and equipment　　　Plant as percentage of total assets
Motor vehicles　　　　　　Vehicles as percentage of total
　　　　　　　　　　　　　assets

Stock　　　　　　　　　　Raw materials, work-in-progress
　　　　　　　　　　　　　and finished goods as
　　　　　　　　　　　　　percentage of total assets

Debtors　　　　　　　　　Debtors as percentage of total
　　　　　　　　　　　　　assets

Cash　　　　　　　　　　　Cash as percentage of total assets
Other　　　　　　　　　　　Other assets as percentage of
　　　　　　　　　　　　　total assets

Total assets　　　　　　　 $\underline{100}$　 $\underline{100}$　 $\underline{100}$　 $\underline{100}$　 $\underline{100}$

11　*Liquidity*
Current ratio　　　　　　　　　　$$\frac{\text{Current assets}}{\text{Current liabilities}}$$

Acid test, solvency ratio,　　　　　$$\frac{\text{Cash} + \text{debtors}}{\text{Current liabilities}}$$
　quick ratio, liquidity ratio

11 *Liquidity* (continued)   1985 1986 1987 1988 1989

Cash flow generation   Cash flow as percentage of sales
                                 Cash flow as percentage of
                                     capital employed

Day's cash available $$\frac{\text{Cash balance}}{\text{Average daily expenses}}$$

12 *Stock Market Statistics*
Share price   As quoted

Earnings yield $$\frac{\text{EPS}}{\text{Market price}}$$

Price-earnings ratio $$\frac{\text{Market price per share}}{\text{EPS}}$$

Dividend yield $$\frac{\text{Dividend}}{\text{Market price}}$$

Dividend cover $$\frac{\text{EPS}}{\text{DPS}}$$

Changes in the above $$\frac{\text{This year's statistic} - \text{last year's statistic}}{\text{Last year's statistic}}$$
    statistics

Inter-Firm Comparison (IFC)

Either by joining a scheme of IFC or collecting financial information on competitors, managers can use ratios to compare performance and probably identify different corporate strategies. For example, a firm with a long debt collection period may be using extended credit as one strategy for increasing sales. A scheme for inter-firm comparison would normally show ratios for the first quartile, median, and third quartile. In a census of 99 companies, the gross profit/sales percentage, for example, for all companies is ranked in ascending order. Company number 25 is the first quartile, company number 50 is the median, and company number 75 is the third quartile. Each company has access to its own statistics and can therefore compare its own ratio with the first and third quartiles, and the median. The members of the scheme do not know the names of the other members, and therefore

Table 12.5   Company Alpha plc

		Company	Industry First Quartile	Industry Median	Industry Third Quartile
Gross profit/sales	%	37.1	27.8	42.3	49.4
Net profit/sales	%	15.9	11.7	17.7	19.8
Cost of sales/sales	%	62.9	52.2	58.8	71.7
Sales per employee	£	15,529	13,627	16,250	20,072
Profit per employee	£	2,059	1,767	2,300	2,714
Value added/sales	%	61.7	49.2	57.6	78.7
Cash flow/sales	%	17.8	11.6	16.4	21.2
Wages/sales	%	44.0	37.2	41.0	49.1
Materials/sales	%	18.9	19.6	21.7	25.2
Bad debts/sales	%	—	0.2	1.3	1.9
Sales/capital employed	Times	0.69	0.6	1.1	1.7
Sales/fixed assets	Times	1.0	0.8	1.3	1.7
Stock turnover	Times	3.3	3.4	4.1	4.9
Debt collection period	Days	100	87	116	141
Creditors payment period	Days	174	107	127	152
Capital employed per employee	£	22,471	19,673	26,540	29,178
Gearing	%	40.2	29.4	34.7	46.2
Fixed assets/total assets	%	67.8	48.0	57.6	68.3
Current assets/total assets	%	32.2	25.0	39.6	61.0
Current ratio	Times	1.2	0.9	1.6	1.9
Liquidity ratio	Times	0.7	0.6	1.1	1.4

do not have access to confidential information relating to specific competitors. Table 12.5 presents ratios which we suggest could be of interest to practical financial managers.

From data which appears in table 12.5 managers can study the performance of Company Alpha plc *vis-à-vis* other firms in the same industry. Attention can be focused on what appear to be the problem areas. The objective of the exercise is to isolate those indicators which suggest that the company is out of step with the industry averages. Extreme care must be taken in interpreting results. As we shall say again later ratios are affected by accounting policies, and the general assumption that year-end figures are representative of the whole period.

Performance Appraisal

We can use ratios to compare actual performance with the budgeted or target performance. A great deal more information is available to the company than appears in published accounts. A great deal of the traditional approach to ratio analysis concentrates on published accounting information since this is usually the most comprehensive information available. Company Alpha plc is aware of its own targets, and can therefore compare actual performance with target.

Example

From the following data relating to Company Alpha plc compare the actual performance with the target performance using ratio analysis.

Company Alpha plc

	Target £		Actual £
Profit and Loss Account			
Sales		250,000	264,000
Opening stock	40,000		40,000
Labour costs	100,000		116,000
Materials	47,000		61,000
	187,000		217,000
Less closing stock	42,000		51,000
Cost of sales		145,000	166,000
Gross profit		105,000	98,000
Other variable costs	31,000		32,000
Fixed office expenses	17,000		19,000
Depreciation	5,000		5,000
Interest on long-term loan	8,000		7,000
		61,000	63,000
Net profit		44,000	35,000
Less dividend		18,000	18,000
Retentions		26,000	17,000
Average number of employees		16	17

Company Alpha plc

	Target £		Actual £
Balance Sheet			
Sources of capital:			
Share capital (£1 shares)		100,000	100,000
Retained earnings brought forward	94,000		94,000
Retentions this year	26,000		17,000
		120,000	111,000
		220,000	211,000
Long-term loans		70,000	65,000
		290,000	276,000
Employment of capital:			
Property at cost		180,000	180,000
Plant and machinery (net)		42,000	44,000
Motor vehicles (net)		33,000	35,000
		255,000	259,000
Current assets:			
Stock	42,000		51,000
Debtors	63,000		72,000
Cash at bank	—		—
	105,000		123,000
Current liabilities:			
Creditors	16,000		29,000
Bank overdraft	54,000		77,000
	70,000		106,000
Net current assets		35,000	17,000
		290,000	276,000

Ratio Analysis: Company Alpha plc

Answer

Profit/Profitability		Target	Actual
Gross profit	£	105,000	98,000
Sales	£	250,000	264,000
$\dfrac{\text{Gross profit}}{\text{Sales}}$	%	42.0	37.1
Net profit before interest	£	52,000	42,000
$\dfrac{\text{Net profit before interest}}{\text{Sales}}$	%	20.8	15.9
Net profit after interest	£	44,000	35,000
$\dfrac{\text{Net profit after interest}}{\text{Sales}}$	%	17.6	13.3
Total capital employed (total assets)	£	360,000	382,000
Long-term finance (net assets)	£	290,000	276,000
$\dfrac{\text{Net profit before interest}}{\text{Total capital employed}}$	%	14.4	11.0
$\dfrac{\text{Net profit before interest}}{\text{Net assets}}$	%	17.9	15.2
$\text{EPS:}\dfrac{\text{Net profit after interest}}{\text{Number of shares}}$	P	44	35
Earnings before interest per employee	£	3,250	2,059
Value added $T = 250 - 45 - 31 - 17$			
$\qquad\qquad A = 264 - 50 - 32 - 19$	£	157,000	163,000
or, Value added $T = 26 + 18 + 8 + 5 + 100$			
$\qquad\qquad A = 17 + 18 + 7 + 5 + 116$	£	157,000	163,000
$\dfrac{\text{Value added}}{\text{Sales}}$	%	62.8	61.7
Value added per employee	£	9,813	9,588
$\dfrac{\text{Profit}}{\text{Sales}} \times \dfrac{\text{Sales}}{\text{Total capital}} = \dfrac{\text{Profit}}{\text{Total capital}}$		$20.8 \times 0.69 =$ 14.4%	$15.9 \times 0.69 =$ 11.0%
$\dfrac{\text{Value added}}{\text{Sales}} \times \dfrac{\text{Sales}}{\text{Total capital}} = \dfrac{\text{Value added}}{\text{Total capital}}$		$62.8 \times 0.69 =$ 43.6%	$61.7 \times 0.69 =$ 42.7%

		Target	Actual
Cash Flow			
Funds from operations (profit before interest + depreciation)	£	57,000	47,000
$\dfrac{\text{Funds from operations}}{\text{Sales}}$	%	22.8	17.8
$\dfrac{\text{Funds from operations}}{\text{Total capital}}$	%	15.8	12.3
Funds from operations per share	p	57	47
Funds from operations per employee	£	3,563	2,764

$$\frac{\text{Funds from operations}}{\text{Sales}} \times \frac{\text{Sales}}{\text{Total capital}}$$

$$= \frac{\text{Funds from operations}}{\text{Total capital}}$$

	Target	Actual
	$22.8 \times 0.69 =$ 15.8%	$17.8 \times 0.69 =$ 12.3%

Costs

	Target	Actual
Sales	100	100
	%	%
Materials	18.0	18.9
Labour	40.0	44.0
Other variable costs	12.4	12.1
Fixed office expenses	6.8	7.2
Depreciation	2.0	1.9
Interest	3.2	2.7
Dividends	7.2	6.8
Retentions	10.4	6.4
	100	100
Value added	100	100
Wages	63.7	71.2
Depreciation	3.2	3.1
Interest	5.1	4.3
Dividends	11.5	11.0
Retentions	16.5	10.4
	100	100

Asset Utilization/Efficiency		Target	Actual
$\dfrac{\text{Sales}}{\text{Total capital(total assets)}}$	Times	.69	.69
$\dfrac{\text{Sales}}{\text{Fixed assets}}$	Times	.98	1.0
$\dfrac{\text{Sales}}{\text{Closing stock}}$	Times	6.0	5.2
$\dfrac{\text{Cost of sales}}{\text{Closing stock}}$	Times	3.5	3.3
$\dfrac{\text{Sales}}{\text{Closing debtors}}$	Times	4.0	3.7
Debt collection period	Days	92	100
$\dfrac{\text{Credit purchases(materials)}}{\text{Closing creditors}}$	Times	2.9	2.1
Creditors'payment period	Days	124	174
Total assets per employee	£	22,500	22,471
Fixed assets per employee	£	15,938	15,235
Sales per employee	£	15,625	15,529
Capital Structure		%	%
Shareholders' funds		61.1	55.2
Long-term loans		19.4	17.0
Bank overdraft		15.0	20.2
Creditors		4.5	7.6
		100	100
Gearing (Balance sheet)			
$\dfrac{\text{Long-term loans}}{\text{Long-term loans}+\text{equity}}$	%	24.1	23.6
$\dfrac{\text{Long-term loans}+\text{overdraft}}{\text{Long-term loans}+\text{overdraft}+\text{equity}}$	%	36.0	40.2
$\dfrac{\text{FFO before interest}}{\text{Interest}}$	Times	7.1	6.7
(FFO = Funds from operations)			

continued

Asset Structure		Target	Actual
		%	%
Property		50.0	47.1
Plant and equipment		11.7	11.5
Motor vehicles		9.1	9.2
Fixed assets		70.8	67.8
Stock		11.7	13.4
Debtors		17.5	18.8
		100	100
Dividend Cover			
Net profit after interest / Dividends	Times	2.4	1.9
Liquidity			
Current ratio	Times	1.5	1.2
Acid test, liquidity ratio, solvency ratio, or quick ratio	Times	0.9	0.7

Managers can use their imaginations to generate vast quantities of statistics. Whilst managers may be eager to find ratios which give the key to corporate success, we must recommend a great deal of caution in making decisions on the basis of a few ratios. The theory of finance teaches that decisions should be based on cash flow and risk. Ratios are all-other-things-being-equal numbers. There may be good reason why stock, debtors, creditors and cash balances are high or low at the year-end. In ratio analysis we usually use year-end numbers because these are readily available. A company going into liquidation will tend to have a low stock figure, giving the company an excellent stock turnover ratio for the year. Another company has difficulty collecting cash at the year-end from two of its largest customers. using year-end balance sheet numbers, this will give a much longer debt collection period than has existed during the year. Balance sheet numbers and profit and loss account numbers are affected by accounting policies relating to stock valuation, depreciation, inflation, research and development, profit on long-term contracts, etc. These policies, and changes in these policies, will have some considerable influence on accounting numbers. If we are sufficiently naive to assume that ratios provide 'answers', then we must give considerable thought in defining the question. Overall, we conclude that ratios help to give managers a 'feel' for the company's performance in relation to its targets and its competitors. We exhort practical financial managers not to seize upon two or three ratios as offering the key to corporate success or failure.

Forecasting

Ratios can provide a useful aid to forecasting. Established financial ratios can be used to forecast next year's profit and loss account and balance sheet. The forecasting of sources and applications of funds can be achieved essentially by taking the differences between the balance sheet at the beginning of the period and the forecast balance sheet at the end of the period. Readers may recall the use of ratios in chapter 11 to forecast financial statements, given the forecast of next year's sales. The cash balance at the end of the year is the balancing figure in the balance sheet. A similar exercise follows.

Arthur Parkinson is managing director of Barnsley Bag Makers Limited. He asks you to prepare forecast statements for an urgent board meeting. The sales director has won new contracts which will add about £100,000 to existing turnover in 1989.

Profit and Loss Accounts		1987		1988
		£		£
Turnover		242,000		250,000
Opening stock	30,000		40,000	
Add purchases	152,000		147,000	
	182,000		187,000	
Less: closing stock	40,000		42,000	
Cost of sales		142,000		145,000
Gross profit		100,000		105,000
Less: other variables	30,000		31,000	
fixed costs	28,000		30,000	
		58,000		61,000
Net profit		42,000		44,000
Less: dividend paid		15,000		18,000
Retentions		27,000		26,000

Balance Sheets

	1987	1988
	£	£
Sources of Capital:		
Share capital	100,000	100,000
Retained earnings	94,000	120,000
Shareholders' funds	194,00	220,000
Long-term loans	90,000	70,000
	284,000	290,000
Employment of Capital:		
Property	180,000	180,000
Plant and equipment (net)	40,000	42,000
Motor vehicles (net)	32,000	33,000
	252.000	255,000

Current Assets:			
Stock	40,000	42,000	
Debtors	60,000	63,000	
Cash at bank	—	—	
	100,000	105,000	

Current liabilities:			
Creditors	25,000	26,000	
Bank overdraft	43,000	44,000	
	68,000	70,000	
Net current assets		32,000	35,000
		284,000	290,000

Use ratio analysis to forecast the profit and loss account and closing balance sheet for 1989.

Answer

Barnsley Bag Makers Ltd

Profit and Loss Account for 1989

		£000
Turnover		350
Opening stock	42	
Add purchases	219	
	261	
Less: closing stock	58	
Cost of sales		203
Gross profit		147
Less: other variables	43	
fixed costs	42	
		85
Net profit		62
Less: dividend paid		25
Retentions		37

Balance Sheet	1989
	£000
Sources of Capital:	
Share capital	100
Retained earnings	157
Shareholders' funds	257
Long-term loans	50
	307
Employment of Capital:	
Property (cost)	180
Plant and equipment (net)	58
Motor vehicles (net)	46
	284

continued

Barnsley Bag Makers Ltd *continued*

Balance Sheet		1989 £000
Current Assets:		
Stock	58	
Debtors	88	
Cash at bank	—	
	146	
Current Liabilities:		
Creditors	37	
Bank overdraft	86	
	123	
Net current assets		23
		307

Workings (£000)
1 In the profit and loss account, turnover = 250 + 100 = £350.
2 Opening stock is 1988 closing stock, £42.
3 Gross profit on sales 42 per cent, £147.
4 Cost of sales, 350 − 147 = £203.
5 Stock turnover = 6 times. Closing stock = 350 ÷ 6 = £58.
6 Purchases = £219, balancing figure.
7 Other variables = 12.3 per cent of sales = £43.
8 Fixed costs = 12 per cent of sales = £42.
9 Net profit = 147 − 85 = £62.
10 Dividend estimated at £25.
11 Retentions = £37.
12 In the balance sheet, the share capital is still £100.
13 Retentions are 120 + 37 = £157.
14 The long-term loans appear to reduce by 20 per annum to £50.
15 Both sides of the balance sheet must total £307.
16 Property stays at £180.
17 Plant and equipment estimated at £58.
18 Motor vehicles estimated at £46.
19 Stock already calculated at £58.

20 Debtors turned over 4 times. Debt collection period 3 months, $350 \div 4 = £88$.

21 Creditors turned over 5.9 times. Credit payment period 2 months, $219 \div 5.9 = £37$.

22 Balancing figure is bank overdraft at £86.

Clearly we have taken a very simple approach to financial statement forecasting. We have assumed that historic ratios will hold in the future. Obviously, this may not be the case. We may change selling prices, costs of materials and wages will change, as will debt collection periods and creditors' payment periods. New fixed assets will be acquired, technological advances will be made and new financing structures and asset structures will either be designed or will emerge. Nevertheless, ratios are widely used throughout industry as a useful and practical aid to forecasting.

Regardless of the method of forecasting financial statements, we suggest that managers should carry out a ratio analysis of the financial forecasts. This should help to identify areas of excessive optimism or pessimism.

A Note on Predicting Financial Distress

Several authors have attempted to use ratio analysis to predict the future. In particular, several attempts have been made to predict company failure. Such predictions would be of tremendous interest to the lending banker, creditors, and competitors, as well as corporate managers and other employees. Perhaps the most well-known prediction model is the Z score of Professor Altman (1968). He examined thirty-three manufacturing companies that failed, these being paired with thirty-three companies of similar asset size and in a similar industry which had not failed. Twenty-two ratios relating to liquidity, profitability, leverage, solvency, and activity were calculated for all companies. Of these twenty-two ratios, five were selected as having the greatest predictive power. These five ratios are:

$$X_1 = \frac{\text{Working capital}}{\text{Total assets}}$$

$$X_1 = \frac{\text{Retained earnings}}{\text{Total assets}}$$

$$X_3 = \frac{\text{Profit before interest and tax}}{\text{Total assets}}$$

$$X_4 = \frac{\text{Market capitalization}}{\text{Book value of debts}}$$

$$X_5 = \frac{\text{Sales}}{\text{Total assets}}$$

Working capital is defined as current assets less current liabilities, and therefore X_1 is a sort of measure of liquidity and asset structure, X_2 is a measure of cumulative retained profitability, X_3 is a measure of profitability, X_4 is a measure of gearing, and X_5 is a measure of the company's ability to turn over its assets. The model is as follows:

$$Z = 1.2X_1 + 1.4X_2 + 3.3X_3 + 0.6X_4 + 1.0X_5$$

A company with a Z-score of 3.0 or more is considered to be safe. Alternatively, a company which scores 1.8 or less is classified as a potential failure. Such a company could go into liquidation during the following three years.

Prediction models based on a ratio analysis have been widely used in recent years. We urge managers not to accept blindly the predictive powers of such models. After all, the Z-score is just one ratio, or rather a combination of five ratios. The models tell us only that which we already know – that firms with poor profitability, poor liquidity, and inefficient use of assets are more likely to experience financial distress than other companies. We do not know whether such models have a higher predictive power than the traditional rules of thumb used by bankers and lenders based on trends in profitability and liquidity. In general, these models are generated using at least five years' data and are not necessarily applicable to shorter periods; most corporate failures, however, occur in the first five years of trading. The models are usually derived from samples of fifty per cent successful firms and fifty per cent failed firms, whereas the bank manager's problem is to identify one or two suspect firms out of one hundred clients. We suggest that firms with poor Z-scores are more likely to fail after a sudden downturn in the economy rather than in a subsequent economic boom. Some firms appear to have the ability to survive long periods of financial distress. Distress models are based on empirical observation, there being no accepted theory of financial distress. In fact, there is no accepted definition of financial distress and many researchers have suggested that financial distress should include liquidation for companies and bankruptcy for individuals, government intervention, the calling of a creditors' meeting, failure to pay interest or make loan capital repayments, bypassing of an ordinary or preferred dividend, the seeking of a merger, a declining market value of the firm, declining market share, and even the existence of a bank overdraft.

Whatever problems exist in the prediction of financial distress, we encourage managers to avoid the costs of financial distress. These include accounting and legal costs, delay in payout to creditors and shareholders, the making of sub-optimal investment decisions including selling off the 'crown jewels', the calling in of a bank overdraft, restrictive covenants on additional borrowings, reduced debt capacity, the departure of major financial institutions as shareholders, a going concern qualification by auditors, restrictions in trade credit, and reduced job security for managers and other employees. Financial distress can be avoided by successful trading, making money satisfying consumer wants in competitive markets, i.e. making successful financing and investment decisions. When firms do experience financial distress, liquidation may be avoided by an uplift in the economy, a turnround by management, turnround by a company doctor, government intervention, or a merger. In anticipation of financial distress in the future, managers should have a strategy for financial emergencies. Such a survival plan would include reorganizing the firm's asset structure and capital structure with a view to generating cash. Financial distress may be forecast by trend analysis, by using ratios to prepare forecast financial statements, by forecasting future financial statements without using ratios, or even by the use of a predictive model.

Study Questions

12.1 From the following data relating to Steeton Water Beds Ltd compare the actual with target performance using ratio analysis.

Profit and Loss Account	Target £		Actual £
Sales		500,000	516,000
Opening stock	90,000		90,000
Labour costs	180,000		230,000
Materials	92,000		124,000
	362,000		444,000
Less closing stock	82,000		107,000
Cost of sales		280,000	337,000
Gross profit		220,000	179,000
Other variable costs	60,000		56,000
Fixed office expenses	38,000		43,000
Depreciation	12,000		12,000
Loan interest	18,000		16,000
		128,000	127,000
Net profit		92,000	52,000
Less dividend		40,000	40,000
Retentions		52,000	12,000
Average number of employees		38	46

Steeton Water Beds Ltd

Balance Sheet		Target £		Actual £
Sources of Capital:				
Share capital (£1 shares)		200,000		200,000
Opening profit and loss account	160,000		160,000	
Retentions this year	52,000		12,000	
		212,000		172,000
		412,000		372,000
Long-term loans		180,000		160,000
		592,000		532,000
Employment of Capital:				
Property at cost		340,000		340,000
Plant and machinery (net)		76,000		82,000
Motor vehicles (net)		60,000		70,000
		476,000		492,000
Current Assets:				
Stock	82,000		107,000	
Debtors	100,000		130,000	
Cash at bank	—		—	
	182,000		237,000	
Current Liabilities:				
Creditors	30,000		35,000	
Bank overdraft	36,000		162,000	
	66,000		197,000	
Net Current Assets		116,000		40,000
		592,000		532,000

12.2 George Wynberg is managing director of the Stoke Electrical Company Limited. He asks you to prepare forecast financial statements for an urgent board meeting late this afternoon. The marketing director has just come up with a sales forecast of £400,000 for 1989.

Profit and Loss Accounts		1987 £		1988 £
Turnover		190,000		240,000
Opening stock	24,000		28,000	
Add purchases	116,000		150,000	
	140,000		178,000	
Less closing stock	28,000		36,000	
Cost of sales		112,000		142,000
Gross profit		78,000		98,000
Less:				
Other variables	22,000		27,000	
Fixed costs	23,000		28,000	
		45,000		55,000
Net profit		33,000		43,000
Less dividend paid		10,000		12,000
Retentions		23,000		31,000

Balance Sheets		1987 £		1988 £
Sources of Capital				
Share capital		60,000		60,000
Retained earnings		104,000		135,000
Shareholders' funds		164,000		195,000
Long-term loans		100,000		100,000
		264,000		295,000
Employment of Capital				
Property (cost)		190,000		190,000
Plant and equipment (net)		28,000		38,000
Motor vehicles (net)		24,000		34,000
		242,000		262,000
Current Assets:				
Stock	28,000		36,000	
Debtors	32,000		40,000	
Cash at bank	—		3,000	
	60,000		79,000	

continued

Balance Sheets *continued*		1987 £		1988 £
Current Liabilities:				
Creditors	36,000		46,000	
Bank overdraft	2,000		—	
	38,000		46,000	
Net Current Assets		22,000		33,000
		264,00		295,000

The data relate to 1987 and 1988. Use ratio analysis to forecast the profit and loss account and closing balance sheet for 1989.

Present calculations for six of your 1989 estimates.

Note: Cash at bank (bank overdraft) is the balancing figure. Make reasonable assumptions such as available capacity, no issues of shares or more loans, dividend proposed £15,000.

Further Reading

Brigham, Eugene F. *Financial Management: Theory and Practice.* New York: Dryden Press, 1985, chapters 22–3.

Schall, Lawrence D. and Haley, Charles W. *Introduction to Financial Management.* New York: McGraw-Hill, 1986, chapter 12.

References

Altman, E. I. 1968: Financial Ratios, Discriminant Analysis and the Prediction of Corporate Bankruptcy. *Journal of Finance*, vol. 23, September.

Bar-Yosef, S. 1977: Interactions of Corporate Financing and Investment Decisions – Implications for Capital Budgeting: Comment. *Journal of Finance*, vol. 32, March.

Black, F. 1976: The dividend puzzle. In Myers, S. C., *Modern Developments in Financial Management*. Hinsdale, Illinois: Dryden Press.

Black, F. and Scholes, M. 1972: The valuation of option contracts and a test of market efficiency. *Journal of Finance*, vol. 27, May.

Black, F. and Scholes, M. 1973: The pricing of options and corporate liabilities. *Journal of Political Economy*, vol. 81, May–June.

Black, F. and Scholes, M. 1974: The effects of dividend yield and dividend policy on common stock prices and returns. *Journal of Financial Economics*, vol. 1.

Boardman, C. M., Reinhart, W. J. and Selec, S. E. 1982: The role of the payback period in the theory and application of duration to capital budgeting. *Journal of Business Finance and Accounting*, vol. 9, Winter.

Clarkson, G. P. E. and Elliot, B. J. 1969: *Managing Money and Finance*. London: Gower Press.

Dimson, E. and Marsh, P. R. 1979: Modern risk measurement. *Managerial Finance*, vol. 5, no. 1.

Dimson, E. and Marsh, P. R. (eds) 1982: *Risk Measurement Service*. vol. 4, no. 3, July.

Donaldson, G. 1969: Strategy for financial emergencies. *Harvard Business Review*, vol. 47, November–December.

Elton, E. J. and Gruber, M. J. 1970: Marginal stockholder tax rates and the clientele effect. *Review of Economics and Statistics*, February.

Fama, E. F. and Miller, M. H. 1972: *The Theory of Finance*. New York: Holt, Rinehart and Winston.

Franks, J. R. Broyles, J. E. and Hecht, M. J. 1977: An industry study of the profitability of mergers in the UK. *Journal of Finance*, vol. 32, December.

Franks, J. R. and Hodges, S. D. 1978: Valuation of Financial Lease Contracts: A Note. *Journal of Finance*, vol. 33, May.

267

Franks, J. R. and Pringle, J. J. 1982: Debt financing, corporate financial intermediaries and firm valuation. *Journal of Finance*, vol. 37, June.

Galai, D. 1977: Tests of market efficiency of the Chicago Board Options Exchange. *Journal of Business*, April.

Graham, B., Dodd, D. L. and Cottle, S. 1962: *Security Analysis*: *Principles and Techniques*. New York: McGraw-Hill.

Jensen, M. C. 1972: Capital markets: theory and evidence. *Bell Journal of Economics and Management Science*, Autumn.

Jensen, M. C. and Meckling, W. H. 1976: Theory of the firm's managerial behaviour, agency costs and ownership structure. *Journal of Financial Economics*, vol. 3, October.

Johnson, R. W. and Lewellen, G. 1972: Analysis of the lease or buy decision. *Journal of Finance*, vol. 27, September.

Lintner, J. 1956: Distribution of incomes of corporations among dividends, retained earnings and taxes. *American Economic Review*, vol. 46, May.

Markowitz, H. M. 1952: Portfolio selection. *Journal of Finance*, vol. 7, March.

Markowitz, H. M. 1959: *Portfolio Selection*: *Efficient Diversification of Investment*. New York: Wiley.

Marsh, P. R. 1980: Measuring risk. Unpublished paper, London Business School.

Miller, M. H. 1977: Debt and taxes. *Journal of Finance*, vol. 32, May.

Miller, M. H. and Modigliani, F. 1961: Dividend policy, growth and the valuation of shares. *Journal of Business*, vol. 34, October.

Modigliani, F. and Miller, M. H. 1958: The cost of capital, corporation finance and the theory of investment. *American Economic Review*, vol. 48, June.

Modigliani, F. and Miller, M. H. 1963: Corporate income taxes and the cost of capital: a correction. *American Economic Review*, vol. 53, June.

Myers, S. C. 1974: Interactions of Corporate Financing and Investment Decisions – Implications for Capital Budgeting. *Journal of Finance*, vol. 29, March.

Myers, S. C. 1976: *Modern Developments in Financial Management*. Hinsdale, Illinois: Dryden Press.

Myers, S. C. 1977: Interactions of Corporate Financing and Investment Decisions – Implications for Capital Budgeting: Reply. *Journal of Finance* vol. 32, March.

Myers, S. C., Dill, D. A. and Bautista, A. J. 1976: Valuation of Financial Lease Contracts. *Journal of Finance*, vol. 31, June.

Myers, S. C. and Stewart, C. 1984: The Capital Structure Puzzle. *Journal of Finance*, vol. 39, July.

Newbould, G. D. 1970: *Management and Merger Activity*. Liverpool: Guthstead.

Pettit, R. R. 1972: Dividend announcement, security performance, and capital market efficiency. *Journal of Finance*, vol. 27, December.

Pike, R. H. 1985: Owner-manager conflict and the role of the payback method. *Accounting and Business Research*, vol. 16, Winter.

Rubner, A. 1966: *The Ensnared Shareholder*. Harmondsworth: Pelican.

Schall, L. D. 1974: The lease-or-buy and asset acquisition decisions. *Journal of Finance*, vol. 29, September.

Sharpe, W. F. 1963: A simplified model for portfolio analysis. *Management Science*, vol. 9, January.

Sharpe, W. F. 1964: Capital asset prices: a theory of market equilibrium under conditions of risk. *Journal of Finance*, vol. 19, September.

Shefrin, H. M. and Statman, M. 1984: Explaining investor preference for cash dividends. *Journal of Financial Economics*, vol. 13.

Tobin, J. 1958: Liquidity preference as behaviour towards risk. *Review of Economic Studies*, vol. 25, February.

Wagner, W. H. and Lau, S. C. 1971: The effect of diversification on risk. *Financial Analysts Journal*, vol. 27, November–December.

Index